The Discipline of Politics

The Discipline of Politics

Jean Blondel
Professor of Government,
University of Essex

Butterworths
London Boston Sydney Wellington Durban Toronto

First published 1981

© Jean Blondel 1981

British Library Cataloguing in Publication Data

Blondel, Jean
   The discipline of politics.
   1. Political science
   I. Title
   320   JA66

   ISBN 0–408–10681–6
   ISBN 0–408–10785–5 Pbk.

Typeset by Scribe Design, Gillingham, Kent
Printed by Mansell Bookbinders Ltd, Witham, Essex

Preface

It is still the case that the discipline, or study, or science of politics attracts in many quarters, not just controversy, but scepticism. There is scepticism among the public and among politicians; many simply do not know that the study of politics is well-developed, but many of those who know continue to believe that there is little point in analysing political life systematically and rigorously. There is much confusion about what a theory of politics is about—whether, for instance, it is about principles or values, or whether it is about 'empirical regularities', that is to say, unavoidable consequences of previous happenings. But there is also some scepticism as well as controversy among those who work in the discipline, between those who believe that the subject-matter can be treated in a 'scientific' manner and those who do not, between those who think it is possible to predict happenings and those who feel that it is more prudent to be modest about claims as these may be disproved by events.

While the controversy is justified and indeed healthy, the scepticism is not. It is right and proper that political scientists should ask themselves how far their inquiries can be rigorous and systematic; it is right and proper that, as other social scientists do, they should be concerned about whether one can discover general laws of human behaviour in politics, when men are so diverse, and the conditions under which they live so varied. But neither political scientists nor the public should doubt the value of political studies: the political world is markedly better known than it was only a generation ago; indeed, by its continuous questioning of the findings which are made, political science improves its understanding of the world of politics—of man as a 'political animal'. Controversies are a sign of liveliness: they are an indication that scepticism about achievements is entirely out of place.

In a sense, therefore, this book is an attempt at 'putting the record right', by showing how political science has progressed, on a wide front, in the course of the post-war period. But this book is, of course, also a personal assessment of the way political studies have grown: although I endeavour to be dispassionate, not just in the coverage of topics but in the description of trends and the analysis of the contribution of major works, I do not wish to pretend that I do more than present my own view of the evolution of political science. Over the last quarter of a century, I have been both affected and fascinated by these developments. Both in my own works and through the institutions I had the opportunity to help build—the Department of Government at the University of Essex and the European Consortium for Political Research, I have tried to contribute to the realization of the potential of political science: I could not therefore be entirely impartial in my reflections over the development of the subject; I can only hope the result is not overly idiosyncratic.

The work is the product of a collaboration between author and publisher—and much of the credit for what is good in it must go to Butterworths and to Peter Richardson in particular. The idea of the book was his; and we had many discussions on content and presentation. But the interpretation is, of course, mine. It reflects the fact that I believe the study of politics to be a very important endeavour, and that I also believe that the study can be conducted with rigour, whatever views are taken about the relative importance of facts and theory, empirical analyses and reflections on values; and I also believe that, ultimately, the better understanding of politics acquired through political science will markedly contribute to the improvement of social life. Political science may not be, despite what Aristotle said, the 'master science': but it is the only means which we have at our disposal to make sense of the way in which man can be governed. This is why it deserves support and those who specialize in it deserve encouragement.

Witham, Essex
November 1980

Contents

Chapter 1
The mystery of politics

Le nez de Cléopâtre, s'il eût été plus court, toute la face de la terre en eût été changée.

Had the nose of Cleopatra been shorter, the whole history of the world would have been different.

Pascal

Cliff-hanger results

On 28 March 1979, a little after 10 p.m., the Speaker of the British House of Commons announced that, on the Motion that 'This House has no confidence in Her Majesty's Government', 311 MPs had voted 'Aye' and 310 had voted 'No'. 'The Ayes have it.' For the first time in over half a century, the House had overthrown Her Majesty's Government. History was being made. But history was being made through a very narrow funnel: the opposition had a majority of *one* over the Government. And it was revealed that Sir Alfred Broughton, a Labour MP, was so ill that the Prime Minister had decided that it would not be proper to insist that he should attend the Chamber. Mr Callaghan could have decided otherwise; Sir Alfred Broughton, who subsequently died, could have felt that he had to come and vote; or the then Leader of the Opposition, Mrs Thatcher, could have been embarrassed at the situation and offered to the Prime Minister that Sir Alfred Broughton should be paired. Had one of these alternative courses of action been taken, Government and Opposition would have had the same number of supporters; the Speaker would have voted for the *status quo*, as he was bound by precedent—that is to say, for the Government. Mr Callaghan's Government would have been saved; and, perhaps, a few months later, he might have won the election. The fate of British political life might have been markedly altered.

1

On 8 November 1960, after a long campaign between the youthful, handsome, rich, Bostonian, Roman Catholic John F. Kennedy and the veteran Vice-President (and still young) Richard M. Nixon from California—a campaign during which Kennedy had exposed the tiredness and lack of imagination of the returning Eisenhower–Nixon administration, and during which he forcefully stressed the need for a change of direction if America was to retain the leadership of the world, be a pole of attraction to its friends and remain a fear to its enemies—the people of the United States were able to give their verdict. They were confronted with two conceptions of the Presidency, one based on imagination, idealism, but also vigour, the other based on the principle of 'business as usual' in which rather sordid deals were not altogether absent. But the people of the United States seemed unable to exercise their choice. They had given large majorities to Eisenhower in 1952 and 1956; but in 1960, the race was very close indeed. By late evening on 8 November everything seemed to hang on the results in Cook County, Illinois, because the State of Illinois, with 27 out of 535 votes in the electoral college, was sharply divided into the urban Democratic masses of Chicago (*alias* Cook County) and the 'suburban' crowds who tended to the Republican. The two elements seemed in balance. In the end, thanks to the efforts of the strong 'machine' politician, Daley, who was then Mayor of Chicago, John F. Kennedy was declared the winner in Illinois; and he thus became President of the United States. The cleavage between two views of society, between two conceptions of America was settled by a tiny number of voters (the difference was under 9,000 votes out of 4,7000,000) in the city of Chicago and in its suburbs.

On 14 August 1949, the electors of the newly established Federal Republic of Germany went to the polls to elect their first Bundestag. The result was somewhat inconclusive. In ways which were somewhat reminiscent of the Weimar Republic, the voters were divided into a sizeable number of parties; and even the top two parties, the Christians Democrats and Socialists, each polled little more than a quarter of the votes. The CDU/CSU obtained 139 seats out of 402, while the SPD obtained 131 seats; the third party, the Liberal FDP, obtained 52 seats. How quickly would the Government be formed and how stable would it be? There were two main contenders for the Chancellorship (that is to say, the Prime Ministership). One was the Rhinelander Konrad Adenauer, 73 years of age, Mayor of Cologne and builder of the new Christian Democratic Union. He had shown force and courage against the Nazis, but he had also shown the Western allies that he was not going to allow his country to become a satellite, although he was a firm supporter of Western values. He had sensed that the new Christian Party had to be much broader than the Pre-war Centrum, whose electorate was exclusively Roman Catholic: the new party had to be an alliance of Catholics and Protestants, and it had also to be centre-right in its policies, Adenauer having seen to it earlier that the zeal for 'progressive reforms' was to be relatively muted. Against him, Kurt Schumacher, the Socialist leader, was also an anti-Nazi resistance leader, but this was the only characteristic that the two men had in common. Schumacher came from East Germany; he opposed big capitalism; he was a German nationalist—and disliked both East and West, wanting his country to avoid being linked to any block, and supporting policies of neutralization and continued demilitarization. As personal animosities between the two leaders combined with policy differences, the idea of a coalition between the CDU and the SPD was unrealistic after 14 August 1949: neither was prepared to serve under the other. In the event, Adenauer was elected Chancellor by a majority of *one*.

One can speculate as to what might have happened if the result had been different. West Germany might have remained neutral— instead of being gradually linked to NATO. Perhaps the European Community might not have been created, as this was born of the profound desire of Adenauer to bring about a reconciliation with France, a policy which was made possible because the French Foreign Minister of the time, Robert Schuman, was close to Adenauer: he came from Lorraine—and thus was a near Rhinelander—and he was a Christian Democrat, and one of the leaders of the French Christian Party. Europe as we have known it since the 1950s might not have existed if some thousands of German voters had preferred the SPD to the CDU or if two deputies from the smaller parties had not voted for Adenauer in the Bundestag. Indeed, one can speculate further. If the Soviet Union had allowed free elections among all four zones things might also have been very different. What is now East Germany had always been proportionately more Socialist and Communist than the rest of the country; thus, had elections taken place across all four zones in 1949, the SPD would have obtained more seats than the CDU and, almost certainly, Schumacher, not Adenauer, would have been the first postwar Chancellor. Thus, by insisting on the separation of East Germany and not opting for an 'Austrian solution' for Germany, Stalin—and almost certainly Stalin alone or with very few colleagues—may have made the European Community possible, clearly not the outcome which he would have wanted.

Longer-term interpretations

Of course, these cliff-hanger results may also be viewed as largely the consequence of longer-term trends. One can remark that Mr Callaghan's Government was on a downward slope and that the events of 28 March 1979 were a 'logical' conclusion. The Labour Government of October 1974 had started with a majority of three over all parties; it lost seats at by-elections; it entered into a pact with the Liberal Party in 1977, but the two parties combined lost their overall majority. The standing of the Government in the country declined over the years, and only the popularity of Mr Callaghan, which was greater than that of Mrs Thatcher, succeeded in maintaining the impression that Labour could continue to hold office. The many strikes of the winter of 1978–79, in particular the lorry drivers' strike, shook the country's confidence in Labour's ability to control the unions. Thus, Mr Callaghan himself seemed no longer able to dominate events; the Government narrowly escaped defeat in February. Had it not lost in March, it might have lost in May, June or July.

One might note that while Kennedy's election in 1960 was an extremely narrow result, fate seemed to have an uncanny way of reshuffling the cards when it was not clear who had won. Thus not only were Kennedy's great plans distinctly less attractive when they came to be confronted with reality; not only did America have to disentangle herself from the rather sordid episode of the Bay of Pigs in Cuba in which intervention in a foreign country was combined with defeat; not only were the policies for the aged and the poor eroded or stopped by a hard-nosed Congress whom Kennedy did not succeed in moving; not only did Kennedy only retain his image of the hero because he encountered violent death in Dallas; but Nixon had his revenge soon afterwards, in 1968. He had the opportunity to try out his policies over a period which turned out to be twice as long as the one during which Kennedy was able to rule. So America had both Kennedy and Nixon: the 'accident' of the Cook County votes in 1960 seemed to be overcome by destiny giving a second chance to the one who had only lost the election by ill-fortune and by a hair's breadth.

It could equally be said that it was no real accident that Adenauer won in 1949: he seemed the more alert and skilful of the two party leaders; he, not Schumacher, saw the need to give Germany a strong economy, based on market forces, and he realized that ties with the West would help Germany to progress; he, not Schumacher, saw that the country's need was one of revulsion *vis-à-vis* the Soviet Union, but also one in which there was a need for a new identity—not based on retrenchment, but based on participation in the rebirth of democracy in Europe; he, not Schumacher, saw that these ideals, combined with skilful manipulation, would make it possible to rally substantial numbers of voters round one party, and Adenauer was master in the manipulation of small parties and of their leaders. Thus Adenauer was perhaps 'bound to win': had Schumacher been elected in 1949 his victory might have been hollow and short, the forces of the centre and right might still have united under Adenauer, and perhaps Adenauer would have become Chancellor a year or two later and built the CDU as a near-majority party in the same manner.

Thus goes a non-ending debate between short- and long-term interpretations, between those who give prominence to daily occurrences and those who look for undercurrents. This debate has long divided historians; it is at the root of the dilemmas facing the discipline of politics. How much importance should be attributed to accidents, to great events, to great men? Indeed, how can one assess the importance of events, even smaller ones, since their consequences may be vast. Two unknown individuals, parading as electricians, break into a hotel complex and bug some offices: the most powerful leader of the world, the President of the United States, has to resign two years later, despite a great electoral victory and great successes in foreign affairs. A few students in a drab and isolated French campus start challenging the University authorities: a fuse is lit which soon sets the whole University of Paris on fire and leads half the country to down tools; the regime almost collapses. By a sudden twist, a few weeks later, the President and his Government enjoy the greatest electoral victory of any French Government. Yet, by a further twist, some months later, the President loses a referendum and resigns. Thus the ball goes from one court to the other: which is more important, accidents or long-term forces? Was Nixon so out of line with the mainstream of American politics that he was bound to lose? Had he been elected on a misunderstanding arising from the Johnson fiasco over Vietnam? Could his election be anything but a hiatus? Was De Gaulle unable to run 'ordinary' French politics? Had he outlived his usefulness once he had solved the Algerian problem in 1962? Was he so lofty that some incident, some day, was bound to bring him down?

The role of 'luck' in politics

Whatever the possible long-term causes of these events, whatever their apparent 'inevitability' in the eyes of some observers—more often distant observers than those who are closely involved—occurrences such as the ones to which we referred suggest that the daily course of political life is heavily dependent on chance. Not surprisingly, many, perhaps the majority, of those who are engaged in politics deeply feel that their career is dependent on the 'wheel of fortune'. They have to accept that it is part of their condition to win or lose, even if the stakes are high. They find 'accidents' at almost every point of their career, from the moment they enter politics to the time they retire. Their fate is decided by small selection committees which might nominate them or reject them by tiny majorities, or by large electorates who vote or abstain, in many cases, on very flimsy grounds. They may then find themselves in Parliament or out of it for reasons which have nothing, or very little, to do with their work in their constituency or for their party. They may become ministers if their party has a majority—but have no chance of gaining office if their party remains for long periods in opposition. Worse still, they may find that there is no outlet for them if no party wants them, or, in tougher political surroundings, if political parties are forbidden and their parliament is closed down. One may win or lose, but, in all cases, there appears to be a large element of luck—and causes of events are in part mysterious. One cannot be sure that some unforeseen circumstance will not upset the best calculations: a small scandal may turn out to be a major topic of controversy which precipitates the downfall of a government. Illnesses, deaths, the weather, the peccadilloes of colleagues are part of the panorama of causes which might make or break a career. No wonder, then, that to remain sane and not to despair a politician should have to be armed with a large dose of fatalism coupled with a deeply engrained belief that some unforeseen opportunity will some day occur! Politics is a profession in which it is dangerous to rely primarily on hard work and sober thinking; it is prudent to believe also in the miraculous.

A strange—and somewhat sad—further comment is that outsiders scarcely feel any sympathy for politicians who follow such a dicey career. For observers, politics is indeed often a mystery, but they usually blame the politicians for this state of affairs. Members of the public seem to want matters to be simple, problems to be rare and solutions to be easy. They commonly believe that politicians 'complicate' questions. They see the glamour of political life—and often resent it—, but do not view this as a compensation for the 'lottery'; they are more likely to laugh at or applaud the downfall of politicians than to grieve at the personal tragedies. Their longing for simplicity, for general and straightforward explanations leads them to pass on to the politicians alone the blame for the unexpected and the mysterious, although they themselves contribute to the unexpected and indeed relish in it: a 'cliff-hanger' result makes more exciting reading than a clear-cut outcome.

How far is it true to say that politics is a profession in which luck and accident have necessarily to play a major part and are the politicians the prisoners of this state of affairs? Long-term interpretations are at least as credible as explanations based on a sudden twist. Not merely historians and academic students of politics, but journalists and pamphleteers, past and present, have looked behind daily events for broad underlying trends. Could the sense of mystery be merely superficial? Could it be an illusion resulting from our closeness to events, from the excitement of the hustings and the passions of the crowds, from our desire to be entertained and from the glamour of power?

The role of 'accidents'

There are apparently some good reasons, truly specific to politics, why mystery and luck loom large in political life. Politics is peculiar, first, in that straightforward 'accidents' uncannily erupt on the political scene. Accidents are those non-political or tenuously political events which come to have a sharp political impact. A natural calamity, such as an earthquake or a landslide, the illness or the death of a leader may produce major ripples. Human error, a rail or ship disaster, for instance, may surge on the political scene. Thus the 'normal' course of affairs may be upset because an event, which leaders could not predict or avoid—or could avoid only at considerable financial cost—largely because it had no political significance, creates a new situation which upsets calculations and modifies the equilibrium of forces.

By and large, however, after some days or weeks, the impact of accidents is seen 'in perspective'. It is rare for the whole political system, or even governmental policies to be markedly altered in view of an 'accident'. The early death of a leader may modify somewhat the course of politics: the death of President Pompidou in 1974 hastened the decline of the French Gaullist Party, but it did not give to French politics a sudden new twist; the death of De Gasperi in 1953 may have contributed to an increase in Italian instability as no leader was to have the same hold on the country in subsequent decades, but De Gasperi had already encountered major difficulties. Meanwhile, more importantly, most leaders seem to be able to 'complete their task' before they leave: Churchill, Adenauer, De Gaulle, all stayed in office for long periods despite their old age. Roosevelt died just before 'his task was completed', in 1945, but at a time when his unique skills of manipulation and leadership were no longer vital; had he died four or five years earlier, the consequences for Western democracies might have been immense, since the American public was very reluctant at that point to become involved in international affairs and to take seriously the danger of Nazism.

'Non-accidents' are thus more numerous than 'accidents': the sequence of events 'normally' follows the course which had been anticipated. There are 'usually' understandable patterns of political behaviour, although these are occasionally interrupted in a manner which limits predictability and reduces regularity. It is right that we be concerned with accidents, since they are practically important, for individuals in particular, and theoretically intriguing, since the size of the ripples is a matter for debate. But they are exceptional and limited in scope. Accidents may give to politics a flavour of mystery and a taste of the unknown: but much of political life remains impervious to accidents, if occasionally close to the precipice.

The shock of revolutions and other 'big events'

If accidents rarely have a major and lasting impact on politics, the same cannot be said of the earthquake which revolutions constitute. The American, French and Russian revolutions did not merely shake the countries in which they occurred, they transformed politics throughout the whole world. Do these commotions not mean that politics is profoundly unpredictable, especially since, alongside these truly colossal events, others, less towering, but very important—coups, riots, 'failed' revolutions such as that of 1968 in France—seem to have a strong impact and yet be almost impossible to forecast, even often to imagine?

Of course, revolutions do not normally occur without warning. The absolutist regime was increasingly in question in eighteenth-century France and in nineteenth-century Russia. It is as if regimes were given time to 'mend' their ways and bring about changes to avoid the final cataclysm. But the exact timing of revolutions seems impossible to predict; nor are the events leading directly to them easy to monitor. It is indeed even more difficult to see why revolutions fail in some countries while they succeed in others. In the 1830s and in 1848, continental European countries had a succession of riots, uprisings, and revolutions. Why two revolutions succeeded in France and very few did so in the rest of Europe cannot truly be 'explained'. One may look at the state of the economy, the development of society, the characteristics of the organization of politics, and the skills of leaders; one can conclude that, here, a peculiar combination of circumstances led to success, while, there, a different combination led to failure. The conditions for revolution may be listed and analysed, but it needs more than these for a revolution to occur and succeed: what this 'more' is remains a mystery.

Yet perhaps the most interesting question raised by revolutions is not why they occurred but what they achieved. At least some of the revolutions transformed politics to such an extent that they seemed truly to alter the 'model' of political life. The new 'model' which emerges is often different, indeed radically different from what the forerunners and precursors might have anticipated: 1789 and, even more, 1792 and 1799 were vastly different from the moderate liberal blueprint which Montesquieu had envisaged in the *Spirit of Laws* in 1748. The events of 1917 led to a political system which was so profoundly distinct from anything which had been anticipated by liberals and socialists before 1914 that it took about four decades for students and observers of politics, except the fully committed supporters of the Soviet Union, to see that the new regime was a truly new experiment in modern government.

Before World War I, it was assumed that 'liberal-democracy' was the only path towards political modernization. European countries had all gradually seen their institutionsed, and in the same manner: the power of kings had been reduced through the increased role of Parliaments; the suffrage had been expanded; parties had emerged to represent new classes. As industrialization progressed, education spread and political participation became increasingly meaningful. What had begun in Britain and north-west Europe seemed to occur everywhere in Europe, first in the German states, and later in southern and eastern Europe; by 1914, it was usually claimed that Russia and Turkey were the only countries which had not been significantly touched by the new style of politics, and the events of 1905 in Russia and of 1908 in Turkey seemed to show that the time was not very far off when changes there would occur.

1917 completely upset these calculations; and the fascist dictatorship which soon became dominant in Italy and parts of central Europe made the course of politics even more difficult to understand. It was as if history was going backwards—although in politics only, not in economics. Orthodox liberals were therefore inclined to interpret Soviet Communism as an accident, and fascism as a reaction to it; others came to despair of the idea of progress, which had been the main undercurrent of political analysis since 1789. The survival of liberal-democracy after World War II gave orthodox liberals, for a while, a respite: fascism had been eradicated. But Communism was stronger than ever: it seemed difficult to treat it, after several decades of liveliness and expansion, as an 'accident' of history.

Yet it was the evolution of the Third World which was finally to force liberal-democrats to rethink their model and to accept that it was not universal. It was evident around 1960 that the new countries were characterized by new political systems (although, for a while, India seemed to provide a 'textbook' example of a new country operating successfully a traditional liberal-democracy). These new political systems were based on the appeal of 'charismatic leaders' backed by the strength of single parties which they had created and aimed at forced 'mobilization' rather than classical representation; the overall goal was collective economic development rather than individual success. These systems became so widespread that they, rather than liberal-democratic countries, constituted the norm. This, in turn, helped to show that the Soviet Union and the other Communist states had been the first of what was becoming a long list of new experiments; indeed, one came to discover other precursors among developing countries, such as Turkey and Mexico after World War I. Politics in the developing countries and in the Communist world was following a different model which needed to be sketched out.

The impact of 1917 on the analysis of government makes it possible to understand the precise character of 'big events'. Big events are, unquestionably, major elements to be reckoned with. They are not 'predictable', first in the sense that we do not know when and how they will occur, although we often realize, more or less precisely, that there are elements of instability in a given country: throughout the second half of the eighteenth century, the difficulties of the French absolute monarchy were repeatedly mentioned, but the French Revolution, as such, was not predicted. The failures of the Tsarist regime were increasingly apparent at the end of the nineteenth century: but the backwardness of much of the country seemed to preclude a rapid move towards 'bourgeois democracy', as indeed many Socialists themselves felt. Neither the timing nor the mechanics of the change were easy to predict. But, in the second place, big events are also 'unpredictable' in that they bring about a new 'model' of politics. It is not, of course, that the ideas which Lenin and Stalin put in practice could not have been conceived by others but, as long as they had not been put in practice, it seemed that they were 'unpractical' because the prevailing 'liberal-democratic' model, which had been proved valid elsewhere, suggested that they were impractical.

Big events thus constitute major challenges to received models of government: this is how they introduce an element of mystery, and this is why they need to be studied with care from the standpoint of political analysis. They are not a challenge to the idea of political analysis as a general proposition: they are a challenge to the models which are currently accepted and which are viewed as the only ways of understanding politics. They are, therefore, stimuli to the development of new ideas and to generalizations about politics; they show that existing models are too narrow, since society can be organized differently—for better or for worse. And if it is suggested that the events of 1917 constituted in some ways a 'regression' as they brought about forms of totalitarianism which had been unheard of and clashed with the ideas of 'progress' of the eighteenth and nineteenth centuries, perhaps it is because not enough effort had been made, prior to 1914, to go beyond models which were currently fashionable, indeed universally adopted, and which were overcomplacent and insufficiently attentive to the problems of industrial society.

Political events and the role of chance

Perhaps the main reason why politics seems based on luck and clouded in mystery is not, however, the very rare, if traumatic, occurrence of revolutions or the incidence of non-political accidents: it is rather the repetition of more ordinary and yet important events where two or more outcomes are almost equally likely to take place. The 'cliff-hanger' situations which we described at the outset are of this type. In the contemporary world, in the West in particular, these cases have become particularly visible because elections provide dramatic examples of close results where it seems impossible to ascribe any satisfactory 'cause' to a very close outcome. And examples of tiny victories and of near-misses are relatively frequent: from the victory of President Kennedy in 1960 to the defeat of the Social Democrats in Sweden in 1979, through the Labour victory in Britain in 1964 and that of President Giscard in France in 1974, to mention only some of the best-known ones, elections have provided a crop of outcomes where luck at the last minute seems to have played a large part.

Elections have this dramatic character because, in one form or another, the selection of leaders—presidents or members of a parliamentary cabinet—entails that there has to be a choice and that only one candidate or only one set of politicians can ultimately be the victors. There have to be winners and losers and, even in a liberal-democratic context, the winner obtains many of the spoils and much of the power while the loser is prevented from sharing in many of the advantages. Politics has discrete consequences, more dramatic than economics, at least most aspects of economic life. The comparison which is often made between politics and economics in this respect is therefore somewhat misleading. One can indeed refer to a 'political market' as one refers to the economic market: electors, like consumers, do choose between 'products', and the choice is made on the basis of millions of independent decisons. But the similarity stops at this point, as politics is a market in which the winner takes all, at least temporarily. The battle between parties is similar to the battle between companies selling a product, but only for the duration of the election campaign: once the electors cast their votes, the result is, in a two- or nearly two-party system at least, that one party wins, has all the governmental prizes, while the other waits on the sidelines. Of course, there are similar cases in economics, as when firms tender for a contract and only one wins; but the comparisons cannot be carried very far on this point either, because the losing firms may then compete for other contracts and win. In politics, the compensations which could be found would have to be at another level, in local government for instance. What makes the outcome of national elections so dramatic is that the election result fixes the situation for a number of years and, in the case of individual candidates, it may fix it for ever, as these candidates may be too old, for instance, to be credible at the following contest.

Of course, there are limitations to the 'winner takes all' situation: in liberal countries, at least, various parties are represented in Parliament, and, in many countries, in the government as well, in the form of coalitions. But there are also limits to the number of parties represented in the government, even with coalitions; and there are situations where there just cannot be more than one winner: there cannot be two Presidents of the United States at the same time. Thus, while it may be possible for a firm to make gradual inroads in the competitor's market and to win gradual victories, victory in politics is basically an 'all-or-nothing' matter: it is not sufficient to do better than last year or last month; one has to do better than the others.

Although elections provide the most dramatic examples of the discrete character of political life, similar situations occur in almost every aspect of political life. We mentioned the example of 'cliff-hanger' votes of confidence at the beginning of this chapter. Occurrences in Parliaments can often be as dramatic as at the polls—and not merely in relation to votes of confidence. The passage of a bill may also depend on tiny shifts in opinion when the two sides have nearly the same strength; these shifts often are unpredictable and seem accidental. And there are instances of a similar type at almost every level of politics—and in every type of political system. Committees provide repeated examples of 'strange' results which are due to the absence of some members, for instance, or, on the contrary, to the 'packing of the meeting' by some who usually do not come.

These examples show that politics has one very special characteristic—which indeed has a profound impact on the nature and the problems of political analysis—namely that it is a process in which *a trend is converted into an outcome*. Politics is based on trends, as everyone knows; working-class electors, for instance, tend to vote differently from middle-class electors. As a result, much political analysis, as economic or sociological analysis, is naturally based on the examination of these trends, often with the help of statistical tools. In such an analysis, it is not necessarily very important to know with assurance how a specific individual votes, provided the trends are known; similarly, it is not very important to know which consumer buys a particular product, provided, in general, the trend is known. But the similarity stops there. Ultimately, what is important in politics is not to know the percentages of party supporters, but which specific outcome will take place at the election, and it is *one* outcome *or* another which occurs in politics, not a trend; the trend may prepare the outcome. It is therefore important, indeed necessary, to know about it, but this is not sufficient; the single, specific outcome is what has to be explained. And, by its very nature, the analysis of trends cannot lead to a precise prediction. Thus, by its very nature, the analysis of political events has at its centre a fundamental element of uncertainty; the marginal uncertainty of one or two percentage points (which remains once the trend has been studied) makes *all* the difference in the outcome.

This uncertainty at the core of the result explains why 'accidents' and 'luck' not only do have, but are also felt by politicians to have, a major part to play in politics. Since the difference between one outcome and the other may well occur at the margin (within the limits of the margin of error, as statisticians often say), luck, chance, unpredictability, once more come back to the fore. We seem dependent on a large number of almost irrelevant elements which may tilt the result in one direction or the other. Hence the strange dialogue between specialists who tend to analyse trends ('Liberals have almost no chance of being elected in Britain, especially outside the geographical periphery', for instance) and the practitioner who feels that, as an individual, he 'may' be able to 'turn the tables'. It matters little to him what his 'probability' of being elected can be; he will, or will not, be elected. It is an 'all-or-nothing' situation to which the answer can be given in the end, only by 'testing fortune'. The gap between political analysts and political practitioners resembles the gap between mathematicians and gamblers. The probability of winning a big prize can easily be calculated; but, for the gambler, the real question is whether *he* will win or lose. And the gamble is even in some ways tougher in politics than at the casinos—and matters of probability seem even more irrelevant—as the game of politics is played at rare intervals only. Chance and accidents loom therefore very large.

The role of individuals

One way of measuring the 'extent' of mystery in politics is therefore to look at the incidence of cases where two or more outcomes seem almost equally likely. But another way of considering this mystery is to examine how individuals come to their decisions. The two are of course closely connected, since political events are in effect the reactions of individuals to certain situations or to other individuals. And one quickly discovers that the analysis of the reactions of individuals poses such problems, either in their attitudes or in their behaviour, that they can easily be labelled as 'unpredictable' or at least 'difficult to predict'.

Politics is, at one level, a game between leaders; but the characteristics of the personalities of these leaders are largely unknown. Although much is written about the major politicians in each country, both in a scholarly manner and daily in the newspapers, the ways in which leaders are likely to behave always retain an element of mystery. And our general knowledge of the elements which combine to form the personality of individuals is still so limited that we are in no real position to predict with accuracy the reaction of individual leaders to a variety of events. Psychological studies and, more recently, psychoanalytical studies have attempted to characterize leaders of the past by looking deeply into their personalities and by attempting to 'explain' their reactions in terms of responses to events which took place in their youth. But while these studies are revealing about potential avenues leading to the analysis of behaviour, they are still so experimental that they scarcely begin to scratch the surface of what seems to be an immense iceberg. We cannot predict why a given individual, in the midst of so many contenders, succeeds in emerging, first, as a credible candidate and, second, as a leader. We cannot then predict with accuracy how this leader will react when confronted by various situations, in large part because his reaction also depends on the reaction of other individuals whose personalities are also far from being 'understood'. Chess takes place in very special conditions between two players who are asked to concentrate on moves among objects with well-established rules; politics takes place, at the top, among a substantial number of players over an almost infinite number of matters which are ill-defined. The stakes are at times so high and relate to such exceptional questions that it is often impossible to rely on experience, while the stress on leaders is often very marked. No wonder it is so often difficult to have a clear idea as to how leaders are likely to behave.

Yet politics is not only uncertain because of the behaviour of leaders: it is also difficult to 'understand' because of the part which the rest of the population plays in the process. There are many degrees of participation—and these vary of course from one political system to another. But, even in closed systems, a large number of individuals is always involved at various levels, and their number is very large indeed in open pluralistic societies, although we know that the bulk of the population is involved only sporadically. Indeed, even if the participation of the population is spasmodic, it is not more easily predictable. Most specialists declared themselves surprised by the sequence of events in Iran in 1978–79; few expected that the demonstrations would continue over such a long period, given the means of repression at the disposal of the government. Specialists were equally surprised by the way in which the students' rebellion in France escalated in 1968; most were further surprised to see how the movement subsided after a few weeks. Some oppositions carry on for a very long time, without apparent success—but eventually break through; others seem incapable of having an impact on the political system—but yet carry on, in the hope that, some day, they will succeed; and others are quickly destroyed by the repression which they have to endure.

Whether crowds are 'rational' or not is beside the point; it would be surprising if they were, as no individual is wholly 'rational', whether he is a politician or not; indeed what 'rationality' precisely means is far from being clear. The point is that there is a need to understand the relationship between the leaders and the led and especially the conditions under which the led give 'support' to leaders. This entails understanding attitudes and the relationship between attitudes and behaviour to a degree of precision which, to say the least, has not yet been achieved. It has often been noted in Britain, since the 1960s, that the majority of the population and even the majority of trade unionists opposed the increased role of trade unions in the political process and indeed wished that trade union power be curbed. And yet, every government—Conservative or Labour—which attempted to curb this power has been defeated in its clashes with the trade unions and has subsequently been defeated at the polls as if the electorate effectively supported the trade unions' stand. This must mean that the electors' 'theoretical' stance and their effective behaviour when confronted with specific actions of the trade unions are at considerable variance or that the link is so complex that the proper solution has not been found by any government. Only when this solution is found shall we be able to pierce one of the major 'mysteries' of contemporary British politics.

These 'mysteries' point to a major problem with respect to the old question of legitimacy. It has been said that 'ultimately all government rests on opinion'. But, while we now know better, for some countries at least, the distribution of opinions among the population, we do not know much about the ways in which opinions intertwine; and we know even less about the ways in which these opinions come to be turned into a response to a particular situation. Some regimes which appear illegitimate are able to remain in existence for decades; some regimes which appear to be very unstable and to totter on the verge of the precipice seem to survive, shaken, but not destroyed, for very long periods: predictions about the collapse of the Italian Republic have been numerous and have hitherto proved to be, like the death of Mark Twain, 'exaggerated'. The nature of the bond which ties individuals to the political system and to the leaders seems to include an element of mystery. Politics thus sometimes appears to be an area where it is better to be wise after the event and not to attempt to give too precise an idea of what the future has in store.

Generalizations and the limits of the 'mysterious'

The element of mystery is therefore substantial; yet, embedded in the mystery is the need and the ability to understand. If we attempt to summarize what we found as we surveyed 'accidents', 'big events', ordinary 'cliff-hanger' events, as well as the underlying role of individuals, we see that mystery and understanding are, so to speak, in equilibrium. Mystery is mystery because we are not able to gauge the rationale of a sequence of events; but we need to know, and want to know. Politicians, observers, the public as a whole want and have to understand politics because they have to plan, to some extent at least, their future actions. And, to do so, they have to generalize about political life.

Generalizations have taken many forms in the course of the history of the discipline of politics. These forms at times appear to be so different as to seem contradictory or exclusive from each other. Yet these forms all stem from a common origin, which is the need to 'structure' the flow of political events if these are to be understood and eventually grappled with by the politicians. Politicians, as we saw, operate in much uncertainty, about their personal career, about the world around them. But they cannot and will not operate in total uncertainty. They therefore look for regularities, both those which they feel to be 'natural' and those which they wish to introduce because it simplifies their life and also that of others; indeed, they often feel that everyone's life would be improved if some patterns were seen to exist and were accepted. Politics is mysterious—but only up to a point: the discipline of politics has to accept that mysteries exist, but it has also to try and understand—and 'regularities' are the ways in which politics can be understood.

Pure accidents cannot of course be made 'regular' in so far as they are natural calamities; but true, pure accidents are rare. Men can reduce the incidence of accidents by taking precautions, by monitoring the environment and by attempting to stop the effect of calamities before this effect becomes too serious. Thus politicians build and use organizations to try and avoid physical disasters which could be dangerous for their prestige and ultimately destroy their power; they also take personal precautions in order to avoid the dangers of violence or of natural accidents from which they might suffer.

But this aspect of the 'domestication' of the environment is primarily administrative rather than political in character. The impact of nature can be predicted with some accuracy in many of its aspects while precautions can be taken to reduce the effect of less predictable calamities. The main difficulty facing politicians comes from man: his behaviour seems less predictable than that of the physical environment; attitudes are unclear and seem to vary widely, the impact of motivations on reactions taking many forms, and it seems far less easy to manipulate men than the physical environment although political leaders are often accused of being manipulators.

The 'domestication' of man, so to speak, is achieved, at least to some extent, by what is variously called 'structures', institutions, rules, arrangements or, even more loosely, 'behavioural patterns'. These have the common effect of ensuring—or of attempting to ensure—that the 'unpredictable' element of politics is reduced to a tolerable minimum. The ways in which the importance of rules, procedures or institutions became manifest to politicians and to observers are unclear; but this importance has been felt for centuries. Self-preservation led many rulers to hire lawyers to defend their claim to govern, for instance. The 'Divine Right of Kings' thus enabled monarchs to be justified in being on their thrones; against them, opponents of various persuasions attempted to 'institutionalize' *their* rights by ensuring that they be represented permanently in a parliament. More generally the determinization of the rights of corporations, of the members of various trades, of various social groups, including families, clans, and tribes, were as many means of maintaining stability among relationships—and thus of reducing uncertainty and 'mystery' in political life.

Rules 'domesticate' politics. It would be entirely wrong to view these rules, procedures or institutions as theoretical constructs imagined in the abstract. The idea of having rules and institutions developed 'naturally': politicians of all types have used them to introduce continuity in politics, and what theorists did was to make these rules more precise and more explicit. In doing so, theorists were often inclined to generalize the rules and to clarify the nature and character of institutions; they thus at times went beyond what the politicians might have liked, and their concerns for understanding the political process has also been more single-minded than that of the politicians. They may therefore have pushed the limits of what was 'explainable' too far and have hoped unrealistically to reduce drastically the zone of the 'mysterious'.

When rules and structures are seen in the context of the 'chancy' character of political life, one can easily understand the reason why it is often a matter of expediency whether these rules are said to be 'descriptive' or 'prescriptive', 'analytical' or 'normative'; in fact, description and prescription are closely intertwined in political theory and political practice. Fundamentally, the mysterious element in politics—that is to say, the role of luck and chance—can be reduced only if individuals—the leaders and the led—behave in a manner which is predictable. Such a predictability can be achieved by exhortation—individuals are asked to behave in a certain manner and they heed to the exhortation for a number of reasons—but it can also be achieved by what might be viewed as 'circumventing' or 'manipulating' the situation—individuals being shown not to be able to play a major part or not to be 'free' to act in more than a limited number of ways—and it can be achieved by a mixture of exhortation and 'circumvention'—individuals being made to recognize that they are not 'free' and therefore being prepared to follow, without complaint, the course which they 'have' to follow. The first type of approach can be said to be 'prescriptive' or 'normative', the second 'descriptive' or 'analytical', while the third—perhaps the most common—is a mixture of the two.

Prescription in politics and in the discipline of politics

The normative approach to rules and procedures assumes that individuals are 'naturally' free. It also assumes that, without guidance, this freedom would lead either to chaos or at least bad organization; the strong might dominate the weak, for instance. There is therefore a need to identify a number of values which mankind should adhere to—and indeed is likely to adhere to once these values are clearly presented—and a number of rules and arrangements will follow in order to implement these values in practice. On this basis, one might appeal to man's reason or to man's fear, or to both. The appeal to man's fear consists of pointing out that very serious personal consequences will follow if the 'chancy' character of politics and society is maintained; there could—would—be chaos, and therefore personal freedom and even personal safety would not be ensured. The appeal to man's reason consists of pointing out the importance of a number of ideals—liberty, justice, equality, democracy—which can be implemented, even if only partially, when a number of rules are introduced and followed by the mass of citizens. Indeed, in a less exalted manner, it can even be suggested that rules have intrinsic virtues, irrespective of content, and without reference to any broader ideals. Rules help to make the game 'comprehensible'; we then 'know where we stand' and can therefore carry out our lives in a secure and more tranquil fashion.

In this approach, rules, procedures, arrangements, institutions, are all constructs of man; they might or might not exist. Man has to be convinced—or coerced into believing—that rules are a good thing, whether good in terms of an ideal or in the narrower sense of being practically useful. But, if man is indeed convinced of the value of these devices, politics does become domesticated: man refrains from behaving in ways which do not correspond to the norms. Politics becomes, *ipso facto*, comprehensible: we know in advance what will be the reactions, since these reactions follow the code which has already been prescribed. The mystery remains only to the extent that the code is not applied, and in the corners in which it is vague. This conception became, of course, increasingly fashionable in the seventeenth, eighteenth and nineteenth centuries, the 'social contract' being the basis of much political philosophy; and only where this contract was not in force, in absolutist countries such as Russia and Turkey, and in the realm of international relations, did politics remain wholly unpredictable.

But this approach is effective only if some important conditions are met: citizens have to believe in the values on which the rules are based and in the adequacy of the rules to implement these values; or they have to be coerced in implementing the rules. If disaffection with the rules becomes widespread and if coercion becomes ineffective (and these two characteristics often reinforce each other), pressure for introducing alternative rules becomes strong; if these demands are not heeded, pressure for a break-up of the system may then be exercised, even in the absence of any other idea of what an alternative system might be. The feeling that some 'miracle' might occur, latent in the minds of many individuals, becomes prevalent and the political system may be shaken in its roots. Revolutions thus take place in the context of the decline in the belief of what has been called by Pareto the 'political formula' on which the existing political system had been based.

Description and the 'inevitability' of political events as a result of the environment

But prescription is not the only justification of rules, institutions, and procedures. It can be shown that some rules simply 'exist', irrespective of whether men wish to have them or not. 'Social contract' theories on which the prescriptive or normative approach was based assumed, as we said, that man was free: he enters into a contract, but if he does not, he can behave in an 'unpredictable' manner. Such a freedom seemed exaggerated: a variety of constraints seemed naturally imposed on man, coming from the various groups to which he belonged. Loyalty to a family, a clan, a religious group, seemed to predetermine the activities of men. While the prescriptive theory was based on individualism, a more realistic approach suggested that a social interpretation of man's predicament would reveal many limitations to man's actions. Rules ceased to be viewed as 'prescriptive' and obeyed by choice: they became increasingly viewed as customs, as practices which man adopted because he was conditioned to do so. Institutions ceased to be viewed as man-made and aimed at a particular purpose—as Parliaments, for instance, could be viewed as being; they became viewed as natural 'structures' within which individuals acted in a broadly 'predictable' manner.

This approach to political theory is descriptive rather than normative; it is sometimes viewed as 'sociological' rather than 'philosophical' and 'legalistic'. It states that, whatever man might want to do, it can only operate in some ways. And these ways are markedly determined, in particular, by the historical context in which man finds himself at a particular moment. Gradually, during the course of the nineteenth century, the increased economic, sociological and anthropological knowledge which was acquired in Western societies suggested that the problem of domesticating politics was more a question of understanding the realistic limits of man's actions as a result of the environment than a question of elaborating institutions which could be prescribed to men.

But, in introducing the environment as a major explanatory variable, 'sociological' approaches were naturally led to go further and further in the direction of reducing man's influence in political life, as the only way to eliminate chance and mystery was, at the limit, to eliminate the individual altogether as a causal element. And no one went further in this direction than Marx who found in the economic 'substructure' the key explanation of political life. The economic determinism which he put forward had the advantage of eliminating chance or at least of suggesting that chance could only affect societies in a superficial and trivial manner, not worthy of 'real' interest. Political theorists of the seventeenth and eighteenth centuries based their analysis of social and political life on the need for man to abide by a number of values if society was to be well-organized; they implicitly accepted that man might or might not abide by these values. Marx and the Marxists, on the contrary, could eliminate the contingency that man might not 'abide by the rules' by stating that the rules were the consequences of social and economic structures, but they could only do so inasmuch as and precisely to the extent that the environment did determine man's actions. Chance and accident remained if there was some leeway in the influence of the environment.

The problem of the 'leeway' was never satisfactorily solved by Marx and the Marxists especially because, in practice, the Marxists in power, and Lenin to begin with, reintroduced 'voluntarism' in a striking manner in political action. Partly because the Russian Revolution seemed to contradict the basic ideas of economic determinism, partly because it seemed counter-intuitive to suggest that man had no influence or only a trivial influence on events, or at best because it seemed impossible to prove satisfactorily that the environment fully determined man's actions, many Marxists, indeed following Marx himself, came to believe in a mixed 'prescriptive–descriptive' approach. Through this approach, men would be exhorted to follow the 'correct path'; that is to say, they would be made to understand the direction which society was taking, become conscious of their own position within it and thereby hasten the pace towards the next development in society. If large numbers of citizens and politicians did follow this advice, the remaining 'leeway' would be abolished and politics would indeed follow the course which the socio-economic analysis of politics predicted.

Psychological analyses of politics

This exhortation has so far not been followed very widely, and chance and mystery have thus not been eliminated from the theoretical analysis of politics based on the environment. Perhaps because socio-economic analyses did seem to leave open the question of the individual, studies of politics began to consider the influence of the individual more directly than in the past. While 'social contract' theories were based on free will and socio-economic interpretations reduced the individual to the group, another descriptive or analytical approach has consisted, not surprisingly of focusing on the individual in order to assess whether, indeed, individuals might not be constrained in a variety of ways—but as a result of their personality. While many political events may seem to occur by chance or result from 'cliff-hanger' situations in which the outcome could go either way, other political events might be accounted for by probing into the personality of the individuals concerned; this would seem to be the case in particular of the great leaders who make—apparently at least—a great mark on their country and indeed on the world.

At the other extreme, big events might also be accounted for by a better understanding of crowds and masses. A socio-economic analysis might tell us that the conditions are 'ripe' for a profound change in the political system; governmental structures may no longer correspond to the types of decisions which have to be made, to the prevailing 'mode of production' (industrial rather than agricultural, for instance) or to the level of participation which the population is beginning to expect. This might create a 'revolutionary situation', but the people might still not be ready to support a revolutionary move. And, unless we understand the ways in which feelings develop in such a context, we may simply have to conclude that 'by accident', 'some day', the fuse will be lit. It would seem that only a socio-psychological analysis of the spread of feelings and of the way in which the feelings are turned into action can help to answer the questions which the timing of big events poses.

Between the two extremes, small group psychology seems able to help categorize the ways in which decisions are likely to be taken in a variety of settings where politics takes place—in cabinets, in parliamentary committees, in local government, as well as between leaders in the international context. Both the timing of decisions and the complicated tactics followed by the actors need to be analysed, unless we are to accept that outcomes are the result of pure chance and can in no way be predicted. In fact, it seems that there are 'rules' followed by committee members; politicians know by experience that some 'tricks' are more successful than others, and they often follow instinctively whatever course of action seems to them most likely to produce the desired outcome. A formulation of these techniques, coupled with a better understanding of small group dynamics, therefore helps reduce the element of accident and the scope of the 'mystery'.

Thus the study of politics has moved from what might be called a 'pure prescriptive' phase to socio-economic analyses and to the examination of human psychology. This does not mean that 'prescription' has been—or has to be—abandoned; nor that 'environmental' pressures need to be discarded in the overall analysis of political life. It means, rather, that the mystery of politics needs to be approached—and is approached increasingly—from a variety of angles. The more it can be explained, the less there seems to be left to chance and accident. Of course, those who like to see politics remain mysterious, even miraculous, can take comfort from the fact that it will take a long time before human attitudes, human behaviour and human personality are so well understood that reactions can be predicted with a large degree of accuracy. But the development of these psychological studies poses, as socio-economic studies already posed, the broader question of the extent to which mystery, chance, luck, play a part in political life.

The answer is so speculative at this point that it is best not given. What the discipline of politics has done—and will long continue to do—is to uncover slowly some corners of the mystery, by looking at a number of aspects which, for some practical or theoretical reasons, seemed particularly important—or easier to tackle. Events have often guided the discipline; this was true when 'tyrants' and 'dictators' led Machiavelli to develop theories of legitimacy at the time of the Renaissance, or when Hobbes felt that 'order' was of such importance that he had to understand and explain how it could be preserved, and this has been true recently when the emergence of new problems seemed to change radically modern societies. At the end of World War II, Western democracies had a new lease of life—but this was on different terms, in that the people, the 'masses' were making a large intrusion in to decision-making. This is perhaps why, in the postwar studies, elections and participation were the first to acquire a major impetus, though new techniques, the survey in particular, were also to give a boost to the whole of the field. This will therefore be the corner of the mystery to which we shall first turn, to see how accidents, big events, and more frequently the cliff-hanger' results can be 'domesticated' or at least more closely analysed and how the discipline of politics has thus contributed, in a dynamic manner, to a better understanding and a better 'handling' of modern mass politics.

Chapter 2
The irruption of mass politics

Man is by nature a political animal

Aristotle

Know your own self

Socrates

Ours is the age of democracy, in spirit if not always in deed. Let us not try and give a date as to when democracy started; in the course of the last 100 years every generation probably said with equal assurance and with much justification that theirs was the period in which mass politics began. But one thing is certain: only after World War II did mass politics become a major subject of *inquiry*. The point may be surprising; if so, it should be remembered. There has still been little time to brood and reflect on the knowledge we acquired. For all intents and purposes, elections and popular participation were simply not studied before World War II.

Then began a period of enthusiasm in which elections and popular participation became thè topic *par excellence*. Everyone who was interested in politics—or almost everyone—did election research: studies were small or large, deep or superficial, repetitive or 'path-breaking'. Election research gave a badge of modernity, a sense that one was part of a great transformation in the field of political studies. It seemed that the whole of the discipline of politics was about to be changed. If this view has had to be toned down in recent years, if some, almost masochistically, decry the value of election studies, it remains true that the rapid development, indeed the explosion of the work on mass participation has transformed political science beyond recognition. The excitement may be followed by an anticlimax—there is always a day when the carnival has to end—but the discipline of politics will never be quite the same again.

Why did it happen in this manner? And where do we stand now, when we seem better able to look wisely and soberly at the effects of the whirlwind which shook the discipline of politics? Why it happened is relatively easy to trace. After 1945, three elements combined: America provided the *skill* and the *power*, while Europe provided at least part of the *occasion* or the rationale. The new skill was the result of a new technique, the sample survey, which took almost 30 years to make a major impact: from the early 1920s to the late '30s, surveys were used in a limited manner, and more outside the field of politics than within it[1]. The irruption of the masses on the scene of political analysis occurred on an October day of 1936 when Dr George Gallup announced, for the first time in a national election, that his measurement of public opinion based on a small sample enabled him to declare that the incumbent President of the United States, F. D. Roosevelt, would be re-elected against his contender Arthur Landon. A generation later, there was to be a cascade of opinion polls telling us the ratings of American candidates before they even entered primaries, of French hopefuls before they declared themselves in the presidential race, or of British governments before Prime Ministers even considered a dissolution. There were also to be ever more sophisticated academic surveys as well as heated debates about the worth and limitations of surveys. But the impact of the 1936 announcement was not immediate: in most of Europe at least, there were to be no elections for a number of years as the war interrupted 'normal' politics.

The intellectual power was provided by a school of thought, behaviourism, which also began in America in the late 1920s and also took some time to come to the forefront. Definitions of behaviourism are many; works on the subject are legion[2]. For our purposes, it is sufficient to note that this great movement conveyed two main ideas. It meant, first, that the stress should be on examining situations as they were, rather than as they should be: it was primarily an impirical endeavour, reacting against what was felt to be an over-emphasis on theory of a normative kind, studying political principles such as liberty, equality or justice, as well as constitutions and rules, rather than the practice. But behaviourism was also a reaction against 'brute' factualism[3]; it urged a systematic approach to empirical analysis. It was scientific in the sense that it suggested that political science should be based on a theoretical approach, by which hypotheses would be elaborated first and facts would then be used to test the validity of these hypotheses. For behaviourists, the empirical work which had taken place previously was mainly a number of scattered comments about the world, not a rigorous analysis making use of logic as well as of data to discover regularities which would lead us to a true understanding, and a prediction, of political events.

The combination of the behavioural approach and of the survey technique was to be particularly useful in the context of mass politics. But, for election studies to develop, method and technique were not sufficient; there had also to be a 'mood' or a consciousness that elections and other manifestations of mass political activity were important problems, and this consciousness was to be widespread among academics and the broader public. The events leading to World War II provided this new mood. Before 1945, the 'mood' did not exist. There had been 'critical'[4] elections before, of course: not only the 1832 and 1867 elections in Britain which led to two Reform Acts or the United States election of 1860 which resulted in Lincoln's victory and precipitated the secession of the South: but also, in the twentieth century, the Liberal landslide of 1906 in Britain or, again in Britain, the 1923 election which brought a Labour administration to power for the first time, or, in the United States, the victory of F. D. Roosevelt in 1932 which was confirmed and indeed reinforced in 1936 in the face of bitter opposition. But the events of the 1930s on the Continent were probably the main cause of a much greater interest in elections: in Germany, the rapid rise of the Nazi party between 1930 and 1932 showed that the people could be lured into being the direct instrument of the death of democracy; the Popular Front election in Spain in 1936 began a process which resulted in the civil war and the Franco dictatorship. Elections could be seen to have a direct impact on the fate of democracy; they needed therefore to be closely examined. And if the reconstruction of democracy following the Allied victory of 1945 was not to lead to the same consequences as the establishment of new democracies after World War I, attention had to be paid to the electoral process and to the means of checking the growth of extremist parties.

The absence of a 'mood' before World War II can be seen by the fact that earlier attempts at analysing elections had been very patchy. As early as 1913, a Frenchman, André Siegfried, had undertaken a pioneering study of 'electoral geography', the *Tableau politique de la France de l'Ouest*, in which he showed the extraordinary continuity of voting patterns, over decades in the various parts of the region, as well as the sharp contrasts between districts, as if electoral behaviour was a consequence of the landscape. He emphasized the relationship between land tenure, patterns of village organization, and voting. Continuities could therefore be explained by, or at least were closely associated with, characteristics of the social and economic structure. But, although Siegfried's study was truly pioneering, it was scarcely followed up, even in France, for several decades. It began to attract interest only after World War II, when a new 'mood' about the importance of elections prevailed. Siegfried's study was then 'rediscovered' and indeed Siegfried himself, who had concentrated in the inter-war period on studies of foreign countries, returned to his earlier interest.

The survey technique, the intellectual thrust of behaviourism, the recognition that elections could be very important, indeed critical, were the three elements which led to the explosion of voting and mass participation studies in the 1950s. It is essential to remember this very peculiar combination since it has now become fashionable to dismiss or at least reduce the importance of all three. We have become so accustomed to elections, in the West at least, that we tend to find that they are somewhat ineffective: parties resemble each other, it is said; they do not achieve what they promise to do. Only newcomers to democracy—Spain, for example, in the late 1970s—seem truly to believe in the import-ance of elections; in other Western European countries, many have come openly to shrug their shoulders; a few are even openly critical.

In parallel, it has also become fashionable in many political science circles to deride behaviourism as exaggerated scientism; even some of those who propounded it in the 1950s and early 1960s have felt obliged to remark that they went too far in the hopes which they entertained for universal systematization[5]. Moreover, it has become very fashionable to point to the limitations of surveys: not or no longer because samples are felt to be unrepre-sentative of populations—these early criticisms (perhaps justified at the start) have now been muted—not even because surveys are said to reveal only what we already knew; this facile criticism is now recognized to be, indeed, facile. It is not true that surveys do not reveal many aspects of political and social life which we simply did not know; moreover, even when surveys confirm what we 'intuitively' knew, they give *evidence* for these intuitions and therefore give us greater assurance that we are not labouring under false impressions. But surveys are criticized for other and 'deeper' reasons. They are said to be superficial, to be unable to probe effectively into man's mind, to force respondents to answer 'off the cuff' to matters to which they often have not given sufficient thought; answers may therefore not correspond to what the people 'really' believe in[6]. For a while, surveys gave us the impression that they would reveal the mystery of mass politics. Alas, for some, and fortunately for others, the mystery remains or, to be more precise, every aspect which is uncovered seems to raise more questions than it is able to solve; the study of mass politics seems to have the characteristics of Sisyphus' effort.

The importance of survey research

What is it, then, which made sample surveys so important in the development of the discipline of politics in the course of the 1950s and 1960s? First, surveys enabled us to know about the background of the electors of the parties; before survey research developed, one could only assume or imagine, but not know, how people voted. There were studies of election campaigns, some of which, especially the British 'Nuffield' studies which began in 1945 (and have continued ever since), gave us a very precise description of what went on at the level of the elite politicians, journalists and interest groups during elections[7]. There were studies of electoral geography, as we saw, which related in broad terms the electoral results in the various constituencies to social background characteristics, and in particular to religious traditions. There were studies of electoral systems and of their impact on party systems, as it began to be noticed that proportional representation, which had been introduced to bring about more fairness, had the apparent effect of dividing large parties and of favouring extremists; a major controversy began, in which one of the major contributions was that of M. Duverger, whose *Political Parties* was published in 1950. But only surveys enabled us to know how managers, farmers, shopkeepers, white-collar workers or industrial workers voted, as well as what precise percentage of Catholics and non-Catholics, men and women, the well-educated and not so well-educated voted for the various parties. And surveys also showed that, by and large, the characteriestics of the voters of the various parties remained relatively stable, at least in terms of broad configurations.

Surveys did not only give us a more precise picture of the background of electors; they also told us much about the views and attitudes of electors. We now take for granted that we can know what are currently the views of electors about the role of trade unions or the death penalty, about price controls or about abortion; this was impossible before the survey. Politicians had to infer what these attitudes were from the circle of activists or other acquaintances whom they might have. This may have given them more freedom at the time, which means that surveys contribute significantly, not merely to the analysis of mass politics, but also to the role played by the common man in politics. Surveys have reduced to a significant extent the freedom of professional politicians and activists to operate as if the common man did not exist—not an unwelcome occurrence for democracy.

And surveys have also enabled us to become better aware of the nature and extent of the influences which operate on all of us.

Before electors could be directly questioned, it was impossible to disentangle the relative role of such long-term factors as home environment from the influence of the workplace and of the daily surroundings as well as from the impact of the media and of the campaigns of politicians. The landscape was flatter; simple explanations based on one overriding 'cause' seemed tenable. It was then possible to state with equal assurance, either that the past moulded the present completely—an inference which electoral geography tended to support, with its emphasis on political continuity in various areas—or that such daily occurrences as a press campaign or more recently a radio or television campaign, could 'completely' transform the mood of the electors. But surveys now showed that all these elements played a part but that therefore each played only a limited part in the overall voting process. They showed that the effects of recent events had to be viewed in the context of predispositions which voters had; the landscape became three-dimensional, as the various elements took their place in the comprehensive picture.

Yet criticisms of surveys continued to be voiced, not just criticisms of detail, or of particular surveys, or criticisms aiming at improving the technique by which the analysis was done, but much wider criticisms accounting to a blanket rejection of the whole approach. And, whatever the intellectual justification given for these criticisms, it is difficult to avoid the impression that part of the problem was that this segment of the discipline essentially developed first in the United States and was only later introduced in Western Europe and elsewhere. The story of election surveys begins indeed in Erie County, Ohio, in 1940, although there had been some attempts before and although, as we noted, commercial opinion polling had begun earlier and, on a nationwide basis, at the 1936 US presidential election. The 1940 Erie County study was a breakthrough; it was a sophisticated attempt in which the authors stated, with some arrogance which the importance of the new technique seemed to justify, that they were embarking on an effort which, over time, would lead to an understanding of the *'People's Choice'*[8].

As a matter of fact, what began in Ohio in 1940 was continued at every subsequent presidential election. In 1954, an election study was published for the first time on the basis of analyses of waves of electors who were interviewed four times between the spring and autumn of 1948 in Elmira County, New York[9]. And 1948 also saw the first nationwide survey conducted by a university team of social scientists, a team which was to dominate the study of elections for two decades, the team of the Survey Research Centre at Michigan. The 1948 and 1952 surveys led to a number of articles; a number of new concepts were elaborated and techniques were refined. This made possible the publication in 1960 of *The American Voter*, based on a survey of the 1956 Presidential election, truly the most acomplished study of electoral behaviour which had been written and which had an enormous impact. It established Michigan as the centre of voting behaviour research; it led directly, often with the help of Michigan scholars, to studies in many countries—Britain, Germany, Sweden, Norway, France, Italy, Switzerland, the Netherlands and indeed outside Europe as well[10]. The story of election studies is by and large the story of the part played by the Survey Research Centre of Michigan, both in the United States and abroad, and, within it, of four scholars: A. Campbell, P. Converse, W. Miller and D. Stokes, with W. Miller in particular becoming the most central figure of the school. But at no time did the four scholars of Michigan do so much for the analysis of mass politics than when they wrote *The American Voter*.

The American Voter and the controversy over the ideology of the 'common man'

The American Voter was a landmark in the study of mass politics: not only was it the first massive national study of an academic king—a panel of 6000 respondents was interviewed—but it was a comprehensive endeavour to look at all the facets of the minds of voters and to see how the act of voting is related to the personality of the elector in general. Previous studies had enabled us to discover the relationship between class and vote, or religion and vote, not just in the United States, but elsewhere, as for instance in Britain. With *The American Voter*, however, it was no longer a question of a still photograph: it was a motion picture analysis, which unravelled the forces which pressed on the elector at various points of his life to lead gradually to the voting decision. Hence the analogy of the 'funnel of causality' which the authors elaborated at the beginning of the work: the voting decision has to be understood in a dynamic manner, and past influences play a large part, but are gradually blended with new influences which are continuously pressing on the elector up to the day of decision.

What gave *The American Voter* a profound unity was the emphasis on the linkage between the various elements of the voting process. The study not only came closer to an understanding of the complexity of the political personality as a whole; it also set the agenda for future investigations by shifting the emphasis from purely sociological antecedents of the vote to a socio-psychological or even psychological frame of reference. Earlier studies had proved conclusively that the relationship between the socio-economic structure of society and voting patterns was much weaker than had been traditionally thought; *The American Voter* confirmed that, in America at least, class was simply not a good predictor of the vote, but it went further. It abandoned altogether the rather mechanistic sociological conception according to which factors such as class, but also religion, language, ethnic group, lead to the voting decision. The authors of *The American Voter* reasserted the point that the individual was the prime object of the investigation and that the individual had a complex history which could not be grasped merely by a listing of factors.

The Michigan authors made clear that, in a real sense, it cannot be the case that electors vote in a certain way *because* they belong to a class or a religious group. The influence must be mediated by various processes, two of which are ostensibly particularly critical. One is the level of the consciousness of electors with respect to political matters, while the other is the consciousness of the political parties. The Michigan school did indeed devote much of its efforts to both of these problems, and in so doing it went beyond what might be called a 'sociological' approach to enter a psychological approach, albeit one which was largely examined in terms of broader groups. Thus *The American Voter* places great emphasis on 'party identification', conceived as the degree of proximity of groups' electors to the political parties. Clearly this 'predisposition' to vote for a party takes time, indeed a very long time to be strong; but once it has become strong, it is unlikely to disappear or even to weaken. And, in the West at least, much of voting behaviour relates to class, religion, or indeed other social factors, through the different effect of 'identification' over many decades.

But party identification does not merely relate to the slow impact of 'reference' groups on the electorate. What needs also to be explored is the extent to which views fit with the characteristics of party predisposition. And this is where the work of the Michigan School—and indeed survey research in general—led to conclusions which, for a variety of reasons, academically good and academically bad, indeed theoretical as well as practical, have remained controversial. It is clear that nineteenth-century party developments, in Western Europe especially, were based on the assumption that there was a strong correlation between party programmes and the supporters' views. But it is also clear that survey after survey showed that the correlation was in fact very low.

The American Voter not only confirmed this general finding; it looked for an explanation—one which led its authors to question the belief, openly stated by some, tacitly admitted by others, that politics is ideological in the mind of the common man. Habit seemed to play such a part, and the distance between electors' opinions and programmes seemed so large in many circumstances that it seemed necessary to conclude that, on the contrary, party identification had, by and large, little to do with views and, ultimately, with right and left, that is to say, with a broad ideology. On this matter, the authors of *The American Voter* answered an emphatic yes. They examined with care the responses of their panel and concluded that only a tiny minority could be said to be ideological in the strong sense of the word, while the great majority did not relate their views to the manner in which they voted. The American electorate appeared primarily to be voting on the basis of habits stemming from generations, rather like a society remains divided into religious groups. The intellectual underpinnings of voting are not programmatic.

Lest it were thought that this was a special characteristic of American electors, studies of British voters which took place some years later—in large part in collaboration with and with help from Michigan—showed also very clearly that ideological predispositions were also very rare.

> ...We asked our respondents if they ever thought of themselves personally as being to the left, centre or right in politics. Only 25 per cent said that they did so; three-quarters of our sample indicated that these concepts were not among their working stock of ideas when they thought about politics. These figures contrast sharply with the fact that 96 per cent of our respondents conceded readily enough to some degree of party commitment. Allegiance to party is one of the central facts of the British elector's political awareness. Identification with the ideological symbols of left and right is clearly one of the more peripheral facets of such awareness[11].

Moreover, only 21 per cent of the sample associated parties with right and left; and once pressed to state what they meant, only about 2 per cent of the sample did give the kind of answer which 'ideologues' would normally be expected to give, namely that the left is for 'more social benefits, the end of private wealth and nationalization', while the right means 'the preservation of private wealth and the reduction of expenditure on social benefits'[12]. The percentages were similar in Britain to those in the United States, despite the fact that in Britain the Labour Party was ostensibly a more ideological party than the Democratic Party in the United States and despite the fact that, overall, socialist 'propaganda' had had more prominence in Britain than in America.

It is therefore no exaggeration to say that the picture of the electorate which emerged from *The American Voter* and other 'Michigan studies' corresponded little to the idealized view of the people which had often been presented on the left, while, on the other hand, it did not suggest that the people were without political commitment or indeed without political views. It showed that the political culture of electors is complex, largely because it is based on deeply engrained habits which constitute a number of layers which are often difficult to disentangle and to assess separately. It showed that ideas, views, let alone ideologies were relatively less important, at least in a direct 'rational' way, than theorists had seemed to assume.

Yet, however large the contribution of the Michigan team has been, questions remained unanswered. By and large, we still do not understand the processes by which change takes place in voting patterns; specifically, it seems very difficult to distinguish long-term movement from short-term reactions. The interpretations of these long-term movements among electors—from the idea of the 'embourgeoisement' of the working class to the new values of the young in the 'post-industrial society'—have given rise to major controversies[13]. Moreover, and deeper down, the understanding of the basic psychology of voters, of the ways in which conflicting ideas and emotions lead them to vote in a certain way, still remains limited; if more progress was to be made, it seemed that one would have to go beyond—or below—analyses at the 'macro-level' to probe deeply into the minds of small numbers of electors. To this extent, voting studies led, and continue to lead, to 'in depth' psychological studies.

'Rational choice' and the role of party competition

While the Michigan studies were examining systematically the ways in which long-term and short-term influences led to individual voting decisions, others had begun to look at voting from a different angle—the angle of party competition. The first important work in the field appeared a few years before *The American Voter*, but its impact was gradual and only from the mid-1960s did the party competition or 'rational-choice' school come to be recognized as an important and fruitful approach. Anthony Downs, an economist, had published his *Economic Theory of Democracy* in 1957, having been struck by the similarities between the political and economic markets in as much as electors are confronted with parties making different offerings between which they have to choose. Thus the prime element in the Downsian approach is the choice exercised by the voters, a choice which is necessarily made on the basis of existing programmes and existing parties. Naturally, the Downsian approach is one which gives prominence to short-term elements over the long-term. Long-term factors can be reintroduced in the sense that electors exercise their choice on the basis of their preferences and of the perception of what is advantageous to them; this 'utility' is moulded by the past and the experiences of electors. But, for Downs and for those who adopt the same approach, it is more important to concentrate on the mechanics of the choice process itself, because these mechanics are what actually takes place and because these mechanics lead to important consequences. In a two-party system, the need to maximize votes induces each party to adopt programmes which come closer to each other. At the limit, in a 'perfect' system, in which the search for the maximization of votes would be the only consideration, the programmes would be identical; they would be located exactly in the middle of the ideological spectrum as each party would compete for the support of the very small band of electors who stand exactly in the middle.

This last conclusion is obviously somewhat extreme and unrealistic, yet the general drift of the Downsian approach appears to correspond to many real world situations. In the 1950s and early 1960s, in particular, parties seemed to be moving closer to each other in many Western democracies: the 1950s were in Britain the era of 'butskellism', one in which both major parties seemed to agree on most issues and on fundamentals in particular; in West Germany, the Social-Democratic Party adopted a markedly more moderate programme in the very year in which Anthony Downs' book was published—1957. It seemed to be the case that the old cleavages, the basic social divisions which had led to political 'sub-cultures' in the past, class and also religion, were losing some of their appeal. Politics appeared increasingly to be concerned with different means of solving the same problems—and Downs' model seemed particularly fitted to cope with this development.

Downs' model was attractive not only for practical reasons, however; it also seemed to provide an explanation of voting patterns and not merely a description of the background of electors. Electors came to a voting decision on the basis of their preferences; naturally, these preferences would vary somewhat from time to time (or the composition of the electorate varied), and what seemed particularly important in elections was the movement, the 'swing of the pendulum', which led to the replacement of one party by another. This ebb-and-flow could be accounted for by fluctuations in preferences; the party which was best and quickest at catching the 'mood of the electorate' (even if it was only that fraction of the electorate, at the centre, which was critical for the result) was the winning party. Conversely parties which departed markedly from the 'centrist' position would be severely punished at the polls. Here again, Downs' model seemed to give a good account of the reality: the US Presidential candidates who did least well in recent years were those whose position was too far to the right (Goldwater in 1964) or too far to the left (McGovern in 1972). The model even seemed able to account for long-term developments in party systems in that it seemed permissible to view the evolution of the last few decades as one in which parties gradually realized more clearly what the 'rules of the game' were if they were to achieve victory. The daily battles between left-wing activists and a more moderate leadership in a party such as the British Labour Party seemed to be surface movements of an erratic character scarcely impeding the gradual move towards 'moderation'.

Yet the Downsian approach also had limitations which became increasingly apparent as attempts were made to extend it beyond the ideal-type of two-party system for which it has been formulated. A simplification of the party system did occur in some countries—in West Germany in particular—but it did not occur everywhere: in many Continental countries, third and fourth parties continued to be strong. Yet the persistence of these parties cannot be easily accounted for by the Downsian model. In part, this is because the model as it was originally developed was uni-dimensional. It might appear in the first instance possible to complicate the model and to introduce a second, third, fourth, dimension of party competition, the problem being seemingly a technical rather than a substantive one. The difficulty is that the 'mechanical' consequences of the model—which, as we saw, formed a large part of its attractiveness—cease to be practically as valuable with more than two parties ordered along more than one dimension. (If the parties are ordered along the same dimension, the consequences are broadly similar to those of a two-party system; in many cases, two of the parties then enter a long-standing coalition against the third, although there are occasional

'reversals' of alliances, as occurred in Germany in the 1960s.)
When there is more than one dimension, the alliances between the
parties become unstable. It is not axiomatic that the parties will
tend to a centrist position; there may be, on the contrary, a very
unstable arrangement somewhat analogous to those which have
been discovered with respect to different preference orderings
relating to three candidates or three solutions to the same problem.

But the fact that the consequences of a two- or three-
dimensional party space may not be 'functional' to the system and
lead, on the contrary, to instability, is not the only reason why the
Downsian model should not be extended with profit to such a
situation. There is a further difficulty, namely that, if there is more
than one dimension, the explanatory power of the model diminishes in that it becomes necessary to account for the very
existence of these dimensions. As long as the electors are ordered
along one dimension only, it is possible simply to assume that this
dimension is 'natural' and corresponds well to the preference
patterns of all individuals; if there is more than one dimension, an
explanation has to be given as to why some electors are more
concerned with some problems than with others. This is to say that
long-term factors have once more to be taken into account. The
difficulty with the Downsian approach seems to be the converse of
the difficulty faced by the Michigan school. The emphasis on
short-term issues is so strong that enduring loyalties cannot be
explained; if these loyalties are 'homogeneous'—that is to say,
operate along the same lines for all—a concentration on the
short-term can provide a satisfactory explanation, but this is not
the case if the basic framework differs among different groups of
electors.

This means that a 'party competition' approach needs to reinte-
grate long-term commitment and long-term influences if it is to
provide satisfactory answers beyond the two-party situation. Some
developments in this direction have begun to take place by looking
at the distance between electors and parties in the most general
fashion. Instead of assuming that electors and/or parties are
ordered along pre-existing dimensions, one can simply note the
extent to which the position of each elector varies from that of the
party over a wide variety of problems; this can be done by
calculating the probability which an elector who has a particular
background characteristic, or who holds a given view or broad
philosophical leaning, has of voting for one party rather than for
another and indeed of abstaining. It becomes therefore possible to
locate electors in a space which is bounded by the parties

themselves and therefore to take into account both the concrete variety of the bonds which link electors to parties and all the parties which may exist in a given system. This method has the advantage of going beyond 'party identification' and indeed of going beyond the more classical Downsian approach[14].

Yet this method remains a descriptive mechanism rather than a new model of voting behaviour; it does not explain the voting decision. In this respect the 'spatial analysis' approach resembles that of Downs. Downs started from the preferences of electors, which he considered as given, in the same way as economists tend to consider as given the preferences of consumers who come to the market. It may be that economists tend to feel that it is not up to them to inquire into the reasons why different consumers have different preferences; perhaps economists feel that monetary mechanisms are so important that they can be analysed in themselves without reference to the consumers' preferences which underlie them. Political scientists have never been entirely satisfied with this intermediate level; moreover, voting, unlike money, does not constitute the basic mechanism by which political activity takes place. It occurs sporadically, often with great intensity when it does occur, precisely because the voting activity is, relatively speaking, so infrequent. Political scientists therefore wish to understand, not merely how people vote and what effects this vote will have, but also *why* people vote and why they vote in a certain way. This means that they have to look into the motivations of the voters and go beyond stated preferences to the reasons why these preferences emerge in the minds of electors. In doing so, political scientists follow the same type of inquiry as the one they follow when they are interested in leaders or other politicians. The point is sometimes obscured by the fact that, with large numbers of voters, it may seem sufficient to note the existence of 'patterns of distribution' as if these patterns were, in themselves, satisfactory explanations. The discovery of patterns is important and often intriguing; it is unquestionably the first step in the analysis. But it is only a first step: why these patterns exist, and not others, or why some patterns occur more frequently than others must be the subsequent steps in the inquiry.

The study of mass politics began with the study of voting, naturally enough, because elections are the most important events in which the great majority of the adult population of modern democracies participates. But the relatively exceptional character of elections does suggest that, if an explanation of voting patterns is what is required, it will have ultimately to be found beyond the voting patterns. Voting is a special case of participation—even if it is of major importance; voting is also a special way in which the people express—and indeed to a large extent form—their views. The solution of the puzzles which voting studies have uncovered will only be found once a long detour has successfully been completed—a detour which involves going into the deepest corners of the personality and into the many manifestations of participation and, indeed, non-participation, which are open to the citizens.

Politics and personality

The study of politics and personality is, of course, very old insofar as it applies to leaders, statesmen, the influential in general. But it came only recently to be concerned with the common man. Admittedly, as early as 1908, Graham Wallas emphasized the complex character of the forces which operate on political man; but his *Human Nature in Politics*, as Siegfried's *Tableau politique de la France de l'Ouest* published at about the same time, did not trigger many followers. It was probably necessary, for personality studies to start in earnest, that a genuinely serious, indeed alarming political matter should have required analysis and explanation: the occasion was provided by the events of the 1930s in Germany. While some political scientists saw the almost mechanical effects of the electoral system as one of the main causes of the rise of the Nazi party, others, mainly sociologists and psychologists, felt the origin was to be found in certain personality traits, which were summarized under the label of *The Authoritarian Personality*, a study directed by Adorno and published in 1950 which had an immense immediate impact and started a major controversy. In subsequent years, aspects of voting studies suggested paradoxes and contradictions which only systematic analyses of the political personality seemed able to answer. In fact, the excursion into some of the deeper aspects of the mind has to date seemed to raise more questions than it appeared to answer.

Voting studies—and indeed studies of mass participation in general—started from what seemed to be the obvious proposition that the main problem was to understand the impact of the environment on the individual. Man being a 'social animal', we needed to assess the various ways in which society reflected itself in man. Indeed, the very first studies, those of electoral geography, were, by the nature of the approach, studies of the impact of the environment alone. With surveys, it became possible to give individuals a somewhat more 'active' role: views were sought on many issues; but the part played by the social background was, as we saw, pre-eminent. Even if the part played by one 'variable' of this social background was not as large as might have been expected, it did seem to exist; and the problem facing specialists appeared to be primarily technical—namely, that of disentangling, by means of elaborate statistical techniques, the specific impact of, say, class, religion, ethnic or national group, and the like. Such an interpretation appeared to assume that it was 'evident' that a factor such as class would have an impact on the individual; and whether the impact was conscious or not seemed immaterial (although the consciousness of class feelings had long been felt to be, at least in a Marxist perspective, an important contributor to political action). In short, no question was asked about the mechanism by which the influence of the social variable was exercised on the elector. Yet a moment's reflection suggests that this mechanism cannot be simple and straightforward as, if it was, everyone would be influenced in exactly the same way. Nor is it a solution to invoke the multiplicity of the 'variables' which exercise influence on the individual, as it is also the case that there is not one formula by which these variables come to be mixed, but rather an infinite number of formulas—as many indeed as there are individuals. Thus the Michigan scholars were right in pointing out that a psychological mechanism was at play, but they stopped short of defining what the machine was which triggered the mechanism; they treated 'party identification' as if it was a 'mixed variable' whose existence was somehow distinct from the individuals who experienced it.

Once it becomes recognized that a 'machine', within the individual, operates the 'blending' among the 'variables' which exercise influence, one is close to asking a fundamental question: is it that the individual is subjected to influence, or does he, on the contrary, select and choose among the various objects which he sees around him? Could it not be that the 'influence' of a particular social factor occurs because the individual 'wants' it to occur or allows it to occur? If the 'machine' which operates this selection is labelled the 'personality' of the individual, could it not be that the personality is at the origin of the influence in the sense that the personality 'lets' some influences occur while it resists other influences? In the early part of his work on *Personality and Politics*, F. I. Greenstein examines the usual objections which are made to the suggestion that 'personality matters': he comes to the conclusion that these objections are not proven. We may only perceive those matters which we want to perceive and therefore class, religion or ethnic group may influence us politically only because and to the extent that our personality wants to be influenced by them. And the point seems increasingly intriguing as voting studies tend to debunk the role of the 'major' variables which seemed 'obviously' to influence political behaviour. We saw that the influence of class was more limited than one might have expected, and it is not increasing—quite the contrary: it has been shown that, in countries such as France and Britain, the religious background was a better predictor of the voting patterns than occupations, despite the fact that religious practice seemed to be on the way out in these two countries[15]. And variations from one election to the next take place across classes, rather than between them. Thus one is inclined to conclude that truly individual factors (whether they are translated into 'issue preferences' or not is irrelevant since, as we said, it remains necessary to account for the issue preferences of individuals), perhaps of a deep psychological character, may have a profound impact on voting and more generally on political attitudes and on modes of political behaviour.

But such comments are more in the nature of a long-term programme of study than in that of a recipe for immediate research. Environmental variables are well-known; they can be listed. They seem to 'exist' in the interpersonal, if not wholly objective sense that everyone knows and understands what class, religion, language, ethnic group, region, may constitute: the same is unfortunately not true of psychological 'factors'. There are no clearly recognized elements in which the individual psyche could be divided; and those which seem to be discovered do not appear to lead directly to marked political consequences. The field appears even more unmapped currently than it was earlier: gone are the moments when psychologists believed that there were 'traits' which could help to differentiate simply among individuals[16]. Thus, while it may well be true that 'personality matters', and while it is clearly true that the environmental impact has to be mediated by means of processes which take place in the individual and which screen or reinforce certain environmental pressures, we know neither what is the process by which the environment comes to have an impact on the mind nor the differences which may well—and indeed almost certainly do— exist among individuals.

We are therefore here in an area in which the mystery almost entirely prevails. It seems that the answer can only be found if we pursue the investigation along lines which are very strange in view of the topic in hand, namely by studying processes within the mind of one or a tiny number of individuals in order to begin to understand 'the political attitudes of the common man' (R. E.

Lane, 1964). Studies of personality and politics are indeed of this kind. Consider the work of Greenstein, of Lane, of Barber: they are not in the conventional sense of the word, indeed in almost any sense which could be reasonably given to the word, studies of mass politics. They are studies of individuals taken individually down the most individual roads which can be found, that of the basic elements of the personality. F. I. Greenstein is anxious to present a model or, perhaps more precisely, a line of inquiry, but the evidence which he collects of this line is one which is almost entirely drawn from biographies of statesmen or other major politicians. J. D. Barber, too, appears to be increasingly concerned with not merely politicians, but the most prominent of all politicians, those who became Presidents of the United States. And while R. E. Lane does inquire into political man in a broad social context, he can only do so by pursuing his analysis into the minds of a small number of individuals in a very personal manner.

The breadth of these studies is therefore very limited; but their depth is considerable. Their authors have shown, for instance, that the relationship of the individual to society and to the political system is one which is strikingly more complex than we tend normally to assume, because the more comprehensive concept of 'meaning' which they use enables them to open up avenues of understanding which a more conventional type of analysis cannot tap. By and large, survey research is concerned with rational or intellectualized aspects of our personality; the emotions which are tapped are the rationalized emotions, those which find their way into conversations which we have at the place of work, in bars, in trains or planes. They are not the truly personal emotions, those which concern our sense of identity or our feelings of adequacy or inadequacy *vis-à-vis* the environment. Psychological studies, through long interviews (or, in the case of some statesmen through the study of their childhood and of their personal correspondence), enable us to appraise the deepest meanings of our actions, meanings which are often obscure to us. Thus for instance, our reactions to parties, to the political system, to the world at large may well relate to feelings of satisfaction or dissatisfaction with our own performance in the past, with our ability or inability to cope with a family or work situation, or to the need to prove ourselves in competition with others.

One can see why studies of this kind can be felt to have more immediate relevance with respect to the influential, to the leaders, than with respect to the common man: leaders influence policies in a major way while the common man acts politically only in a spasmodic manner and the weight of the actions of each individual is very limited. But there are occasions in which the actions of the common man can be important, traumatic even, for society; as we noted earlier, it is not surprising that the Adorno study of *The Authoritarian Personality* should have taken place in the wake of the concern which the Nazi takeover aroused. The calmer manifestations of political behaviour of the 1950s and early 1960s made it less obviously necessary to examine forms of 'hysteria' of this type. But, even if this type of experience were never to be relived (and events since the late 1960s make it more difficult to believe that this will be the case), it remains that more conventional voting studies leave major uncertainties untouched, uncertainties which the analysis of the deeper aspects of the personality seem at least potentially able to reduce.

The difficulty is methodological, however, and it is a substantial one. The inner self is like a fortress which can be progressively besieged only after long and patient efforts. Neither the concepts nor the techniques have as yet been devised which would enable us to explore the personality of the common man in such a manner as to give clues on how a community, let alone a whole society will react. Studies of personality have shown how mysterious is the simple remark that man is a 'social animal' because the linkages between this man and the society are numerous, complex, and extremely difficult to interpret. They have shown the need to 'know one's self' better: but they have not as yet devised mechanisms by which we can do so on a wide scale. In the last analysis, these studies remain pilot studies. We cannot blame their authors for not having discovered the means to move from 'micro-' to 'macro-analysis'; we are left with essential clues. But we are left only with clues which have not as yet provided us with the full answer.

Political culture, socialization, participation and political behaviour

The analysis of politics and personality probes deeply into the individual's views to discover his attitudes; this is, to some extent, at the expense of breadth of coverage. Another avenue towards the understanding of attitudes and behaviour has been explored, however, which is primarily concerned with assessing the variety of patterns which can be found in contemporary societies. Because voting studies concentrated on behaviour in the electoral context, they encountered serious difficulties at the comparative level. We noted that there had been major controversies about the impact of electoral systems on party systems; even if Duverger's conclusions were exaggerated, it has been conclusively shown since that all electoral systems do have some impact, and that differences between the impact of majority systems and the impact of other systems are substantial. What is increasingly debated is the direction of the relationship: while electoral systems shape party systems to some extent, it seems that there are also wider reasons, related to the nature of political conflict and the 'rules of the game', which militate for the maintenance of one or other type of electoral system; this introduces the matter of 'political culture' which seems to colour many aspects of political life—and which may well characterize the attitudes of electors as well[17]. But, even if this were not to be the case, the direct comparison between voting patterns will always be hampered by the fact that party systems, and the relationship between seats and votes differ markedly from one country to another.

What seems therefore necessary is to compare directly the attitudes and patterns of behaviour of citizens outside the voting context. This was of course always a concern of those who were primarily interested in citizens' attitudes in the Third World, since it seemed that the political culture in these countries was vastly different from that of Western countries and since election studies were, in most countries, precluded or meaningless. What was needed was to discover a number of 'problems' common to all citizens which are not expressed in the form of abstract concepts and yet do not constitute issues of a momentary kind. Many elements of the most successful voting studies, those conducted by Michigan in particular, could be assessed generally: interest in politics, sense of efficacy of citizens with respect to the political system, assessment of distance of leaders and other politicians. Indeed, if taken together, the reactions to questions of this type might lead to assessing in a comprehensive manner the way in which citizens reacted to politics; and if one were to discover major variations between the citizens of different countries, one could at least assess precisely the validity of statements made for generations about the 'national character' of political life.

This was one of the main aims of the study of *The Civic Culture*, by G. Almond and S. Verba, which, since its publication in 1963, was both highly criticized for many of its conclusions and repeatedly used in a wide variety of contexts. Based on similar surveys conducted in five countries, one of which, Mexico, could legitimately be said to be part of the Third World, it did reveal profound differences in the political culture of citizens and helped to build a typology of various political cultures. It showed that survey research can enable us to confirm or invalidate propositions which are commonly made about the specificity of the political culture of countries and specifically about differences in the ways in which citizens both expect things to be done and are themselves inclined to act. It is, of course, too early even to begin to assert what these differences would be on a world-wide basis; it is also too early to assert to what extent differences change over time, although, as we are about to see, there are now some indications about the causes of some of the changes. But as a descriptive analysis to begin with, *The Civic Culture* provided evidence about variations in degree of efficacy or about distance between state and citizen which are of significance to our understanding of the meaning of the political process in different societies.

Studies of political culture are not merely descriptive, however: they have endeavoured to look at least at some of the 'causes' of the differences which they found to exist. By and large, and to begin with, they stressed primarily the role of the environment. But, because they have a wider catchment area, so to speak, because they are concerned with the exploration of the whole of the political attitudes of citizens and not merely with how they vote, let alone with how they voted at a particular election, studies of political culture have been able to go far back into the basic political attitudes of those whom they are concerned to study. This led to looking at the earliest possible point in time when views about the political system and political processes can be expected to be formed, namely during childhood and adolescence. The study of political culture thus became concerned with the study of the 'socialization process' and, increasingly, with the study of child socialization[18]. This revealed that many clusters of attitudes, many primary attitudes were already formed at a very early age: beliefs in democratic relationships, in the authority of leaders or in individual efficacy seemed therefore to be deeply engrained, at least as deeply as party identification. It seemed to follow that change was unlikely to take place rapidly, and therefore that the characteristics of different political cultures were unlikely to be altered appreciably; if the political cultures around the world differ from each other today, they are also likely to be dissimilar tomorrow.

How far does change occur in a political culture? Specifically, do the major social and economic transformations occurring in a society affect markedly, a little, or not at all, the basic political beliefs which the study of political culture helped to identify? The question has only begun to be explored, partly of course because the time span during which studies of this kind have been undertaken is still very short, partly because the range of countries studied remains rather limited. Early works, such as that of D. Lerner on the Middle East seemed to confirm the intuitive view that the impact of modernization was substantial on many aspects of the political culture. But there seemed also to be substantial evidence to the contrary: it is, for instance, frequently suggested that, despite its revolution, Russia is still characterized by many of the same political processes as those which prevailed before 1917; and there is, to say the least, considerable debate as to whether the 'cultural revolution' did change the political beliefs and behaviour of the Chinese to quite the same extent as has sometimes been claimed—changes in ideological direction in the late 1970s seem to suggest the contrary. Yet recent studies have begun to throw some light on at least some of the 'cultural changes' which are occurring in the West.

Many voting studies, and many studies of political culture, were undertaken at a period when consensus and instrumental politics were on the ascendant. Events in the late 1960s and of the 1970s in the West suggested that calm was not a permanent feature of Western societies: 'dissatisfaction' and 'protest' became strongly voiced, even to those societies which were economically and socially most successful. The Downsian model of the ebb and flow of parties was seriously challenged by the protesters: a form of 'new politics' was emerging. Was this development a sign that the most advanced industrial societies were increasingly leading to a new form of psychological stress among their citizens as if steady and peaceful progress was not sufficient to satisfy the inner drives of individuals increasingly relieved from physical effort?

Evidence collected by a group, in part led by Michigan scholars, about what came widely to be described as 'post-industrial societies' and published in *The Silent Revolution* seemed to suggest that there was at least some truth in the proposition that values were changing as a result of greater material ease[19]. Those who were still engaged in traditional occupations tended to be more concerned with material progress; those who belonged to the 'new classes' were more concerned with democratic participation, with the environment, with the quality of life. And a similar distinction could be made among countries as well: in those which had 'advanced' more quickly, a greater part of the citizenry was characterized by the attitudes of the 'new classes'.

With a study such as *The Silent Revolution*, the blending of environmental influences with psychological charactèristics seems almost complete; it may become—it is to be hoped that it will become—a prevailing characteristic of future studies. The changing environment prompts certain reactions in the minds of the individual; attitudes are the interpretation which the individual gives of the world as he sees it, and of the changes in the world as he copes with these changes by attempting to understand the place which is going to be his.

Studies of political culture have also contributed to a better understanding of the role of ideology in the mind of the common man. The voting context is somewhat unsatisfactory because it led to an over-concentration on issues as they are defined by the political parties and on political philosophies as they develop from generation to generation among the elite groups. Psychological studies showed that we needed to stay much closer to the individual and to his basic reactions to the political system and to society in general. What is engrained in the mind of the individual is not a set of concepts which the individual sees almost as 'objects' in front of him and which he explores; the living ideological framework of the common man is one which does not separate the conception of society from the part which the individual plays in it. This is yet another indication of the important part which psychological analysis must play in the assessment of the attitudes of the common man.

The ultimate aim of studies of political culture is to account for political behaviour, and not merely for political attitudes and political beliefs. The description of the various forms of participation is now precise, especially in the United States and in other Western countries, but the reasons why it remains so low are still obscure. Nor is it only low; it is evidently also spasmodic, taking the form of outbursts, usually rather disciplined and 'civilized' in Western countries, often 'anomic' elsewhere, but indeed occasionally in liberal-democratic societies as well. Nor is it clear why some participate to a very intense degree, whether in a pluralistic 'associational' context or in the secret and illegal forms which it takes both in large parts of the Third World and, by periodic outbursts, in Western countries as well.

The description of various forms of participation in its more peaceful and conventional forms has not gone appreciably beyond the recognition of the apparent role of a number of background characteristics, and of education in particular, in increasing participation levels. Yet, as studies of revolutions have shown for a long time, psychological characteristics of leaders and active followers are of critical importance. 'Anger' is related to violence in politics,—as the title of a work in this field indicates[20]—and anger requires both an outside stimulus and a particular psychological framework. But the broader question of the reasons why the ordinary citizen does not become an activist has only begun to be explored. The fundamental question which we raised at the beginning of this chapter remains so far unanswered: we do not know what it is that pushes some, but not others, to become involved in one or another form of political activity. What is still missing is a clear perception of the 'weight' of political matters in the psyche of the common man and, further, an analysis of the different frames of mind which trigger different levels of involvement.

Clearly, for the majority of citizens everywhere, the 'weight' of political matters is very slight. No doubt this is closely related to socialization which often has the effect of reducing the expectations of success; but this has also to do with the fact that individuals are ultimately more concerned with their personal well-being, with their family and the small groups within which they live, than with the larger body politic. Why exactly this is the case needs to be understood. And lest it be thought that the question is of academic interest only, it is important to remember that one of the main reasons for the misunderstandings between the active and those who are inactive politically stems from the inability of the active to perceive the 'temperature' of the population; the active usually mistake outbursts of discontent for the beginnings of much larger and more persistent forms of involvement. We do not know why involvement quickly evaporates. We can only surmise at this point that politics is too distant, too complex, too mysterious and therefore too frightening for the common man to be prepared to be involved even if he is momentarily convinced (intellectually, but not truly emotionally) that it is in his interest to be involved.

This is only a general hypothesis which appears broadly consistent with the obviously low levels of participation; it is not a conclusion based on the systematic collection of evidence, either on a broad cross-cultural basis or in the context of studies in depth relating to a few men. The question does need to be explored fully: we must arrive at a point when we can understand what politics really means to each and all of us. It does seem that, to begin with, only in-depth psychological studies can provide some of the clues, by helping us to discover the mechanism of involvement, not among the active only, let alone among politicians only, be they revolutionaries or liberal-democratic politicians, but among ordinary men and women. It is therefore reasonable to conclude that, although there have been great, indeed astonishing strides in the post-war period, the study of mass politics has only begun. We have markedly advanced in our understanding of one form of involvement—the voting process; we have begun to detect the type of linkage which relates individuals to the political system and to map out variations across different types of societies. But, to achieve a real knowledge of mass political activity, we must endeavour to understand what politics really means and why there is a retreat from, or fear of politics. This is the direction in which studies of mass politics must go in the coming decades.

Notes

1. An early study was that of S. A. Rice, *Quantitative Methods in Politics*, which was published in 1928.
2. A concise presentation of the history of behaviourism in political science can be found in R. A. Dahl, 'The Behavioural Approach in Political Science', *American Political Science Review* **55**, Dec. 1961, pp. 763–772. *See also* D. E. Butler, *The Study of Political Behaviour,* 1959 and A. Ranney, *Essays on the Behavioural Study of Politics*, 1962.
3. The expression which was sometimes used was 'hyperfactualism', for instance by D. Easton, in *The Political System* (1953), p. 66. We shall return to this point in Chapters 4 and 7.
4. The idea of critical elections was popular at some point in the United States to distinguish between durable and transient realignments. *See* V. O. Key, Jr, 'A Theory of Critical Elections', *Journal of Politics* **17** (1955), pp. 3–18.
5. *See*, for instance, D. Easton's address to the American Political Science Association, published in the *American Political Science Review*, **63** (4), Dec. 1969, pp. 1051–1061, under the title 'The New Revolution in Political Science'.
6. *See* H. Hyman, *Survey Design Analysis* (1955) and M. Rosenberg, *The Logic of Survey Analysis* (1968) for a balanced presentation of the value and problems of survey research.
7. The Nuffield election studies began in 1945 with R. B. McCallum and A. Readman, *The British General Election of 1945* (1947), London; Oxford University Press. They were continued in 1950 by H. G. Nicholas and have been authored or coauthored by D. E. Butler since 1951 and published by Macmillan.
8. R. Lazarsfeld *et al.*, *The People's Choice* (1944).
9. *Voting* (1954), by the same team.
10. The study which has resulted most closely from this collaboration is that of D. E. Butler and D. Stokes, *Political Change in Britain* (1969); other studies have been more indirectly, but yet profoundly, influenced.
11. D. E. Butler and D. Stokes (1969), p. 206.
12. *Ibid.* p. 208.
13. The thesis of the embourgeoisement of workers was fashionable, particularly in Britain, in the 1960s. It was heavily criticized by J. H. Goldthorpe *et al.*, in *The Affluent Worker* (1971), Cambridge: Cambridge University Press; but their critique was in turn criticized: *see* I. Crewe, 'The Politics of "Affluent" and "Traditional" Workers in Britain: An Aggregate Data Analysis', *British Journal of Political Science*, **3**, Jan. 1973, pp. 29–52.
14. I. Budge, I. Crewe and D. Fairlie (1976), pp. 383–393.
15. *See*, for Britain, W. Miller (1977), and for France, G. Michelat and M. Simon, 'Systèmes d'opinion, choix politiques, pratique religieuse et caractéristiques socio-démographiques', *Achives de la Société des sciences religieuses* **37**, Jan.–Jun. 1974, pp. 87–115.
16. *See*, for instance F. E. Fiedler, 'Personality and situational determinants of leadership effectiveness', in D. Cartwright and A. Zander, *Group Dynamics* (1953), London; Tavistock, pp. 362–380.

17. The concept of political culture remains vague. See. L. W. Pye and S. Verba, *Political Culture and Political Development* (1965).
18. *See* in particular the works of F. I. Greenstein, D. Easton J. Dennis and A. Percheron.
19. R. Inglehart, *The Silent Revolution* (1977). *See also* the studies by S. Verba and N. H. Nie (1972) and with J. O. Kim (1978), and by A. Marsh (1977).
20. I. K. Feiearbend, R. Feiearbend and T. R. Gurr, *Anger, Violence and Politics* (1972). *See also* T. R. Gurr, *Why Men Rebel* (1970).

References

ADORNO, T. W. *et al.* (1950). *The Authoritarian Personality.* New York; Harper and Row

ALMOND, G. A. and VERBA, S. (1963). *The Civic Culture.* Princeton, N.J.; Princeton University Press

BARBER, J. D., (1972). *The Presidential Character.* Englewood Cliffs, N.J.; Prentice Hall

BUDGE, I. CREWE, I. and FARLIE, D. (eds.) (1976). *Party Identification and Beyond.* London; Wiley

BUDGE, I. and FARLIE, D. (1977). *Voting and Party Competition.* London; Wiley

BUTLER, D. E. (1959). *The Study of Political Behaviour.* London; Hutchinson

BUTLER, D. E. and STOKES, D. (1969). *Political Change in Britain.* London; Macmillan

CAMPBELL, A. *et al.* (1960). *The American Voter.* New York; Wiley

CAMPBELL, A. *et al.* (1966). *Elections and the Political Order.* New York; Wiley

DOWNS, A. (1957). *An Economic Theory of Democracy.* New York; Harper and Row

DUVERGER, M. (1950). *Les partis politiques.* Paris; A. Colin (English trans. 1955: London; Methuen)

EASTON, D. and DENNIS, J. (1969). *Children in the Political System.* New York; McGraw-Hill

FEIERABEND, I. K. FEIERABEND, R., GURR, T. R. (eds.) (1972). *Anger, Violence and Politics.* Englewood Cliffs, N.J.; Prentice-Hall

GREENSTEIN, F. I. (1965). *Children and Politics.* New Haven, Conn.; Yale University Press

GREENSTEIN, F. I. (1969). *Personality and Politics.* New York; Markham

GURR, T. R. (1970). *Why Men Rebel.* Princeton, N.J.: Princeton University Press

GYMAN, H. (1955). *Survey Design Analysis.* Glencoe, Ill.; Free Press

INGLEHART, R. (1977). *The Silent Revolution.* Princeton, N.J.; Princeton University Press

LANE, R. E. (1964). *Political Ideology.* New York; Free Press

LANE, R. E. (1969). *Political Thinking and Consciousness.* New York; Markham

LANGTON, K. P. (1969). *Political Socialization.* New York; Oxford University Press

LASSWELL, H. D. and LERNER, D. (1965). *World Revolutionary Elites.* Cambridge, Mass.; M.I.T. University Press

LERNER, D. (1958). *The Passing of Traditional Society.* New York; Free Press

LIPSET, S. M. and ROKKAN, S. (eds.) (1967). *Party Systems and Voter Alignment.* New York; Free Press

MACKENZIE, R. T. and SILVER, A. (1968). *Angels in Marble: Working Class Conservatives in Urban England.* Chicago: University of Chicago Press

MARSH, A. (1977). *Protest and Political Consciousness.* London and Beverly Hills; Sage

MILLER, W. (1977). *Electoral Dynamics in Britain since 1918.* London; Macmillan

PERCHERON, A. (1974). *L'univers politique des enfants.* Paris; A. Colin

PYE, L. W. and VERBA, S. (1965). *Political Culture and Political Development.* Princeton, N.J.; Princeton University Press

RANNEY, A. (1962). *Essays on the Behavioural Study of Politics.* Urbana, Ind.; University of Illinois Press

RICE, S. A. (1928). *Quantitative Methods in Politics.* New York; Knopf

ROSENBERG, M. (1968). *The Logic of Survey Analysis.* New York; Basic Books

SIEGFRIED, A. (1913). *Tableau politique de la France de l'ouest.* Paris; A. Colin

TINGSTEN, S. (1937). *Political Behaviour.* London; Bedminster Press

VERBA, S. and NIE, N. H. (1972). *Participation in America.* New York; Harper and Row

VERBA, S., NIE, N. H. and KIM, J. O. (1978). *Participation and Political Equality.* Cambridge, Mass.;

WALLAS, G. (1908). *Human Nature in Politics.* London; Appleton-Century-Crofts

Chapter 3
Coping with bureaucracy

*More and more throughout the world, thoughtful men are realizing
that the development, if not the survival of civilization depends on
organization, coordination and the responsible and purposeful handling of human affairs; that is, on the science and practice of administration.*

L. Gulick

Future historians may describe the twentieth century as the age of
the common man: for the first time, millions of men and women
were asked to decide who their rulers would be and, occasionally
at least, what should be the laws by which they would be governed.
But future historians will surely also describe the twentieth century
as the age of bureaucracy. The signs of the importance of public
bodies are everywhere; the growth of government, both central
and local, has been massive. It has been paralleled by the
development of an outer zone, the 'public sector', which includes
large numbers of social, commercial, and industrial undertakings
owned or controlled, wholly in part, by states, regions or local
authorities. And the regulatory powers of governments extend
deeply into the fabric of society and thereby markedly reduce the
autonomy of private organization and of private citizens, even in
countries which claim to be organized on a 'free enterprise' basis.

How is one to cope with bureaucracies, in an age in which the
role of the common man is being emphasized? Specifically, how is
one to ensure that bureaucracies act in the most efficient manner
to further the 'interests' of the population? These are pressing
questions, to which no simple answer can be given. It is no solution
to follow past practice: history is of no use and historians provide
no guidance. In the past, they helped each generation by passing
judgement on the decision-makers of the previous periods. They
examined individuals—kings, Prime Ministers, a few advisers—
and found these worthy of praise or deserving condemnation. But
what does it mean to praise or condemn a whole bureaucracy?
And even if such a judgement were meaningful, it could not be

sensibly arrived at by a casual, or even scholarly look at one or a few men. Bureaucracies are vast and anonymous; they develop an almost infinite number of hierarchies, of branches, of sub-groups which may or may not work in unison. They are also often secretive, sometimes out of a conscious desire to keep outsiders in the dark (typically by stating that it is not in the 'national interest' that outsiders should know what happens), but more frequently because they develop a 'style' which only insiders seem to grasp. To discuss the accomplishments of bureaucracies meaningfully, a whole new branch of learning had to be invented, with a methodology, concepts, general aims and more specific objectives. Thus, begins the story of the branch of the study of politics known as public administration: it is as protean as the subject it has to cater for. It is concerned with the structure of the civil service and the accountability of public corporations, with the organization of huge departments such as ministries of defence or social security and with tiny local communities, with decisions of truly world-shattering magnitude such as the Cuban missile crisis of 1962 and with 'parish-pump' matters.

Naturally, such a subject attracts—is bound to attract—men with different viewpoints and different aims. Ambitious model-makers wish to establish the principles on which all organizations are based. More modest, but infinitely curious scholars wish to examine how organizations operate in detail. Some are impatient with matters of 'mere' organization and want to find out what seems to be the 'real' object of the game—namely what bureaucracies achieve. A few want to uncover conspiracies, or at least self-indulgence, among administrators. Perhaps the most widespread desire is practical: most wish to improve the *status quo*, because administrators ask them for advice, as administrators are the first to be puzzled about the organizations in which they live, and more than occasionally want to be or appear to be responsive to public demands. To cope with bureaucracies, large and small, in developed industrial societies and in the new developing world means, therefore, many different things to scholars looking at different problems in many different ways.

Curiously, the resulting picture is not one of total confusion. There is even less confusion, and less opposition among scholars than there used to be. Debate has been profitable; the most extreme positions have been abandoned. A synthesis is in progress. There is not *a* school of public administration: this would be stultifying. But there has been a movement towards greater unity as a result of the progress which has been made. Fifty years ago, studies of administration seemed to some to be incredibly simple, to others impossibly difficult. Both groups have had to work and in so doing they not only learned more, but they became more rigorous and more realistic.

Early discord

The study of public administration began in the inter-war period but the narration of the story of the first 20 to 30 years of the new discipline is best done if we do not follow the chronological order too closely. Rather one must see the period as a number of variations on two principal themes. Specifically, developments were ordered around a permanent debate between the general approach and the specialist approach, between those who were eager to look at administrative structures systematically and indeed formally and those who preferred to describe arrangements as they saw them. At first, the two types of studies developed in parallel, but general analyses became rapidly more prominent; they then lost some of their appeal, only to be revived, at least to some extent, in the late 1950s, by the call for the modernization of bureaucracies in the developing world. Meanwhile, major criticisms of the early general approach had come to be published, while countless detailed works on central and local government had begun to appear.

In the early period, belief in the potential of general administrative studies grew very quickly. Some did, admittedly, mainly want to describe the structure and style of particular branches of administration. They were mostly prominent in Britain, which was the European country where public administration was most developed; H. E. Dale's work on the *Higher Civil Service*, published in 1941, was a good example, emphasizing by implication the need to study the particular context in which bureaucracies operated. But this approach was not, for a while, the most popular. For a decade or more, general and systematic studies were most prominent, as many, mainly in the United States, but also to some extent in Britain, wanted to go much further and set up a 'science' of administration. This new branch of study did not owe much to the earlier attempts of Max Weber who had truly been the first to analyse the general characteristics of the bureaucracies' ethos; his work was still then largely unknown outside the Continent. The idea of a 'science' of administration owed more to the American 'frontier spirit' according to which solutions can be found to problems if enough effort is made; it owed also much to the fact that, in the American tradition, there

was scarcely any distinction between public and private administration—what was needed was good management. In the private
sector, guidelines were being discovered to ensure the efficiency of
management; it seemed that these should be applied to the public
sector. Administrative science was thus primarily normative: it
aimed at stating the principles which should be observed if
organizations were to be effective. Considered with hindsight, and
on the basis of the greater knowledge which we have since
acquired of what is admittedly a much larger and more complex
bureaucracy, the enterprise seems to have been based on an
amazing belief that relationships between individuals could be
reduced to a somewhat mechanical set of rules. But these rules
were at the time elaborated, listed and expressed with great
authority. The two most prominent members of the 'scientific'
school, the American L. Gulick and the Englishman L. Urwick,
whose *Elements of Administration* were published in 1943, had
considerable influence. They asserted a number of general principles from which bureaucratic organizations should not depart if
they were to be efficient. It was claimed, for instance, that the
unity of command was an absolute necessity; it was also stated that
the span of control of any superior should not exceed five or six
subordinates as otherwise these could not be relied on to obey.

This type of approach was too simplistic not to create much
opposition, but it did meet a need, especially at a time when new
organizations were being created, almost from scratch, often to
deal with what were viewed as extraordinary functions of government. In the 1930s and 1940s in America, it seemed appropriate to
have 'principles' of organization when the Federal Government
was setting up new agencies to handle, first, the economic
depression, and the war afterwards. The staff of these agencies
had often to be brought together hurriedly from many corners of
the private sector, the appointment of private businessmen to
public agencies being a common American practice which has
persisted to this day; as late as 1960, J. F. Kennedy's appointment
of R. MacNamara to the Department of Defense led to major
development in administrative thinking.

A similar view was to be at the root of many efforts made to
assist the development of administrative bodies in newly independent countries. While the new Indian republic adopted the ideas of
the Imperial civil service, many other nations did not show much
respect for the colonial traditions which they inherited; many also
believed that the new emphasis on economic and social goals
meant that administrative bodies had to be organized on wholly
different lines. Thus when calls began to be made, in the 1950s, on

both administrators and public administration specialists to help reorganize the civil services of many developing countries, the need to follow guidelines seemed once more to prevail. The special character of the Third World had, of course, to be taken into account. By then, interest in the general aspects of development had begun to grow and broad political models were being elaborated to provide a framework for this new interest; we shall consider these models in the next chapter. But administrative analyses retained their identity, in part, to be sure, because of the specific normative traditions of administrative studies and the practical needs of administration. The volume on *Bureaucracy and Political Development*, published in 1963 and edited by J. La Palombara with articles written manily in the 1950s reflects both this tradition and the coming of new models, with F. W. Riggs being perhaps the scholar most anxious to merge concern with administrative principles with the political problems of the developing world.

Meanwhile, however, the mainly British empirical administrative school had become firmly established. By the 1950s, British specialists of public administration rejected the general normative approach, despite the fact that Urwick's work had considerable influence on some sectors of administration. One reason was that in Britain, in contrast with America, the distinction between private and public administration was sharp. Only in the 1960s did the general idea of 'management' begin to be adopted as a yardstick for good public administration; and, even then, the distinction continued to be strongly stressed, even though the conception of public administration had become more 'theoretical' and 'general'. As P. O. Self was to say:

> It is natural enough to conclude that the differences between large and small organization are generally more significant than those between public and private. And up to a point the conclusion is a true one—far truer than it was 50 years ago. Yet the differences that remain are also enormously significant, and perhaps more inclined to be lost sight of in the current enthusiasm for organization theory and common management practices[1].

The 1945 Labour Government's reforms increased the public sector—indeed, were largely instrumental in giving major importance to the developing concept of the public sector. There were so many new agencies; the relationship between central and local government, and between the central government and the public corporations was becoming so complex that it seemed wholly unrealistic to hope to find principles at least until a good mapping of existing arrangements was described. So much was unknown and so much was deliberately hidden (by Official Secrets) as well as by the sheer size of the administrative machine, that the first and most urgent task was to find out what happened in the many tentacles of the bureaucratic octopus. Most British specialists of the time would have agreed with F. M. G. Willson who stated about the period:

> Can there be . . a set of rules so clear, so mechanical and so certain, applicable to a structure of government which is the result of centuries of growth and which is so liable to be affected by the needs and the public opinion of the moment?
> Our study of the experience of the years between 1914 and 1964 has convinced us that scepticism of this kind is thoroughly justified. There is no simple or single formula by whose application all the problems or adminstrative arrangement can be solved[2].

If this caution may sometimes have gone too far, it enabled British specialists of public administration to study in great detail their own institutions. Piecemeal but periodic reforms as well as the age-long practice of the Royal Commissions and of departmental committees of inquiry also helped. As a result British public administration studies excelled in being concerned with the precise description of the structure of central and local government as well as with an analysis of the flavour of bureaucracy. The main developments occurred under the leadership of D. N. Chester, at Nuffield College and in the Royal Institute of Public Administration; they occurred even more at Manchester University whose Department of Government under W. J. M. Mackenzie was for a decade perhaps the most active political science centre in Britain, not least because of the importance it gave administrative studies. The tone was strictly empirical; in the 'Preface' to *Central Administration in Britain*, published in 1957, W. J. M. Mackenzie and J. W. Grove state:

> In imposing unity in our material, we have been concerned more with the needs of potential readers than with theories about the nature of the British Constitution or of the modern state. Our main object is to explore the work of the great central departments of British government and of the various organs of administration which are directly subordinate to them[3].

The work then goes systematically through the characteristics of the civil service, the organization of departments, the central control of administration, the place of central administration. At one level, the study is a textbook, as the authors modestly claim; but, at another, the work is a declaration of intent: it reveals the spirit of the study of public administration which the Manchester School of Government developed at the time.

The approach was outspokenly, aggressively descriptive; but it was far from being narrow. It was concerned with an understanding of the processes and the spirit of administration as well as with institutions. But it was also concerned with an attempt to compare and contrast, and in the first instance to learn about, administrative practices in other countries. Perhaps the most ambitious cross-national study of the civil service in Europe was undertaken during this the period by B. Chapman, under the title *The Profession of Government*, published in 1959. Efforts were also made to appreciate the characteristics and the problems of the emerging bureaucracies of the new states of the Commonwealth; the tradition has been kept to the present day.

Herbert Simon's *Administrative Behaviour*

By the late 1950s, however, the overall setting for administrative studies was in the process of being transformed through the development of sociological studies aimed at studying power in local communities. However, part of the groundwork had been done, over a decade before, by Herbert Simon's study of *Administrative Behaviour*, first published in 1947. This book is squarely in the tradition of general analysis, but its concern for the environment of administration, for the concrete situation in which decisions take place, for the analysis of organizations as living groups, announces the synthesis of approaches which was to come. Simon stated clearly the reason why general studies were for him essential. In the 'Preface' to the second edition of the work, in 1961, he wrote:

When I attempted twenty years ago (around 1940) to find some answers to some questions of municipal organization, e.g. whether a recreation department should be administered by the school board for the city government, or how city planning functions should be organized . . I discovered that no theory existed that could provide the answers and I was forced into an analysis of the ways in which the organization affects human choice[4].

Like the earlier works of Gulick and Urwick, Simon's work was therefore triggered by the desire to find general criteria of administration: it was, as the studies of his predecessors, a 'normative' analysis. By then, the development of many new organizations during Roosevelt's presidency had increased rather than decreased the need for general guidance in the organizational field. Moreover, the traditional unity between private and public administration was still upheld: private managers were deeply involved in many of F. D. Roosevelt's new developments. Indeed, significantly enough, Simon himself was Professor of Administration and Head of the Department of Industrial Management at the Carnegie Institute of Technology and he was very aware of the trends towards general theory in the field of organizations.

But Herbert Simon's aim was to go further than the simple principles of administration of the pre-war period, which were general, but very vague. He was concerned with seeing that we understood what he called 'administrative situations' in the concrete context of a particular administration. He was conscious that administration was about decision-making, and decision-making in a detailed and sophisticated way. Therefore the decision-maker is at the centre of his work. And, naturally, enough, Simon introduced elements of psychology and of group relationship which should supersede the abstract principles which existed in his time:

> Administrative theory must be interested in the factors that will determine with what skills, values, and knowledge the organization member undertakes his work. These are the limits to rationality with which the principles of administration must deal[5].

He then goes on to examine the limits which operate on the individual, in particular his skills, knowledge and values. He is particularly concerned with attempting to define realistically the concept of 'rational choice' open to individuals and he states that rationality has clear limits due to lack of knowledge, imperfect imagination, and the fact that choices only take place among some, not all possible alternatives[6].

The picture of individual decision-making is complemented by the view that organizations are bodies in which decisions have a group character: 'Almost no decision made in an organization is the task of a single individual[7].' Subordinates participate in the decision in that they have considerable leeway in how to carry out the task. Thus Simon's work is a major effort to change the perspective of analysis by bringing real life and concrete resonance to studies which were previously dry and exclusively based on abstract principles: 'It is the central thesis of this study that an understanding of administrative principles is to be obtained from an analysis of the administrative process in terms of decision[8].'

Herbert Simon's work was almost prophetic, in that he was calling for a blending of sociology and psychology going much beyond the mechanical or mechanistic analyses which were prevailing in his time. His approach was also leading to a reconciliation between particular and general studies; the examination of detailed cases could be seen as one way—the best way—of examining how decisions were taken in practice and of understanding the group context within which administrative processes developed. But it had appeared at a time when too little was known about administrative structures, especially in Europe, when many new institutions were set up and indeed an almost entirely new public sector was created: these institutions and this public sector had first to be better understood; internal relationships had to become clearer; above all, there had to be a motive, an urge, a 'mood'. This mood was to come when dissatisfaction with the new arrangements began to spread. Interestingly enough, the first signs of dissatisfaction came from America and at the very point where America was thought to bring about democracy and autonomy—in local communities.

Sociological studies: elitism *v.* pluralism and the question of the bureaucratic ethos

In 1953, the sociologist Floyd Hunter published *Community Power Structure*, a little book which was devoted to the study of the way in which Atlanta, Georgia, was ruled. On the basis of interviews of a substantial number of local 'influentials', he thought that he could conclude that the city was dominated by a 'power elite', almost at the same moment as C. Wright Mills was concluding that the United States as a whole was dominated by a power elite composed of businessmen, civil servants and military men (Mills, 1959). Although Hunter's study was only marginally a study of administration, it had a profound effect on administrative studies, largely because the work was extremely controversial in its findings and seemed even to be controversial in its methodology. Hunter's work—like that of C. Wright Mills—attacked the prevailing belief in the democratic and open character of American politics; in Atlanta, it was said, a tightly-knit group controlled decisions and thus frustrated demands coming from outside the group. This seemed counter-intuitive: America was surely the land of opportunities. Many were therefore inclined to refute the conclusion of the book, and one way of refuting it was to look more closely at the method which had been adopted. The method was ostensibly scientific: the conclusion had been reached by interviewing members of the elite groups of the city and by asking them whom they thought were the most influential; the power of elites was inferred from the *reputation* which members of elite groups had among others. But on closer look the method did not seem as rigorous as might have at first appeared. For instance, local influentials may have misjudged or simply not known who had power. And many decisions may be taken outside or against members of the elite groups, but local influentials may have refused to assign importance to these decisions.

Accidentally, it happened that, at the same time, major reforms were under way in the Connecticut city of New Haven, where Yale University is located. These reforms were put forward by a dynamic new mayor who had been elected as part of a movement to rejuvenate the Democratic Party. Could these reforms be described as merely the by-products of the action of a power elite? Was it not the case on the contrary that, if one looked patiently at *decisions*, at outputs, one would find many instances where a variety of groups competed—successfully—for power. America had always been viewed—as early as the 1830s by de Tocqueville—as the land where bodies created at the grassroots could affect the course of politics. Were not the New Haven reforms a clear indication that this was the case? By studying decisions in various areas, one would come to a more realistic assessment of who indeed governed. This required a detailed, careful monitoring of the decision process in many areas, but this was worth doing as the goal was no less than the assessment of whether America was, or not, ruled by a power elite. Yale had one of the finest political science departments in the country; Yale had to undertake the study.

From this emerged another major work which was to be extremely influential on both democratic thought and administration studies, R. A. Dahl's *Who Governs?* After a close analysis of Mayor Lee's activities, in part taking place within the City Hall itself, coupled with a wide-ranging examination of the various pressure groups which were active in attempting to modify the mayor's proposals, as well as after a very detailed historical scrutiny of the development of policy-making in New Haven since the foundation of the city, Dahl and his associates concluded that power was shared among a number of distinct groups. It was probably true that, *at the origin*, there was a power elite, but this monopoly power had been broken; elite groups still had social status, but they had little political power. There were different sectors of government, and different groups had power in these different sectors. New Haven was, as Dahl was to say, a 'polyarchy', if perhaps not a democracy. The reputational method had led to the wrong conclusion because it had looked at status, rather than at decisions; those who had status tended to believe that only members of their group had power because they ignored much of what was happening in other sectors, although, of course, the situation in Atlanta may have been different from that of New Haven. At any rate America was open to pluralism and polyarchy.

The controversy between 'power-elite' supporters and 'pluralists', with its undertones in the methodological conflict between members of the 'reputational' school and those who felt that the best way to locate power was to study policy areas, was to have a major impact on the whole of political science. We shall have occasion to see how the approach to the study of power had considerable influence on the development of formal analysis. Indeed, it might even seem that the impact on public administration as such should have been relatively limited, since the object was more to assess the distribution of power in society than to examine the structure and effectiveness of bureaucracies. In fact, it is in the field of public administration that the debate produced the greatest advance, because it provided the occasion, the *raison d'être* as well as the methodological tool, for the type of studies which Simon had called for. After the Hunter–Dahl controversy, it was no longer possible to claim that studies of local government were mere descriptions of details. Local studies were transformed almost overnight, becoming part of an ongoing—indeed almost indefinite—research programme designed to discover whether, and, if so, the ways in which various types of groups in the local communities had access to power. Local government studies—in America and elsewhere—became 'community studies', taking into account social relationships as well as administrative arrangements. Moreover, as a result of Dahl's approach (though not of Hunter's—but we saw that Dahl's methodological approach was largely triggered by the desire to respond to Hunter and to combat what was viewed as a major methodological flaw), the emphasis shifted from the examination of organizations to that of decisions, of the content of the policies which local government adopted. In doing so, Dahl was also giving genuine intellectual status to a method of investigation of administrative practices which had existed for some time but which had been to some extent disapproved of both by the generalists and by the specialists, the case-study method. We would still have to wait until the 1970s to find a way (indeed a double way—normative and empirical) in which the study of cases could be truly integrated in the study of administration; but Dahl did make the first and most crucial move by attempting to demonstrate that pluralism existed in America. The cases were cornerstones in the intellectual edifice because it was from the variety of experiences emerging from these cases that evidence for pluralism could be found.

Thus a great part of Simon's programme of action was being achieved in the early 1960s. There was emphasis on the study of decisions and of the particular context in which decisions were taken, while the overall purpose was general. But it does remain true that Hunter and Dahl were not primarily concerned with public administration, and that they had a major impact on the course of administration studies almost by accident and clearly indirectly. This impact was due to the fact that governmental and administrative elements merge at the top of the bureaucratic structure and that the ripples of political decisions extend down the bureaucratic hierarchy. But the core of the administrative apparatus was not studied *per se*, even by Dahl, although his concern for the description of policies and his method of close observation placed him in direct contact with administrators. Thus one further step had to be taken—and it had to be taken by scholars directly concerned with the bureaucratic machine as such. Perhaps it is not suprising that these scholars should have come from France, one of the countries—indeed *the* Western country— which had always been renowned for the part which bureaucracy played in its historical, but also its recent, development. Renewing the Weberian tradition of studying bureaucracy, but in much greater detail and with perhaps a more systematic approach, Michel Crozier published, in 1964, *The Bureaucratic Phenomenon* which linked the analysis of bureaucracies to the overall ideological concern for understanding how bureaucracies ruled us—or at least ruled the French. The answer was a pessimistic one.

The question which Crozier wished to tackle was that of the impact of bureaucratic structures and processes on members of the bureaucracies. Is it not the case that bureaucracies shape individuals in such a way that their behaviour becomes as much the result of the bureaucratic ethos as that of their own personalities? In particular, is it not the case that the middle management in bureaucracies can benefit from anonymity and exercise power in a negative and irresponsible fashion, using the structure and the rules to establish their supremacy over subordinates and, indeed, the public? As Simon had correctly noted, decisions are not 'taken' at the top and mechanically implemented down the line: they are taken at every point in the hierarchy, and implementation is in itself a series of decisions. But the view that administrative decisions are taken on the basis of general rules has the effect of giving to those who are down the line an arbitrary power because, as long as they are out of the public limelight, they can always hide behind the rules to claim that they are only applying literally the decisions of the organization.

Thus one comes to a point of contact between studies of organization and studies of individual and group psychology: the organization and the rules of procedure give opportunities to members of the bureaucracy; individual and group psychology suggests how the decision-makers will use these opportunities. Crozier does not claim that the effect of organizations or that of individual and group psychology needs to be the same everywhere: his work is based on the study of specific organizations in the French administrative context. He no doubt feels that the institutions which he studied in depth were fairly representative of types of French administration, but he does not state that all French administrative organizations are identical, let alone that all administrative organizations everywhere are identical. He indicates a common tendency among bureaucracies, a tendency which is reinforced in the French context since centralization has prevailed there for centuries and the bureaucratic ethos has been particularly strong. He looks for the underlying effects of some types of arrangements, suggesting that reforms will only be effective if profound structural and procedural changes—including of the group relationships within the bureaucracy—are gradually introduced.

Crozier's study of *The Bureaucratic Phenomenon* (and indeed the studies which were conducted later in collaboration with a team from the Centre for the Study of Organizations[9]) have all the characteristics which had been required by Simon to help advance the analysis of bureaucracies in the desired direction. It is a detailed study, based on concrete examples which are examined in depth; but it also has the general aim of attempting to account for the characteristics of bureaucracies in general. It marries the impact of structures and of organizations in the sense of purely legal arrangements (with their rules, their procedures and in particular their centralized aspects) with the environment and with the personality of the administrators. And it is concerned with reform as much as with description: the description is given in order to assess exactly where reforms could be introduced and have maximum effect. It is no good reforming an administration 'by decree'—the title Crozier gave to one of his later works devoted to the structure of research and higher education in France (Crozier, 1979); genuine reform has to be at points where the most stultifying effects of bureaucracies occur, namely at the points where the structure of the organization gives to some individuals an anonymous—i.e., irresponsible—power of a negative kind, thereby making it always more advantageous to reject demands than to engage in imaginative action.

Yet Crozier's studies suffer from two major limitations. They are *potentially* general—their aim is to uncover at least some of the directions in which bureaucracies can go and to examine what should be done to avoid the excesses resulting from the bureaucratic 'ethos'—but they are not general in practice; they are deeply embedded in the French context, and Crozier has little to say about administrative organizations elsewhere. Although he compares organizations, the comparisons are always within the French context, and it is therefore difficult to know precisely from his analysis how far different arrangements, in a different context, would lead to different consequences and therefore how truly general is the 'Bureaucratic Phenomenon' which he describes.

Moreover, Crozier's work has an exclusively structural or organizational character. He studies cases of decision-making because they reveal the ways in which the individual and group psychology of the decision-makers are moulded by structures, not in order to find out what, in practice, the decision-makers achieve. Outputs are not his concern, although he must assume that a healthier administrative environment would lead to better outputs. To this extent, Crozier remains close to the first wave of administrative studies, of the tradition which began in the 1920s and 1930s and examined organizations in detail (as in Britain) or claimed to provide guidelines for the setting-up of new 'rational' structures. Crozier's contribution to the development of administrative studies has been a major one because a way was found of relating psychological analysis to the study of structures. But a further step had to be taken before administrative studies could be said to achieve their full potential.

Policy studies, case studies and the problem of studying outputs

It would, of course, be exaggerated to claim that, in the 1960s or even now, our knowledge of administrative structures is comprehensive. The formulas are too numerous: there are large numbers of ways of organizing central government departments; the civil service can be recruited, trained and posted in a variety, of manners; the forms and organization of local authorities can differ markedly; the control of these authorities by the central government can vary; there may or may not be a philosophy of decentralization leading to the setting up of regional agencies, of 'states' in a federal context; and there may or may not be a widespread tendency to create independent corporations to manage substantial segments of the economy. All these aspects of public administration need to be studied more, and more systematically than they have been done up to now.

Yet there comes a point when such studies may appear esoteric. They may be general, but they are also purely descriptive. Their multiplication may not seem justified. The value of these inquiries depends on the extent to which the descriptions help to provide clues to the understanding of the administrative process as a whole. Bureaucracies exist to elaborate and implement policies; their success of failure must therefore be judged by the policies which are elaborated and by the smoothness of the implementation of these policies. The worth of administrative structures lies in the worth of the outputs: administrative studies must therefore be ultimately concerned with studies of outputs.

The point may seem obvious, but it is not easy to analyse outputs and to relate outputs to organizations. So far, difficulties have not been fully or even largely overcome, for what is missing is an instrument by which to describe policies within a comparative framework. By and large, policies are described through the 'case study' method (as no other method is available); but this is unsatisfactory because either the cases are described very closely and cannot be compared, or they are overviewed broadly but the concrete reality of the problem is overlooked. Moreover, it is difficult, if not impossible, to assess the precise impact of structures on policies: one knows in general that centralization will lead to fewer variations between units, but which aspect of centralization will lead to this result is far from clear. And, ultimately, policies and structures are embedded in a specific cultural context, so that the study of each structure seems to entail the study of all the others. The description of a case dealing with relations between central and local government has no real meaning unless the procedures of central control, the area of local autonomy, the relative position of central and local officers are well-known or described. The aim of assessing structures through the outputs which result from these structures is scarcely brought closer by the use, even a repeated use, of the case study method.

Nor can the case study method enlighten us on what is typical; indeed case studies have often been used in relation to events which are examples of excesses of administrative behaviour. The 'Crichel Down' affair, for instance, has often been mentioned; it showed how entangled the various subdivisions of the British Ministry of Agriculture had been in the late 1940s and early 1950s and how limited was the control that the top decision-makers in the department could exercise on their subordinate agencies[10]. But this was an extreme case. Clearly, extreme cases of this kind should not be allowed to occur, but they do not enable us to pass judgements on the British administrative system any more than a few infanticides enable us to pass judgements on the behaviour of parents. Case studies do not provide guidelines by which to abstract from reality the 'critical' elements which would provide the material for comparisons on a large scale: we are thus precluded from passing judgements on 'average' levels of effectiveness.

An instrument has therefore to be found which will help the specialist of administration to take some distance from the reality while taking into account the broad characteristics of policy developments. This instrument does not exist. But two developments occurred in the 1960s and 1970s which seem to have brought us a little nearer to the ultimate goal. The first was a reaction at the opposite extreme to that of the case study: since what seemed necessary was to obtain an instrument which could produce large numbers of examples which were comparable, a solution seemed to be to assess the results of adopted policies by a whole class of administrative bodies. Budgetary appropriations can be compared in this manner; so can the decisions taken by central and local governments in a number of fields. Without examining how a given council decides to introduce fluoride in water or, in the British context, to adopt a comprehensive scheme of secondary education, one can relate the decision which has been taken to a number of factors, social and economic on the one hand, political and administrative on the other.

This idea led to a number of general studies which related outputs to a number of antecedents and which helped to assess more precisely than before the importance of social, economic and political characteristics in the development of policies. At first only local government was studied in this manner; some studies of central government followed later. At first—like the 'community' studies of the early 1960s—they were almost exclusively concerned with the role of politicians and parties, but the potential for administrative studies is slowly being perceived, particularly in order to examine the consequences of centralization or decentralization on the effectiveness of decision-making and implementation[11].

Yet general studies of outputs based on the 'budgetary' method are insufficient from the point of view of administrative studies as they do not enable us to assess whether particular arrangements, in a given administrative agency, lead, and lead speedily, to the desired effect. It is essential to find out what happens during the 'administrative' part of the decision-making and implementation processes, and this is clearly the objective of policy studies which have gained considerable support in the 1970s.

Policy studies are in essence half-way between case studies, which are too detailed, and general 'budgetary-type' analyses, which jump too quickly over the very problem which needs to be tackled. Policy studies are of the same nature as the studies of policy areas in which Dahl was interested, although they stress, more than Dahl did, the administrative context in which the policy process develops. Their main contribution to the study of administration comes from the fact that they look at a group of decisions in one field, not, like the case study method, at one problem only. This has three main advantages. First, it is not likely that policy studies will lead us to consider examples which are untypical; any untypical case, within the policy area, will soon be discovered and either discarded or treated as what it is, i.e., untypical. Second, it becomes possible to look at dynamics: one can see whether an administrative agency changes its methods over the years, how far it adapts to new problems by adopting new techniques or even new administrative arrangements. Third, policy studies can be comparative in character, a result which the case study method does not enable us to achieve. The ability to draw comparisons is essential, as we shall see more and more in the course of this book, if only because, in situations in which there is no clear yardstick by which to discover what is the 'best' that can be achieved (as well as the 'worst' that can occur), comparisons enable us to see at least whether others have done better or worse or have achieved about the same results. Comparisons are also essential because they enable us to see whether those better, worse or similar results were achieved by similar or different methods—similar or different administrative arrangements, for instance. Indeed, it is because the case study method does not allow for comparisons that it is so liable to lead us to examine untypical cases, even unwittingly. And, by comparisons, one means not only those which can be made among different agencies of the same government, or among different regional or local authorities in the same country, but between different countries with widely differing goals[12].

In principle, therefore, policy studies enable us to pass a more informed judgement on administrative bodies, their structure, the socio-psychological context within which administrations work, and the effect of these bodies on outcomes as these occur. But this remains at this point an ideal, rather than a reality; despite some successes, comparative studies are still rare[13]. Policy studies are still a programme of action, rather than a methodological instrument. There are no guidelines helping scholars to distinguish between broad trends and unimportant events. As long as this is the case, policy studies will run the risk of being too detailed or too general or, if they are comparative, of looking at similar problems from a different perspective. But, as an approach, policy studies constitute an important advance over previous types of analyses.

The concern for administrative overload in industrial societies and elsewhere

Perhaps the instrument which is needed will come indirectly from the concern for the structural inefficiency of administrative bodies which grew in the 1970s. Hunter and Dahl were debating where power was located; Crozier examined whether certain bureaucratic practices did not have the effect of stultifying the administration. None of them was fundamentally pessimistic about efficiency. More recently, however, scholars have been questioning the ability of governments and administrations to cope with demands in industrial societies.

The idea that administrative bodies are 'overloaded' is not entirely new; it has been used in the past to characterized some organizations and the bureaucracies of some governments. But it was associated then with specific situations and with ills which were diagnosed; for instance, the pre-1958 French politico-administrative machine was felt to be overloaded because the political decision-makers were unable to agree among themselves or were too transient to have the time to address themselves to most problems. For instance, too, local authorities covering small areas or with small populations, or only empowered to deal with some matters were often felt to be overloaded because their administrative machine was unsophisticated and their personnel insufficiently trained or competent. For instance, also, some industrial and commercial services of the State were felt to be overloaded because their decision-making machinery was too clumsy to be able to cope with the need for speedy action in the industrial field. But there seemed to be solutions to such problems. The ills of the Fourth Republic could be cured by changes in the political arrangements and the party structure. Local government reforms—of areas, of population catchment, of powers— seemed to provide answers to the choking of local decision-making. The hiving-off of administrative agencies, through the creation of national corporations, seemed to provide solutions to the difficulties experienced by administrative bodies attempting to compete with the private sector.

As long as reforms of this type were felt sufficient to meet the problems, there were specific situations of administrative overload but no consciousness that here was a general difficulty which modern societies would all have to face. Indeed, it may be that, up to the 1960s, the administrative structures and procedures which had been devised were still experiencing some slack and therefore could cope with the demands coming from the society. It is interesting to note that R. A. Chapman and A. Dunsire's comprehensive study of *Style in British Administration*, which was published in 1971, does not discuss the problem.

The idea of administrative overload arose in the 1970s as it seemed clear that reforms undertaken along the same lines as those which had previously been introduced did not have the desired effect of increasing the number and speed of decisions. Reforms of local authorities and of the social services which were introduced in the 1970s were followed by widespread disillusionment about results: administrative costs seemed to soar, manpower seemed to increase, but decisions were not taken apparently more easily. The 'limits to growth' appeared to have been reached, in administration as well as in the society at large[14].

The characteristics of modern societies appeared to suggest that the problem could not easily be alleviated. First, overload seemed a direct consequence of the democratization of Western countries: more were aware of their needs and were more sanguine about attempting to fulfil these needs by putting pressure on the administrative machine. There were more 'voices' and these voices were louder[15]. It had been suggested earlier by political scientists that 'apathy' was needed for the political system to be able to operate smoothly; they seemed to be proved right, as greater participation led to more problems. For the first time, it seemed that the conflict between bureaucracy and democracy was a structural one, not the result of the desire of bureaucrats to cling to power: it appeared to result from the cacophony of the world outside. It seemed impossible to avoid conflicts and delays, as many demands were presented as 'non-negotiable' and the satisfaction of someone's requests led to somebody else's counter-demand.

Administrative overload seemed also due to internal technical problems within bureaucracies. The increased size and complexity of organizations was leading mechanically to increased communication problems within organizations and between organizations. Gulick's precept that the span of control of administrators should not be too wide seemed to take a new validity: the multiplication of agencies, often autonomous in order to benefit from the apparent advantages of democratization, led to a clogging of the administrative machine because decisions were contradictory or, in order to avoid these contradictions, huge amounts of time and large numbers of civil servants were used for the sole purpose of improving 'communication'. Parkinson's statements no longer seemed amusing and extreme; they seemed to have been prophetic and to have identified what was potentially a major crisis. As K. Hanf says in his introductory chapter to *Interorganizational Policy-Making*, significantly sub-titled 'Limits to coordination and central control': 'Territorial and functional differentiation has produced decision systems in which the problem-solving capacity of government is disaggregated into a collection of sub-systems with limited tasks... At the same time, however, governments are more and more confronted with tasks where both the problems and the solution tend to cut across the boundaries of separate authorities and functional jurisdictions...'[16]. And F. Scharpf and his associates warn: 'If however problems should increase much beyond present levels, political processes in the Federal Republic (of Germany) are more likely to be characterized by conditions of overload than would be the case in political systems with either less need for consensus or greater consensus-building capacity'[17]. But it seems that modern industrial socieities are precisely characterized both by a 'need for consensus', as this appears to be what we mean by democracy, and by a low 'consensus-building capacity', as more democracy means more contradictory demands.

It has clearly become widely accepted among practitioners and among the public as well as among specialists of public administration that administrative organizations and processes have reached saturation point; if we do want to achieve more, organizations and processes will have to be altered. It does therefore seem that Western industrial societies are facing the difficulty which has long been felt to be characteristic of developing societies or, according to Western observers at least, of Communist societies[18]. The level at which saturation has been reached in Western societies (if it has been reached) is different from the saturation level in other societies, but the problem is identical. Yet, while it was possible in the past to solve the saturation problems of some societies by examining practices in other countries, this strategy is not open in the case of the overload of Western administrative agencies. Inventiveness and imagination are required. It seems that the only practical way out is to follow a plan of normative and empirical studies, using, as there is none other, the policy study approach to assess current results. This is the programme which F. Scharpf suggests in conclusion to the work on *Interorganizational Policy-Making*[19]. It is a programme which may yield results only after many comparative studies have been undertaken and many arrangements have been found to be inadequate to the task in hand.

Studies of public administration are therefore deeply involved in problems of reform; practical preoccupations have perhaps been the most common goal of specialists from the start, as we said, and it seems to have remained a major preoccupation. But, in the process, the various branches of and approaches to public administration have come closer to each other: studies of outputs are linked to studies of organizations; general questions are raised, but they are examined in the concrete context of 'cases' and policies; and the comparative dimension is used as widely as possible, both to discover whether problems are common and to find solutions. Not surprisingly, public administration has remained a somewhat special branch of political science. It has benefited less from technical advances than has the study of mass politics; it sometimes seemed concerned with matters of little general interest, such as the organization of local authorities or independent agencies; it seemed occasionally to move to abstract generalizations about organizations which had little relevance to politics in general. Both dangers now appear avoided, although much advance is still needed to improve the instruments by which policies can be recorded and compared. But, by and large, studies of administration have developed smoothly and in a cumulative manner; they will continue to improve as they do not seem to require, as do studies of mass politics, and indeed other parts of the discipline of political science, the broad underpinnings of a general theory to which we are now coming.

Notes

1. P. O. Self, 'Bureaucracy and Management', in R. A. Chapman and A. Dunsire (1971), p. 62.
2. D. N. Chester and F. M. G. Willson, 'Administrative Change', in R. A. Chapman and A. Dunsire (1971), pp. 293–294.
3. W. J. M. Mackenzie and J. W. Grove, *Central Administration in Britain* (1957), p. v.

4. H. Simon, *Administrative Behaviour*, 2nd edn. (1961), p. xiii.
5. *Ibid.*, pp. 39–40.
6. *Ibid.*, p. 81.
7. *Ibid.*, p. 221.
8. *Ibid.*, p. 240.
9. Perhaps the most interesting of these studies is P. Grémion, *Le pouvoir périphérique* (1976).
10. *See* R. D. Brown, *The Battle of Crichel Down* (1955), London; The Bodley Head.
11. *See* for instance the studies of T. R. Dye (1966), (1973) and (1976), I. Sharkansky (1970) and, for Britain, J. N. Danziger (1978).
12. *See* A. Wildavsky, *The Art and Craft of Policy Analysis* (1979) for a comprehensive view of the state of policy studies. He states (p. 3): 'Policy analysis, however, is one activity for which there can be no fixed programme, for policy analysis is synonymous with creativity, which may be stimulated by theory and sharpened by practice, which can be learnt but not taught.'
13. An outstanding example of such comparative analyses is that of H. Heclo, *Modern Social Policy in Britain and Sweden* (1974). See also D. Ashford, *Comparing Public Policies* (1978).
14. The title of the first Report of the Club of Rome.
15. From the title of A. O. Hirchman's *Exit, Voice, and Loyalty* (1970), Cambridge, Mass.; Harvard University Press.
16. K. Hanf and F. Scharpf (1979), p. 1.
17. *Ibid.*, p. 17. *See also* R. Rose (1980).
18. *See* C. Beck, 'Bureaucracy and Modernization: the Russian and Soviet case', in J. La Palombara (ed.) (1963), *Bureaucracy and Political Development*, pp. 268–300.
19. K. Hanf and F. Scharpf (1979), pp. 166–167.

References

ASHFORD, D. (ed.) (1978). *Comparing Public Policies*. London and Beverly Hills, California; Sage
CHAPMAN, B. (1959). *The Profession of Government*. London; Allen and Unwin
CHAPMAN, R. A. and DUNSIRE, A. (eds.) (1971). *Style in British Administration*. London; Allen and Unwin
CROZIER, M. (1964). *The Bureaucratic Phenomenon*. Paris; Grasset and London; Tavistock
CROZIER, M. (1979). *On ne réforme pas la société par décret*. Paris; Grasset
DAHL. R. A. and LINDBLOM, C. E. (1953). *Politics, Economics and Welfare*. New York; Harper and Row
DAHL, R. A. (1961). *Who Governs?* New Haven, Conn.; Yale University Press
DALE, H. E. (1941). *The Higher Civil Service in Britain*. London; Oxford University Press
DANZIGER, J. N. (1978). *Making Budgets*. London and Beverly Hills; Sage
DYE, T. R. (1966). *Politics, Economics and the Public*. Chicago; Rand McNally
DYE, T. R. (1973). *Understanding Public Policy*. Englewood Cliffs, N.J.; Prentice-Hall
FULTON COMMITTEE ON THE CIVIL SERVICE (1969). *Surveys and Investigations* **3** (1) and (2). London; H.M.S.O.
GRÉMION, P. (1976). *Le pouvoir périphérique*. Paris; Seuil

GULICK, L. and URWICK, L. (1937). *Papers on the Science of Administration.* New York; Institute of Public Administration

GULICK, L. and URWICK, L. (1943). *Elements of Administration.* London; Pitman

HANF, K. and SCHARPF, F. (eds.) (1978). *Interorganizational Policy-Making.* London and Beverly Hills; Sage

HECLO, H. (1974). *Modern Social Policy in Britain and Sweden.* New Haven, Conn.; Yale University Press

HUNTER, F. (1953). *Community Power Structure.* Chapel Hill, N.C.; University of North Carolina Press

LA PALOMBARA, J. (ed.) (1963). *Bureaucracy and Political Development.* Princeton, N.J.; Princeton University Press

MACKENZIE, W. J. M. and GROVE, J. W. (1957). *Central Administration in Britain.* London; Longmans

MILLS, C. W. (1959). *The Power Elite.* New York; Oxford University Press

POLSBY, N. W. (1963). *Community Power and Political Theory.* New Haven, Conn.; Yale University Press

ROSE, R. (ed.) (1980). *Challenge to Governance.* London and Beverly Hills: Sage

SHARKANSKY, I. (1970). *Policy Analysis in Political Science.* Chicago; Markham

SCHARPF, F. and HANF, K. (eds.) (1978). *Interorganizational Policy-Making.* London and Beverly Hills; Sage

SIMON, H. (1947). *Administrative Behaviour.* New York; Macmillan

WEBER, M. (1947). *The Theory of Social and Economic Organization.* Glencoe, Ill.; Free Press

WILDAVSKY, A. (1979). *The Art and Craft of Policy Analysis.* London; Macmillan

Chapter 4
Global models for one world

After Rousseau, and, in a decisive manner, Marx has taught us that social science cannot be built at the level of events any more than physics from what we observe with our senses: the aim is to build a model, to study its properties and the different ways it behaves in the laboratory, in order to apply these observations to the interpretation of what takes place in the empirical world.

C. Lévy-Strauss.

In the last quarter of the twentieth century, it seems particularly banal to state that the problem of development is the 'number one' question in the world. The expression 'developing countries' is in very common use; the problems of developing countries loom large in the minds of Westerners, even if Westerners often have no idea of how to tackle these problems and usually little real inclination to do something about them. In various vital ways, these problems are now forced on all of us: the crises of raw materials, famine, poverty and hunger, racial disturbances, military coups and great power involvement, overt or covert, are among the occurrences which contribute to make the developing world present in the minds of even the least travelled and most 'parochial' of Western Europeans and North Americans.

While it is quite commonplace to mention the current overwhelming importance of developing countries, it is perhaps not as commonplace to remark that the problems which these raise emerged suddenly, almost overnight, in front of a Western public opinion which was wholly unprepared for them and in front of a scholarly Western opinion which had never before even considered them. It may seem strange to note that, as late as 1960, two scholars, G. A. Almond and J. S. Coleman, could proudly assert, in the opening statement of their work, *The Politics of the Developing Areas,* that 'this book is the first effort to compare the political systems of the developing areas'. The discipline of politics had just never thought about the problem—nor had indeed the neighbouring disciplines of sociology and economics; the questions raised by 'development' were indeed entirely new, so much so that even the notion of development remained for a long time a very unclear concept more pregnant with emotional undertones than with logical content.

What were the problems which agitated scholars in the study of politics in the 1940s and 1950s before 'development' emerged as a major area of study? Some of them were small 'house-problems'; they concerned the organization of liberal-democracy, the content of constitutions, the relationship between government and parliament, the 'decline' of parliaments. The underlying endeavour was to find means of better implementing the great proposals of the thinkers of the past, from Aristotle to Rousseau. At the time, when Western democracies had been under very serious attack from dictatorships and had almost died, these 'house' problems did not seem unimportant either to scholars or to practitioners.

Their importance seemed indeed on the increase because, while the threats of fascism and Nazism had disappeared with the Allied victory in 1945, the threat of Communism was stronger than ever. Not surprisingly, one of the central themes of political science in the early post-war years was the analysis of Communism. It was now clear that 'socialist' or 'popular democracies' were here to stay, and with Mao's victory in 1949, the Communist 'model' of government was ruling a third of mankind. This situation posed, not merely an enormous economic and military challenge to democracies, but an intellectual challenge as well. Was the Communist system a genuinely acceptable alternative model—indeed, one which might even be superior to liberal-democracy and which would, as Communist writers suggested, eventually replace 'bourgeois democracy'? Political scientists found it hard to handle the question—in large part because the claims made by Communist states were so ostensibly at variance with the reality. There was perhaps more equality in the Soviet Union than in Tsarist Russia, but there was also as much tyranny, if not more. Most political scientists seemed to adopt the view, put forward by Carl Friedrich and many others, that the Communist system was merely a 'totalitarian model'—an 'evil' system which could in no way be presented as a model[2].

Meanwhile, an alternative view was beginning to be presented, according to which differences between Communist and advanced capitalist systems were perhaps not as large as was usually claimed. In his book entitled *The Managerial Revolution,* James Burnham put forward a 'convergence' thesis; he pointed out that both types of societies were increasingly run by anonymous managers with similar backgrounds, characteristics and outlooks. Perhaps both liberal-democratic and Communist 'models' were about to be replaced by a new 'bureaucratic' model, with sets of effective arrangements different from those of the systems from which both proceeded. But this view was shared by very few at the time: for the large majority, the Communist system was morally entirely wrong—and therefore not a 'model' in the true sense of the word.

The 1940s and 1950s were thus dominated by the attempt to understand what was going on in the world as a result of the confrontation between the two models of liberal-democracy and Communism. Few were meanwhile realizing that another intellectual challenge with immense practical implications was about to erupt from an entirely different quarter, that of the newly independent countries. But it is not surprising that this challenge should not have been foreseen, let alone carefully analysed. As late as 1960, almost all of Africa was still under colonial rule; the countries which had become independent in the 1940s and 1950s seemed ready, to begin with, to adopt the model of government of Western countries: the largest of these countries, India, had a system of government which, on the surface at least, was indistinguishable from those of Western countries. And it must be remembered that, for over a century, the first group of 'new' countries, those of Latin America, had readily adopted the principles of liberal-democracy, even if the practice was often very different. There had been, admittedly, here and there, some attempts at 'new'—populist—forms of government; Mexico and Turkey after World War I, Brazil perhaps in the 1930s, Argentina with Peron in the 1940s—all had undergone somewhat novel experiments attempting to move away from the broadly accepted blueprint of liberal-democracy. But these events had not been considered with care; they were viewed either as accidental or as bearing similarities with pre-war fascist endeavours.

Perhaps the first political development which truly announced the new challenge was the Egyptian Revolution of 1952 and the take-over by Nasser in 1954. The new Egyptian leader proclaimed that he was embarking on a new path, combining aggressive anti-Western policies on the international front with efforts at uplifting the Egyptian nation and the whole Arab world. He was, of course, still regarded by many Europeans as a 'conventional' dictator; but some observers at least began to realize that here was a development of a different character from military coups of the past. And the Egyptian Revolution was quickly followed by a number of similar events elsewhere: traditional monarchies began to tumble in the Middle East (the Iraqi was the first to fall in 1958); North Africa was fighting for its independence; colonial rule ended between 1960 and 1965 for almost the whole of the African continent. While Latin America had adopted for decades at least the trimmings of constitutional government and liberal-democracy, the newly independent states of the 1950s and 1960s were often quick to dismiss the political framework which they inherited from the 'mother countries' and set up what came to be described as 'mobilizing' regimes based usually on charismatic leadership, single party systems and a 'developmental' ideology.

These changes posed major problems for Western governments, public opinion and scholars. The first reaction had often been—as with respect to Nasser—to dismiss these experiments as mere tyrannies, not intrinsically different from the many tyrannies which had periodically taken roots in Latin America since the 1820s. But this was not the only reaction; and it soon became less prevalent than the opposite one, which looked at events in developing countries with greater interest. This interest was partly due to the economic ties between the West and what came to be known as the Third World, partly to the desire of the West to see that the new states did not come in the Communist orbit, but partly also to a genuine desire to work for the 'development' of these states (a desire which was, of course, in turn a consequence of guilt feelings in many sectors of Western public opinion). The new Third World forms of government were therefore considered at least with sympathy. Since Western countries attempted to advise the Third World in the administrative field, there was also considerable interest in the broader governmental experiments on which these countries embarked. By and large, it was believed that time should be given for the new systems to 'mature'.

This situation had a profound effect on political science, as indeed on other social science disciplines. To take seriously the forms of government emerging in the Third World meant that one needed to rethink the models which had hitherto prevailed in political science. A place had to be made for Third World systems alongside Western liberal-democratic and Eastern Communist systems. But this could not be done merely by juxtaposing the Third World to the other two 'worlds', because it seemed that Third World systems could not be understood merely in terms of 'conventional' political 'structures' as Western states and even Communist states could be analysed. Third World countries were often entirely new states; their economies were often rudimentary by Western and Eastern standards, and they aimed at catching up very fast with the West, but they were usually adamant to preserve their own culture, as well as their own social and even political structures. This meant that, to a large extent, 'conventional' studies of government began to look narrow because liberal-democracy was not applied in many parts of the world, narrow also because studies of government concentrated on purely political aspects and allowed little room for the relationship between government and society, narrow, too, because they appeared based on a static conception of the world, while what was required was an understanding of the movement of social and political forces. Thus, at the very moment when technical advances occurred in specialized subjects such as elections and administration, the core of the study of government seemed to be in need of almost total reconstruction.

Not surprisingly, the efforts made in political science to understand the characteristics of the processes of Third World countries had slow and uneven results. Not surprisingly, too, they led to considerable scholarly controversies which in many ways were the replicas of ideological and even emotional controversies raised by the condition of the Third World states and by the inequalities between these and the Western countries. The search for a global model enhanced the level of the intellectual debates within the study of government; but it also led to a maze of somewhat esoteric questions and to a large number of different 'approaches'. It must be remembered as we are about to examine at least some of these approaches that the magnitude and novelty of the problems could not but lead to these academic controversies and will indeed lead to similar controversies for a long time to come.

The *Politics of the Developing Areas* and the heyday of structural-functionalism

The first of the endeavours devoted to integrating the Third World within a global model of government was that of G. A. Almond and J. S. Coleman in *The Politics of the Developing Areas*. This work was to achieve rapid notoriety, only to be heavily criticized soon afterwards. Perhaps because it was the first, the scheme was extremely ambitious and made exaggerated claims. The model may have come too early, many important problems posed by the development of the Third World countries were simply ignored, many concepts were insufficiently analysed and practical difficulties were overlooked. Almond and Coleman may have embarked in too precipitous a manner on a scheme which seemed intellectually satisfying. Yet *The Politics of the Developing Areas* did exercise a marked influence; and the importance of the book is considerable, as it opened up a line of inquiry without which studies of government might have appeared irrelevant or at least unconcerned with the new problems of the world.

The aim of Almond and Coleman was to provide a framework for analysis which would do justice to the way in which the new countries of the Third World were governing themselves; but a major stumbling block was the fact that we had come to associate 'modern' political life with the institutions of liberal-democracy— with parties competing at elections, with legistlatures, with governments giving 'orders' to a neutral civil service. A century of belief in constitutional government had led scholars and the public to the conclusion that the representation of the people, for instance, could take place only, or only relatively well, through the medium of an elected legislature in which parties expressed the different shades of opinion. This therefore made it impossible to believe that effective representation was taking place within Communist systems, where the legislature was totally ineffective and where one party seemed to monopolize power. The belief in constitutional forms was also making it difficult to understand the workings of many of the new countries, since legislatures were often weak and parties either did not exist or had little real hold over the population. Bodies such as tribes or the military played a major part in the life of these governments, but these organizations did not fit in the framework within which liberal-democratic politics operated: did *tribes* 'correspond' to *parties* in the West? Did the military play the part of parties? A new framework had to be devised by which one could describe the part played by the institutions and processes of Third World countries: only then would it become possible to assess in an 'objective' manner whether these systems were more or less 'effective' than the liberal-democratic governments based on interest groups, parties and legislatures.

Almond and Coleman felt that 'structural-functionalism', which was enjoying great success in the 1950s in American sociology, especially because of the reputation of Talcott Parsons, might help them to achieve their aim[3]. For, if the problem was to find a framework to analyse countries which would not be based solely on the analysis of and the comparison between similar institutions, such as parties or legislatures, what was needed was a means of relating institutions—'structures'—to a general, indeed universal frame of reference. This frame of reference seemed to exist: it appeared to be constituted by the 'purposes' or 'functions' which institutions or structures fulfilled. While there were specific institutions—specific to a country, or specific to a type of political system—the functions were general, in that every political system attempted to do the same thing—namely, govern. Basically, the proposed scheme was dependent on three points: first, that all societies had institutions of government; second, that each of these institutions fulfilled some 'function' in the process of government; and third, that the political process everywhere fulfilled identical functions.

We need to consider these three points a little more, in view of the controversies which arose, some of which were due to lack of precision and even exaggerated claims on the part of the authors of *The Politics of the Developing Areas*. At one level, none of these three points was controversial, but, at others, they were; they needed therefore to be made very carefully (more carefully than they were indeed made). First, it seemed reasonable to state that every country had institutions of government in the very broad sense; as a matter of fact one cannot see how a society could maintain itself without governmental institutions of some kind. What was often the case, of course, was that the *political* institutions were not necessarily distinct from social institutions: the tribal leadership could, for instance, provide both the basis for 'social control' and be the source of political decisions. Thus if one were to note that the institutions of government could either be specific political institutions or be 'social' institutions also involved in 'non-political' aspects of society, it was certainly permissible to state that there were institutions of government everywhere. In passing, one had discovered the matter of institutional 'differentiation'—a point on which Almond and others were later to lay much emphasis.

It seemed equally sensible to state that all institutions fulfilled some purpose or function, although one should be careful, because of the many meanings attached to the word 'function'[4]: neither Almond nor other 'functionalists' seemed always to have been sufficiently precise in this regard, and much criticism ensued as a consequence. What is non-controversial is that institutions result in certain things being achieved and achieved in a certain way. *Ex post facto*, once one has looked at an institution, one can conclude that a given purpose has been achieved; for instance, one can note that a pressure group for the defence of old people results in the needs of old people being articulated and taken care of. And the 'functions' can be considered at various degrees of abstraction. An organization promoting the interests of old people can therefore be described in terms of its practical achievements; it can also be described in terms of the way in which it gives a say to a section of the community and therefore achieves an element of representation. Not surprisingly, efforts to elaborate a general model will result in greater concentration on the more abstract and the more general of these functions. This may lead to practical difficulties because, of course, it is sometimes difficult to be sure of what the achievements of a particular institution are; but this is a matter of careful empirical analysis, not a theoretical problem. Having established what the achievements of a particular institution are, and given that institutions last over time, one is then permitted to state generally that a particular institution fulfils a given function. In passing, one has to note, however, that institutions may achieve this function more or less well: old people may be taken care of more or less satisfactorily by an interest group concerned with old age.

Yet while it is permissible to examine an institution and to conclude that it achieves a certain function (more or less well), it is not permissible to assume that it is *in the nature* of this institution, so to speak, to fulfil a given function, nor is it permissible to claim that an institution exists *in order* to fulfil a given function; these are points where functionalists have been rightly criticized, because they introduce an element of 'inevitability' which we have no right to introduce. All we know is that the institution happens to fulfil a particular function. Perhaps, at the end of the day, and after exhaustive analyses, we might be able to conclude that a particular function is always achieved in a certain manner; but this cannot be stated *a priori*, especially because, as we noted earlier, we do not know in advance whether a given function is performed well or badly by an institution.

Some confusion does arise, however, because it is also true that institutions are sometimes set up with a particular aim in mind— for instance, organizations for old people are set up *in order* to further the interests of old people—and it would then seem reasonable to conclude that such institutions exist to fulfil that function. Yet, even then, we do not know to what extent the institution does actually fulfil the 'function' for which it was set up; it may do so so very badly, be small, or irrelevant, or be more concerned with other matters. It still cannot be claimed *a priori* that if fulfils the function of representation of old people. Moreover, not all institutions are set up *in order* to achieve a function: specifically, the broad institutions which have existed for generations may fulfil some functions without having been 'set up' in a conscious, purposeful manner. Indeed, it seems that, by and large, while many political institutions in liberal-democracies are set up with a 'function' in mind (legislatures, for instance), the broad social institutions have usually emerged without any clear 'purpose'. Social scientists remain entitled to look at all these institutions and state *ex post facto* that they do fulfil some function, but they are not entitled to go further and claim that the function is 'inherent' in the institutions or that the institution exists 'in order' to fulfil that function.

We have therefore already discovered many dangers with respect to the relationship between institutions and the functions which they fulfil. But there are even greater problems with respect to the third point on which the framework is based, namely the view that the functions, or purposes, are universal. Clearly, it would not be very useful to state that each institution fulfils a function, if each function was different; one would come out with an enormous list of functions alongside the various institutions. The idea becomes useful only if one can reduce the number of 'functions' to a small number existing everywhere. While such an endeavour seemed in principle theoretically and even practically feasible, it turned out to raise difficulties which the authors of *The Politics of the Developing Areas* did not succeed in overcoming.

Easton's contribution to the structural-functional framework

It seemed that these universal functions existed and Almond and Coleman did indeed believe that they could elaborate a tight scheme on the basis of these functions. They relied heavily on the work which David Easton was independently in the process of elaborating and which was to be fully developed in *A Systems Analysis of Political Life*, which was published in 1965. Easton's effort aimed also at discovering a general model; in the 1950s, he had been complaining bitterly about 'hyper-factualism' in political science at the time[5]. But Easton's starting point was not to find a framework within which Third World countries could be analysed alongside Western liberal-democracies; the aim was more general: it was to understand the nature of all political systems in a deductive manner. Easton therefore started by a definition of politics based, not on institutions, but on the activity of politics which, he showed, was universal; it consisted of a process by which 'values' were allocated in an 'authoritative manner', that is to say, of decisions by which goods (physical and moral goods) were distributed in a way 'acceptable' to the society.

This activity led to a 'cycle' or 'sequence', starting with demands for certain policies or programmes, which were then elaborated in greater detail; they were 'adopted' and turned into laws and regulations which were implemented, only to give rise to further demands which were eventually to follow the same sequence. Political activity thus occurred everywhere according to the same broad pattern—irrespective of the institutions which would help to elaborate, adopt and eventually implement the decisions.

Since political activity followed a universal sequence, it followed that one could subdivide the political process into a number of elements which would also exist in all political systems. And Easton proceeded to indicate what these elements were. One was the elaboration of inputs, during which policies were suggested and pressed on the political system; the other was the development of outputs, during which policies were formally adopted in the name of the state and then implemented by agents appointed for this purpose.

Easton's analysis stopped at this point, because he was concerned with a theoretical presentation of his model. But Almond and Coleman had to be more precise because, for them, the Easton cycle was the reference frame which they needed in order to be able to relate the institutions of the various countries to a general framework. By discovering a universal cycle of political activity, Easton had given Almond and Coleman the starting point which they needed: the elements of this universal sequence could constitute the 'functions' of every political system to which 'structures' would then be related. But, as it was not sufficient to subdivide the sequence into only two elements, Almond and Coleman proceeded to re-examine these and found that they were indeed made of a succession of aspects, of 'sub-functions', which they named 'articulation', 'aggregation', 'rule-making', 'rule-implementation', 'rule-adjudication'. Articulation was the phase during which demands were presented; during the aggregation phase, demands were brought together in the form of policies. Then came rule-making, followed by implementation and by adjudication when there were conflicts over the implementation of rules. This description seemed universal; it seemed also to make the model of Easton more practical. One last hurdle had to be overcome, however, namely to relate existing institutions to the various 'functions' or phases of the political process which Almond and Coleman had outlined. This was to prove a major stumbling block.

As Almond and Coleman themselves pointed out in what was perhaps the most perceptive section of their work ('Towards a probabilistic theory of the polity'), institutions are multi-purpose[6]; they cannot therefore be related to a function on the basis of a simple one-to-one linkage. The scheme must be more elaborate; to be precise, it must be based on the proportion of the activities of each institution which is related to each function. A political party, for instance, is concerned with the articulation and the aggregation of demands; it may even dictate to the government the rules to be made and eventually oversee the implementation of these rules; and the point is even truer of bodies such as tribes which, being 'undifferentiated' social groups, probably cover almost all the activities of a political character in a traditional country.

Although Almond and Coleman recognized the problem, they could not overcome the empirical difficulties which stemmed from the multi-purpose character of institutions. They had found a way of describing the political system, but only provided they could measure precisely the extent to which a given institution performed simultaneously or successively the various 'functions' in which it was involved: it did not seem possible to undertake such a measurement. Consequently, one might say vaguely that a party such as the Communist Party of the Soviet Union is 'more' involved in the implementation of rules than a party such as the British Labour Party; one might go further and claim that Communist regimes are characterized by a higher level of involvement of parties in the 'implementation process' than is the case in liberal-democracies. This is already an achievement; but this is not sufficient to elaborate a precise model which would help to locate different countries in a general 'space'. Structural-functionalism seemed to have considerable potential; but it was in practice of little use, given the level of empirical knowledge of the workings of institutions in the countries of the world and given the tools of analysis available to political scientists.

The analysis of the development process through 'institution-building'

Whether Gabriel Almond realized that a global model based on the relationship between structures and functions could not be constructed in practice is not clear; but a noticeable shift of emphasis occurred in the subsequent years, both in Almond's work and in that of other American political scientists who were broadly associated with the 'structural-functional' approach. Instead of exploring further the line which he had opened in *The Politics of the Developing Areas* by attempting to specify which functions institutions 'fulfilled' in given societies, Almond became increasingly concerned with a different problem which may have seemed to him to provide more swiftly the means of building a global, but also practically useful model. This approach consisted in attempting to assess whether institutions were effective or performed their functions 'well'. The idea seemed potentially fruitful—indeed very sensible. It appeared reasonable to claim that institutions were likely to be more or less successful in achieving their goals, that they were, to use Almond's expression, more or less 'capable' of handling the problems which had to be solved; and it seemed equally sensible to argue further that some configurations of institutions were more 'capable' than others to provide a solution to the problems facing a society.

Indeed, such an approach had the advantage over the descriptive presentation of the earlier analysis of coming more closely to grips with the problem of development. Both Easton's framework and the adaptation made to it by Almond and Coleman could justifiably be criticized for being 'static': they attempted to present a comprehensive picture of political life in various types of societies, but they did not give an idea of the directions in which institutions were moving. Conceivably, if and when the picture had been completed, differences among societies from the point of view of their institutional arrangements might have enabled us to infer differences in development. But the method did not by itself focus on the process of development, or on the ways in which institutions changed over time. It seemed, on the contrary, that, by examining the 'capabilities' of institutions and of a configuration of institutions, the process of development could be studied directly.

In a second formulation of his model, published in 1966 in *Comparative Politics*, Almond considered therefore a number of elements which seemed particularly important to determine the capacity of political systems. Similar ideas were developed by S. P. Huntington, whose work, *Political Order in Changing Societies*, appeared in 1968. Four characteristics seemed particularly relevant. The first was, naturally enough, the process of institutionalization. It seemed reasonable to state that, to be effective, a political system needed to have a network of well-organized political institutions. 'The level of political community a society achieves,' said Huntington, 'reflects the relationship between its political institutions and the social forces which comprise it'[7]. And he added: 'The level of political development of a society in large part depends upon the extent to which ... political activities belong to and identify with a variety of political institutions'[8]. Otherwise, demands will remain diffuse and the processes by which they can be handled will remain unsatisfactory.

But it is not sufficient for institutions to be set up for them to acquire importance in a political system. They have to be 'recognized' as having importance, they have to be credible; this is what the process of 'institutionalization' achieves. Over time, the purposes of the institution become accepted, with the result that those who wish to achieve an aim—for instance, introduce a demand—will use the institution as a necessary step; citizens use interest groups in order to put pressure on the government. On the other hand, as long as institutions are not recognized, it is difficult to know where pressure can be put in order to make a demand, and the overall capacity of the political system seems reduced. It seems therefore quite reasonable to conclude that political systems will be 'improved' through the development of the institutionalization process.

One related aspect of this move towards a more 'mature' political system is 'differentiation'. Traditional political systems are undifferentiated; for instance, in a primitive system, a tribe may be an 'all-purpose' body which is equally in charge of running the local affairs of the tribe, of putting pressure on the political system of the nation, and of implementing decisions. Such a state of affairs would appear to be 'inefficient', and to become increasingly inefficient as the society becomes more complex. On the contrary, 'developed' or 'advanced' political systems appear to have a multitude of political institutions each of which is in charge of only a limited part of the whole of the political process. Some institutions (such as pressure groups) deal with demands, others (such as bureaucracies) implement policies; indeed, bureaucracies are composed of a large variety of differentiated sub-units, central as well as local. The division of labour within the political system would appear to be a prerequisite of increased capacity. And, consequently, a desire to develop the political system would seem to entail greater differentiation among political institutions.

The requirement to have differentiated political institutions had to be balanced against another requirement, which is in some manner contradictory, that of integration, often discussed in terms of 'nation-building'. One of the major problems which new states have to face is the low level of allegiance of the citizens to the national unit, while the allegiance to some of the component parts—tribal, ethnic, religious bodies—is much greater; in some cases these 'component' bodies cut across the boundaries of states created along the lines of colonial administrative divisions, as occurs often in Africa. Clearly, the decisions of the state will not be implemented easily in such a situation; and clearly, too, the demands of certain members of the community coming, for instance, from a minority tribe, may often simply not be passed on to the central governmental machine, let alone be the basis of future decisions.

Thus the problem of national integration has attracted the

attention of those who wished to see developing countries 'move' towards a state of more advanced development. Evidence from many countries, in Africa and elsewhere (Zaire, Chad, Nigeria and Uganda, but also Iraq and Iran, as well as ethnically divided Latin America countries) has shown with regular monotony that 'plural' societies were unable to achieve high levels of 'political' development[9]. Indeed, evidence drawn from Western countries in the past and at present also shows that the difficulties encountered by ethnically or linguistically divided countries are often unsurmountable; there is often a paralysis of the political system or at least a low 'capacity' of the political system (Belgium and Canada seem to be good examples of this state of affairs).

If institutionalization, differentiation and integration seemed to be important factors in the development process, they seemed to be more generally encompassed in a fourth and more general question: the political systems of developing countries seemed to lack legitimacy, while, on the contrary, Western institutions and Western political systems appeared to be supported by the population. There is therefore a need to increase the legitimacy of the new states; it is important, consequently, to discover ways of building institutions designed to achieve this purpose.

The unsolved problem of the improvement of the 'capacity' of political systems

A number of problems were thus identified and these helped to distinguish between 'developed' and 'developing' societies. But, as with the earlier formulation of 'structural-functionalism', it soon became clear that there was little practical way of measuring the extent to which individual countries scored in terms of institutionalization, differentiation, integration or legitimacy. To begin with, these concepts were never defined with precision, and it was therefore difficult to test their importance operationally. What institutionalization means, for instance, may be clear intuitively, but what it means specifically is much less clear. It has been said that 'institutionalization is the process by which organizations and procedures acquire value and stability[10]. But value is a vague word which refers in a general fashion to 'recognition' and therefore indirectly to legitimacy and 'stability' is a concept which, while ostensibly very simple, becomes very difficult to define as soon as one notices that one characteristic of organizations is to change a little every day and yet remain 'the same': does a party change if it changes its name? Conversely does it remain 'the same' if its membership, leadership structure, even goals become different? And what is true of institutionalization applies equally to differentiation, to integration, to legitimacy. While these concepts are manifestly important in the evolution of societies, their definition is so elusive that they are, in practice, extremely difficult to use in order to build a precise model of the development of societies.

If it is difficult to define these concepts precisely, it is therefore difficult to provide a real proof of the impact which they have on the evolution of societies. It does seem to be the case that institutionalization helps a political system to become more advanced; but this general impression does not constitute a proof. It does seem to be the case that integration is an important prerequisite of development, but, as a matter of fact, some highly developed countries such as Belgium or Canada are not markedly integrated. As one cannot, at least as yet, measure degrees of integration precisely, it is not possible to say whether the level of integration of, say, Sri Lanka or Nigeria is markedly lower than that of Belgium. But, unless it is proved that this is the case, one has either to show that low integration can be compensated for by other elements, as yet undetermined, or to conclude that integration may not be as important a factor in political development as it seems ostensibly to be.

Moreover, it is usually felt that time is a requirement for the 'improvement' of political institutions, in that only with time do all the factors which we have discussed result in an effect on the political system. But the way in which time has this effect is unclear; and we are not as yet in a position to say how long it takes for significant improvements to occur. The examination of past cases does not seem to provide much guidance; variations in time are considerable, as far as one can judge, between the process of 'legitimization' or 'institutionalization' in one country and the same process in another. Indeed, even when much time has elapsed, levels of integration or legitimacy do not always improve significantly. Examples drawn from the history of European countries show that levels of legitimacy may remain low over generations (France is a case in point) while elsewhere (as in post-war Germany) there appears to be a rapid, almost instantaneous improvement from a very low level to a very high level of legitimacy of political institutions.

This suggests that the effect of time can be altered by the presence of some further factors. It is indeed often suggested that some institutions can play such a part, although this brings about a further element of imprecision. A strong single party, military rule, a charismatic leader are often said to help improve levels of integration or legitimacy: indeed, one of the main reasons given for the imposition of a single party system is that the divisive influence of tribes and ethnic groups has to be broken. Similarly, military rule is often justified on grounds of integration. It would therefore seem that these institutional arrangements can cut the time needed for integration to take place. But these hypotheses still need closer examination before they can be adopted as valid and form one of the cornerstones of a general model of develop-ment—a point which led some scholars, more recently, as we shall see in Chapter 7, to concentrate on a middle-range analysis rather than on a 'global' undertaking.

Finally, perhaps the major difficulty of this global approach is its lack of overall goals. Almond is concerned with the improvement of the capability of the political system; so is Huntington, who wishes to prevent decay as well as ensure progress. But for what purpose? To achieve which results? Are the goals 'self evident'? In the early 1960s, many thought probably that they were; but it soon became obvious that this was not the case. Thus from the mid-1960s onwards, the study of development led to a reassess-ment of the real meanings of development—and underdevelop-ment.

Development and underdevelopment

The studies which we examined up to now have been American. It is in the United States that the search for a new model occurred, but it occurred, as we saw, by gradual modifications of the 'traditional' approach based on the analysis of liberal-democratic institutions. The first model attempted to discover a more general yardstick which would, so to speak, avoid loading the analysis against Third World countries and their institutions; the second model attempted to list the various ways in which new societies were likely to differ from 'developed' societies, these being, by implication, the liberal-democracies. Thus there was more than a grain of truth in the view which began to be expressed, among Third World scholars in particular, but also among some Western scholars, especially European, according to which analyses of 'development' on the 'structural-functional' model were essential-ly Western-based.

Critics claimed that there was no justification for such a state of affairs, all the more insidious because it was implicit. They noted, for instance, that the original functions in the first structural-functional model were so closely related to the part played by interest groups, parties, legislatures, governments, bureaucracies and courts in Western societies that Almond and Coleman were simply giving new names to a political process directly borrowed from Western arrangements. And they also remarked that, not surprisingly, the 'development' towards institutionalization, differentiation or integration was one which made Western countries appear necessarily more 'developed'; Almond's presentation at the end of *Comparative Politics* of a two-dimensional diagram of the development process places liberal-democracies at the 'developed' end on both dimensions, while Communist countries score low on one dimension and Third World countries also score low on one or even both of the two axes[11].

It may, of course, be the case that Western liberal-democracies are more advanced than Communist or Third World states; but this conclusion seemed more often held as axiomatic by the writers on political development of the early part of the 1960s than argued on the basis of systematic evidence. What evidence there was was often circumstantial or very vague. For instance, Western liberal-democracies seemed to be regarded as the most politically developed countries because they were advanced economically—at any rate highly industrialized—and because they seemed to 'score high' on a battery of social indicators, such as numbers of doctors, percentage of the population in schools and universities, etc. But, independently from the fact that some radical critics of the West claimed that these social and economic benefits were due in part at least to the exploitation of the Third World, it did not seem right to claim that political development followed automatically—axiomatically almost—from social and economic advance. Admittedly, evidence of political advance was also given, in part, in terms of the extent of freedom and political equality prevailing in Western countries, and in part in terms of the efficiency of the institutions which seemed to characterize these countries. But, while it was obviously true that Western countries were industrial countries and Third World countries, in the main, were not, the claims made by Western countries about the levels of freedom and even more equality were somewhat more doubtful. The institutions on which structural-functionalists based their assertion of the greater political development of the West were often recognized to be undemocratic, weakly organized or very bureaucratic: this was the case with many interest groups and parties. Business groups and financial organizations often seemed able to manipulate the political system of Western countries to their advantage although they did not belong to the official structure of government and were not responsible to the electorate. It was felt that, conversely, the part played either by tribes or by new single parties and other more modern social organizations of the Third World were not regarded in a sufficiently positive manner by Western political scientists but were dismissed as either wholly traditional or insufficiently implanted and therefore contributing to a low level of political development.

These criticisms were pointing to the conclusion that the discipline of politics had embarked collectively, so to speak, on a study of political development without being at all clear as to what was meant by the concept, not merely precisely, but even in a broad manner. With hindsight, it may seem surprising that the question of the definition of political development had not been raised earlier, at the very moment when the matter of development arose. This may have been because, at the time, Western political scientists, and American political scientists in particular, were implicitly and even explicitly convinced that Western liberal-democracies were unquestionably more advanced than other political systems; indeed, even supporters of Communist regimes recognized then the advanced character of industrial capitalist societies by comparison with others. There was therefore little or no questioning of the developed character of Western systems; and the institutional arrangements of Western countries were also felt to be more advanced.

Under the impact of criticisms made by Third World social scientists and by Western social scientists who associated with the Third World, the need to elaborate more rigorous criteria became patent. But it then became also quickly clear that these criteria were difficult to elaborate. Surveying the field in his work on *Aspects of Political Development* published in 1966, L. W. Pye listed ten different definitions of political development covering such goals as social and economic development, democracy and administrative efficiency. He concluded that it was not reasonable to adopt a single criterion only, but that one should take into account a number of factors, including equality, the 'massness' of the society, capacity and differentiation[12].

Gradually, the efforts undertaken to discover a precise meaning to political development as such led to the need to distinguish it from its social and economic counterparts; social or economic progress could be viewed as linked to, but different from political progress. Moreover, it was also gradually realized that political development had to be kept from institutional improvements: institutions may be the instruments of political progress; they are not ends in themselves. Political development, in its deepest meaning, had to be related to an ideal image of society and to the values which society should embody. It was D. Apter who saw most clearly the need to relate political progress to an overall goal; in his *Choice and the Politics of Allocation* (1973), he defined political development as the endeavour to expand the opportunities for choice given to citizens: societies which offered more choice were on the way to political progress[13].

One merit of this definition stems from its close connection to a broad societal goal: a political system which offers more choice is 'bigger', so to speak, in that it incorporates more of the values, desires, of more individuals. But the definition has a further merit: it succeeds in circumventing the main difficulty arising from the link between development and the values of the society, for such a link makes the definition subjective in that one man's value may not suit another man. For instance, if political development is based on equality, or 'massness', or indeed freedom, one may retort that other goals have an equally good claim to become societal aims. By stating that political development relates to the expansion of choice opportunities, Apter links the concept to all the values of all the individuals, whatever they are: the aim of politics is to give everyone as much chance as possible to do what he or she wishes to achieve. The concept is 'value-loaded', but in the direction of giving maximum importance to what individuals want.

So far, Apter's idea has not been used in empirical analyses, but it does provide guidelines towards operationalization: it seems possible to assess whether citizens have or not a variety of choices. Institutions can also be measured according to this yardstick, but they are not part of the definition. And social and economic progress remain distinct from political progress. Finally, as this approach does not presuppose, explicitly, that Western societies are 'better' than others, Apter can be said to have provided political science with a very valuable conceptual tool for future studies of development.

Why and how does the development occur?

Yet the studies which we have discussed up to now left unanswered one set of important questions: why does development occur? Why are some countries more developed than others? And by what processes does development take place? In one form or another, all the models which we examined tended to *describe* development; they did not attempt to give reasons for development nor to detail the stages through which countries may have to go. And yet these are perhaps the most fundamental questions, both in theory and in practice. If we do not know how development occurs, it seems difficult to see how developing countries and their leaders can be advised about how to move towards further advance. These 'models' did not therefore amount to a genuine 'theory'.

A piecemeal theory of political change

Indeed the approaches which we discussed did not concentrate on a theory of the development process. They started from a standpoint, which they inherited, of what might be called 'instantaneous voluntarism', with respect to improvements of political life. Liberals had believed that political change was to be introduced by constitutional reforms; more recently, the setting-up of parties and interest groups and the organization of the civil service on a 'merit' basis were included among the reforms which were required for 'good government'. But all these changes could be achieved either immediately, or very quickly, if there was sufficient 'will' on the part of the population. The legacy of traditional liberal-democracy was that political change was a matter for action by 'good men', not a long 'process' of social transformation.

Not surprisingly, this view lingered on in political studies in the early post-war period, especially because liberal-democratic reforms still seemed to depend largely on legal change. What experience had shown, however, was that a number of 'conditions' had to be fulfilled if liberal-democratic institutions were to be maintained and lead to political stability. The analyses of S. M. Lipset and others, for instance, to which we have already referred, had indicated that a certain level of economic development was required to avoid the return of authoritarian government or the recurrence of military coups[14]. It followed that those who wanted to ensure stability had also to ensure that economic development was steady and substantial. To this prerequisite were gradually added other conditions, which we examined earlier; it seemed that legitimacy, integration, institutionalization could only be achieved relatively slowly; thus institutions were felt to remain fragile for a period, although, as we also saw, structural-functionalists were not able to specify the precise duration during which, nor the exact conditions under which institutions remained, so to speak, in a state of 'probation'.

Structural-functionalists thus had only an embryonic 'theory' of development: it was vague; it emerged piecemeal; it included a mixture of voluntarism and 'inevitability', as the will to introduce reforms was needed, but there had also to be a 'sound' economic substructure over which political reforms had at best very little control. Some achievements could be immediate, others depended on an (unspecified) time sequence. The result was therefore more in the nature of a number of recipes than in the form of a coherent theory. And while these recipes might lead to 'political development', they were so vague about the character and timing of the result that they offered only limited hope to those who desperately wanted to bring about a brighter future.

As the problem raised by the need to improve the economic substructure and to strengthen institutions was better explored, a variation was added, which was specifically concerned with the Third World. This variation was due to the recognition that developing countries had (or often had) to undergo a period of 'modernization' or 'mobilization' during which institutions designed specifically to improve the economic performance, on the one hand, and to achieve better integration and greater legitimacy on the other were to be set up. Apter, in his earlier work on *The Politics of Modernization*, published in 1964, examined in particular the role of the 'mobilizing' single-party system; this was to reintroduce an element of 'voluntarism' in those aspects of the model of development which was previously outlined and which were characterized by apparent 'inevitability'. Since liberal-democratic institutions could not be expected to lead to a stable system unless the economic substructure was modern enough and unless the integration and legitimacy of the state, to begin with, were sufficient, it was helpful for the model of development to be able to show that these results could be attained more quickly if certain institutions were set up. On the hypothesis that a country would perform better if the 'will to perform' was present, one could conclude that a truly mobilizing party would lead to greater and quicker performance because it would pull the energies of the population towards the improvement of the country. Thus developing countries might short-circuit some of the difficulties which they faced. Admittedly, the setting up of a single party and of a number of peripheral organizations (such as trade unions, cooperatives, youth organizations) also posed a problem: these bodies had to become legitimate. This is why a strong charismatic leader was always, or at least very often, needed to help put in orbit the 'mobilizing' institutions which might lead the country towards development.

A 'theory' of political development thus emerged in the 1960s alongside and partly in conjunction with the efforts of the 'structural-functionalists' to elaborate a general model of politics. This development theory gave a mixture of hope and despair. Despite some additions and amendments, it still combined 'voluntarism' and 'inevitability' in a rather vague manner; indeed it could be said that the theory had to resort to a *deus ex machina* (the charismatic leader) when it could provide no logical way out. And the theory remained Western-based: the 'reconciling' system (Apter) of Western liberal-democracies was felt to be 'better', although it was not applicable, for a period at least, in the developing world.

The Marxist theory of development and the notion of dependence

Not surprisingly, this piecemeal approach to political development attracted substantial criticism, both for its lack of intellectual coherence and for its 'paternatlistic' Western arrogance. It seemed that developing countries were advised to show patience in order to build gradually the foundations of a stable political system; upheavals were felt to have the effect of preventing improvements in legitimacy, integration and institutionalization, and they should therefore be avoided.

Yet such a reformist view is at best controversial, if one judges by past political developments, including the past developments of many of the contemporary liberal-democracies. Change had often taken place through revolutions, a state of affairs which liberal-democrats often chose to forget since it did not tally with the reformist and constitutional principles of liberal-democracy. But, to the extent that a change of will had to occur for reforms to take place, it was *prima facie* at least as sensible to claim that such a change of will would not take place unless a break in the 'natural sequence' also changed the outlook of many of the leading members of the polity. And, if this view was felt to be acceptable, it seemed that the main problems were to forecast when the revolution would take place and to hasten its occurrence by discovering the conditions leading to it.

Marxism provided apparently the best answers to both these problems. The Marxist analysis of revolutionary situations arising out of successive stages of development clearly constituted a 'theory' in the strong sense of the word; and it seemed to meet the ideological and practical requirements of developing countries. It gave an explanation of poverty and backwardness—the domination by the capitalist bourgeoisie; it constituted a dynamic approach, as the increased concentration of capital was leading to increased exploitation but also to increased resentment; and it provided hope, as the revolution was considered to be inevitable.

But Marxism in Marx's presentation concerned industrial societies only. Lenin had to make an important addition, by stressing that developing (then colonial) countries were the new proletariat. This made it possible to achieve a double aim. First, the conditions of developing countries could be accounted for; and, second, the fact that Western industrial societies were richer ceased to be viewed as an argument in favour of the West's advance but merely the consequence of the exploitation of the developing countries. A major flaw in the Western 'theory' of development had always been that it did not provide an explanation of the backwardness of the Third World, except in so far as some blamed the colonial system for underdevelopment. On the contrary, the Leninist argument about exploitation by imperialists does provide an explanation and leads to the corollary that only an abolition of world-wide capitalism could create the prerequisite for the development of the Third World. It is, of course, arguable as to whether the impact of capitalism on the Third World has been either so profound or indeed so negative. But it is, on the other hand, rather difficult to find any explanation for underdevelopment, and indeed for poverty among Western countries, except by claiming that there are intrinsic cultural and socio-psychological reasons for this underdevelopment and this poverty, a line of argument which unquestionably leads directly to a form of 'racism': poorer countries are poor because they are simply not enterprising enough. While it seems plausible that some countries are, on the whole, less technologically or even commercially inclined than others, it seems difficult to claim, as there is no clear evidence in this direction, that such a proposition relates to the whole of the Third World. And, since this is the case, supporters of the Western theory of development are left, as the Marxists suggest, without an overarching explanatory argument.

Given what they see as a marked distance between claims and reality, Marxists are also particularly anxious to demonstrate that much of the legitimacy of Western institutions and of the constitutional model lies in the ideological stranglehold by which Western citizens and indeed many Third World elites are subjugated. Freedom is used, in the Marxist interpretation, in a cynical manner in order to legitimize modes of political, social and economic behaviour which benefit only a minority. It is the Darwinian freedom by which the rich, the clever, the powerful have the ability to dominate the rest. And peace and reconciliation are viewed as ideological devices by which the poor and the oppressed are made to keep quiet while others can benefit from the situation. History seems to suggest that nothing in the past has happened without major conflict; it is a 'trick' of capitalism to make people believe that conflict can now be superseded by peace and harmony.

From these analyses emerged, especially in the 1960s in the Third World, the theory of the 'dependence' of developing countries on Western industrial societies: this dependence is inherent in the nature of world capitalism because capitalism needs world-wide markets to maintain itself; it can be abolished only through a revolutionary break from capitalism on the part of countries suffering from underdevelopment. In these circumstances, the aim of Marxist and other radical scholars is to fill in the global model which they inherited from Marx and Lenin with detailed analyses which help to show the circumstances under which the revolution is likely to occur and therefore to be hastened. It becomes essential to study the relative strength of groups in different societies, because, in the Marxist interpretation, only when groups representing the oppressed have a certain objective dimension can society reach a crisis point at which the conflict can end in the victory of the oppressed group. This was what made Marx suggest that capitalism would disappear only once property was concentrated in a very few hands indeed. This prognostication proved wrong in a variety of ways, and not least because capitalism was so weakened by World War I in the Soviet Union that a strictly political take-over was possible before industrialization had reached its peak, but the idea of conflicts among groups is so central to the Marxist and neo-Marxist interpretation that it still constitutes a major element of the academic analyses which are conducted from a Marxist standpoint; it is also a constant theme addressed to those who wish to undertake a struggle against political, social and economic establishments. It is a central part of the concern of Marxists and neo-Marxists to achieve a 'correct' analysis of the specific position of groups in the different societies: the result is that, paradoxically enough, an approach which is based on the highly abstract theory of group conflicts between oppressed and oppressors, leads to large numbers of detailed studies of a historical character designed to find out whether a particular situation indeed corresponds to a strong group conflict and is therefore likely or not to lead to an overall crisis. This was the approach already adopted by Marx himself, for instance when he examined the abortive revolutionary movements of nineteenth century France[15].

These analyses are often too detailed to lead to clear conclusions and, being historical, they do not facilitate prediction. But they play a crucial part in the analysis because one problem for Marxists is to be able to assess whether a situation is 'objectively ripe' for revolution. However, as another problem is the degree of 'consciousness' of the 'exploited' classes, Marxist analysis is also directly concerned with the extent to which 'dominant' ideologies can be expected to undermine this consciousness. This is why much emphasis is placed on the need to 'unmask' the underpinnings of these ideologies and to demonstrate that the credibility or legitimacy which characterizes Western systems, for instance, is based on contradictions of which those who suffer from these ideologies are not aware. The efforts of Marcuse and J. Habermas are devoted in large part to this problem, the latter's general approach being that there is a systematically distorted communication resulting from 'legitimation of the ruling system of norms' and from 'the anchoring of the belief in legitimacy in systematic barriers to well-forming communication'[16]. Habermas looks for the legitimation crisis points in advanced capitalist societies; he seeks to demonstrate that constitutional democratic societies, far from being an 'advance' on authoritarian systems, are in some ways more dangerous because they succeed in providing the capitalist system with an appearance of legitimacy which reduces the desire of the underprivileged to complain and react against the system. But he also points out that change may make it more difficult—ultimately impossible—to avoid a legitimation crisis.

The major instrument by which Marxist and neo-Marxist intellectuals seek to achieve change in society appears to be an increase in the awareness of the characteristics of group configuration at every point in the history of these societies and to identify the hegemonic character of some of them to use Gramsci's expression; they wish not to be caught morally and politically by the 'rationalizations' which are given by proponents of constitutional democracies. To the extent that there is a residual view in Marxism that politics results from the economic substructure and that ideologies reflect the politico-economic arrangements, it is always somewhat difficult for Marxists to claim that they can be sufficiently outside their own objective condition to perceive the somewhat specious character of prevailing ideologies. Yet they have to rely on at least the possibility of analysing the impact of ideologies as there would otherwise be no way at all to move out of the situation in which they are in order to assess the effect of ideologies. And it is only by so doing that they feel that they can hope to help the advance of societies beyond what they consider to be the fundamental hypocrisy of constitutional democracies[17].

The neo-Western theory of crises of development

Marxist and neo-Marxist theories of crises based on the global model of dependence have in their favour a powerful intellectual base and a substantial amount of evidence. But not all the evidence is in their favour. And, perhaps like any social science theory which is organized around one overarching explanatory factor, Marxist theories need often to undertake operations of 'reductionism' in order to show that the overarching factor—the economic exploitation of capitalism—is indeed overriding. Thus Marxism, despite its unquestioned popularity among social scientists from the late 1960s and early 1970s, not just in the Third World but in Western Europe and even to some extent in the United States, has not been able to account truly satisfactorily for some of the movements which are occurring or did occur in the past. Even if it is granted that the first view of development was simplistic because it did not take into account the role of crises and their revolutionary consequences, it has also to be recognized that these crises often stem from causes which are only remotely connected with capitalism and imperialism, such as tribalism or ethnic antagonism.

Moreover, the refusal to accept the possible autonomy of political values and of political institutions makes it difficult for neo-Marxists to consider with care the characteristics of the instruments by which improvements can occur. Hence a further paradox—or 'contradiction'—which leads to almost no analysis being devoted to the institutions—parties, trade unions, for instance—by which change can and does take place in the societies which profess to wish to move from constitutional democracy towards socialism[18]. The poverty of Marxist analysis with respect to the political institutions of countries which claim to adopt a Marxist model is an indication, not merely of the limited legitimacy of these institutions and of a possible fear of neo-Marxists that any detailed analysis would reveal this low legitimacy, but indeed of the fundamental difficulty of a model which continuously attempts to undermine the autonomy of political institutions and yet has led to the emergence of political systems in which institutions such as the party and its ancillary organizations are important, indeed paramount, in the society.

Yet neo-Marxism has nothing at all to say at the theoretical level about how the party should be organized and should behave, either in terms of its tactics or in terms of its moral and political goals. While the first wave of Western development models had been relatively weak with respect to the means by which institutions could be strengthened, they had at least attempted to show that the role of these institutions was essential. A line of inquiry into institutional effectiveness had been opened. Thus, not surprisingly, empirically minded observers of development have attempted to look in an 'open-minded' manner at the development crises which have taken place, and specifically at the crises which occurred in those countries which are now normally viewed as developed. Historians and historically-minded political scientists have endeavoured, especially in the 1970s, to detail 'crises' of development and to examine the routes which countries took towards development. Perhaps the first truly successful study in this vein was that of Barrington Moore, in which the author showed successfully how the bureaucratic characteristics of some countries led to specific consequences in the developmental evolution of these countries[19].

The combined efforts of historians and political scientists did lead to an even more systematic analysis of crises. While political scientists identified the types of crises which did occur or constructed models in which countries could be located[20], historians attempted to look at the evolution of European countries systematically to see how far these crises were related to each other, whether they followed each other chronologically according to the same sequence, and how far development was hastened or slowed down as a result of the way the crises were handled. The most advanced result of this approach was published in 1978 in the last volume of the 'Princeton series' on political development (*Crises of Political Development in Europe and the United States*, edited by R. Grew). This work succeeds in combining case studies and systematic analyses of types of 'crises management' while taking into account both revolutionary change and piecemeal evolutions.

The need to think about the characteristics of developing countries, about the ways they might 'progress' and about the meaning of this 'progress' led political scientists, from the 1960s, to a marked deepening of our understanding of society and of the relationship between politics and society. Before 1960, the core of the discipline—the study of government—could justly be called 'parochial', since non-Western societies were scarcely examined. The first steps made by political scientists in the outer world of developing countries were difficult ones; the characteristics of these countries were often misunderstood—usually with the best intentions. The result was, a few years later, a debate, often acrimonious, between what has sometimes been labelled a 'pro-Western' approach and a more 'radical' approach favouring the Third World. This debate continues. It is not likely to cease, partly because emotional standpoints underlie the debate, partly also because, as we have seen, the definition of development has to be based on values. There is therefore always room for disagreement, in bulk or in detail, about the components of development. But the confrontation between scholars over problems of development has markedly broadened the approach to the study of politics. It has also made it relevant to those who are concerned with the future of their country in every part of the world. It has brought back the need for 'grand models' in political science and shown their usefulness as a spur to new thinking even if models are partly unsuccessful and have to be discarded or drastically amended. At the time, by a dialectical process, the grand models have made political scientists more aware of the need to look for precise empirical indicators—some of the more recent studies of development 'crises' are a move in this direction—but the urge for precision has also been felt in other ways. Because grand models were needed, but were vague, some felt inclined to fill in the gaps by starting at the other end and building, step by step, the elements on which a general study of politics could be based. Hence the movement towards quantification, which also began in the 1960s at the very moment when grand models were beginning to emerge.

Notes

1. G. A. Almond and J. S. Coleman (1960), p. 3.
2. C. Friedrich and Z. Brzezinski (1956), *Totalitarian Dictatorship and Autocracy*, is an example of this approach.
3. T. Parsons' *Toward a General Theory of Action*, Cambridge, Mass; Harvard University Press, first appeared in 1951.
4. *See* E. J. Meehan (1967), *Contemporary Political Thought*, pp. 111–116 for an analysis of the various meanings of the word 'function'.
5. D. Easton (1953), *The Political System*, pp. 66ff.
6. G. A. Almond and J. S. Coleman (1960), pp. 58–64.
7. S. P. Huntington (1968), p. 8.
8. *Ibid.*, p. 9.
9. *See* for instance, A. Rabushka and K. A. Shepsle (1972), *Politics in Plural Societies*. *See also* R. Rogowski (1974), *Rational Legitimacy*.
10. S. P. Huntington (1968), p. 12.
11. G. A. Almond and G. B. Powell (1966), p. 308.
12. L. W. Pye (1966), Chapter 2, pp. 31–48.

References   103

13. D. E. Apter (1973), p. 10.
14. S. M. Lipset (1960), *Political Man*, London: Heinemann. *See also* analyses by P. Cutright, 'National Political Development' in N. W. Polsby *et al.* (1963), *Politics and Social Life*, Boston; Houghton Mifflin, pp. 569–581, and of R. A. Dahl (1971), *Polyarchy*, New Haven, Conn.; Yale University Press.
15. In the *18th Brumaire of Louis Bonaparte*, and in *Civil War in France*, for instance.
16. J. Habermas and N. Luhmann (1971), *Theory of Society or Social Technology?*, p. 120.
17. J. Habermas (1973), *Legitimation Crisis*.
18. Of course, Marx himself was not interested in depicting the society of the future, in constrast with the 'utopians' such as Fourier or Proudhon. For a concise presentation, *see* M. Duverger (1980), *Les orangers du lac Balaton*.
19. B. Moore (1966), *Social Origins of Dictatorship and Democracy:* T. Skocpol's more recent *States and Social Revolutions* (1979) is on the same theme.
20. For a concise summary of these models, *see* S. Rokkan (1970), *Citizens, Elections, Parties*, pp. 46–71.

References

AKE, C. (1967). *A Theory of Political Integration.* Homewood, Ill.; Dorsey Press

ALMOND, G. A. AND COLEMAN, J. A. (1960). *The Politics of the Developing Areas.* Princeton, N.J.; Princeton University Press

ALMOND, G. A. AND POWELL, G. B. (1966). *Comparative Politics.* Boston; Little, Brown

APTER, D. E. (1964). *The Politics of Modernization.* Chicago; University of Chicago Press

APTER, D. E. (1973). *Choice and the Politics of Allocation.* New Haven, Conn.; Yale University Press

BURNHAM, J. (1942). *The Managerial Revolution.* London; Putnam

DUVERGER, M. (1980). *Les orangers du lac Balaton.* Paris; Seuil

EASTON, D. (1953). *The Political System.* New York; Knopf

EASTON, D. (1965). *A Systems Analysis of Political Life.* New York; Wiley

FINKLE, J. L. AND GABLE, R. W. (1966). *Political Development and Social Change.* New York; Wiley

FRIEDRICH, C. AND BRZEZINSKI, Z. (1956). *Totalitarian Dictatorship and Autocracy.* Cambridge, Mass.; Harvard University Press

GREW, R. (ed.) (1978). *Crises of Political Development in Europe and the United States.* Princeton, N.J.; Princeton University Press

HABERMAS, J., AND LUHMANN, N. (1971). *Theories des Gesellschaft oder Sozialtechnologie?* Frankfurt; Suhrkamp Verlag

HABERMAS, J. (1973). *Legitimationsprobleme in Spätkapitalismus.* Frankfurt; Suhrkamp Verlag (English trans. 1976: London; Heinemann)

HUNTINGTON, S. P. (1968). *Political Order in Changing Societies.* New Haven, Conn.; Yale University Press

JACKSON, R. AND STEIN, M. (eds.) (1971) *Issues in Comparative Politics.* New York; St Martin's Press

MAYER, L. C. (1972). *Comparative Political Inquiry.* Homewood, Ill.; Dorsey Press

MEEHAN, E. J. (1967). *Contemporary Political Thought.* Homewood, Ill.; Dorsey Press

MEEHAN, E. J., (1971). *The Foundations of Political Analysis.* Homewood, Ill.; Dorsey Press

MILIBAND, R. (1969). *The State and Capitalist Society.* London; Weidenfeld

MARCUSE, H. (1964). *The One-dimensional Man.* London; Routledge and Kegan Paul

MOORE, B. (1966). *Social Origins of Dictatorship and Democracy.* Boston; Beacon Press

POULANTZAS, N. (1973). *Political Power and Social Classes.* London; New Left Books

POULANTZAS, N. (1978). *Power and Capitalism.* London; New Left Books

PYE, L. W. (1966). *Aspects of Political Development.* Boston; Little, Brown

RABUSHKA, A. AND SHEPSLE, K. A. (1972). *Politics in Plural Societies.* Columbus, Ohio; Merrill

ROGOWSKI, R. (1974). *Rational Legitimacy.* Princeton, N.J.; Princeton University Press

ROKKAN, S. (1970). *Citizens, Elections, Parties.* Oslo; Universitetsforlaget

SKOCPOL, T. (1979). *States and Social Revolutions.* Cambridge; Cambridge University Press

Chapter 5
Can politics be quantified?

> *Though it cannot be pretended that the principles of moral and political knowledge have, in general, the same degree of certainty with those of the mathematics, yet they have much better claims in this respect than, to judge from the conduct of men in particular situations, we should be disposed to allow them.*
>
> A. Hamilton, in *The Federalist*.

It may seem something of an anticlimax to descend from the examination of grand models and ask: can politics be quantified? The fact that the two problems have agitated the discipline of politics at the same time in the post-war period may not be regarded as sufficient justification. There is a stigma attached to methodology. Insiders may feel that it is vital to know how one can achieve knowledge, but outsiders are usually more impatient. Indeed, outsiders are right in many cases, as methodological analysis can have an esoteric twist to it, and sometimes becomes parasitic as it burns the energies of those who might have devoted their talents more profitably to the study of specific problems or the discovery of concrete trends. And this esoteric character of methodological work is more marked in the social sciences than in other disciplines. As E. J. Meehan says:

> Long before there were philosophers of science to define the meaning of 'theory', the physical scientists had developed quite sophisticated and powerful theories. The meaning of 'theory' was learned operationally, in the same way and at the same time as the student learned how to carry out his investigations. Some few physical scientists have been much concerned with methodological or 'philosophical' problems, but abstract discussions of methodology have played little part in the development of the meaning of 'theory' in science or in the training of scientists[1].

Yet, justified or not, the discussion of the role of mathematics and quantification did agitate political science in the post-war period. And, in a certain sense, it is not so much a question of

105

methodology as a question of approach, or even of style. In fact, it is not a new problem: in the late eighteenth century in particular, at the time when 'reason' was felt to provide the key to the understanding of the environment, at the time, too, when the idea of democracy began to seem a practical propostion, a spate of mathematicians and physical scientists, in France in particular, examined a number of political problems with the help of mathematics[2]. And, throughout the nineteenth century, at periodic intervals, the idea of 'political physics', of mathematical politics, or of 'polimetrics' has been, for some, the promised land[3].

For others, admittedly, this idea—or ideal—has been a mirage, an absurd obsession, because they felt that politics could not be a science, let alone a fully fledged quantifiable science based on mathematics. Accidents, mysteries, individuals, unique events such as the French or Russian Revolutions seemed to preclude a scientific approach. There is therefore here a basic controversy—and one which no doubt would have died out if a simple answer could be given. For, in reality, contrary to what may be believed, there is no somple answer. It is easy on the surface to dispose of the most extreme 'pro-quantitative' view since, as a matter of fact, much of daily politics seems to be beyond the realm of quantification, although we do not know whether a better understanding of 'causes' or relationships could not narrow down markedly the scope of the 'unquantifiable'. It is even easier to dismiss the extreme 'anti-numbers' position, which suggests that quantification is either impossible or pointless or both. What we have noticed in analysing voting studies should be a sufficient answer: it is clear that here is at least one area of politics in which numbers figure prominently and are, so to speak, 'natural'; it seems plainly absurd to want to discuss electoral politics without considering turnout levels and the share of the votes going to the parties; and it seems equally absurd not to look at trends over time and variations in space. It is, of course, true that electoral analysis also entails examining such apparently unquantifiable matters (apparently, since it may be that quantification is in reality possible) as programmes, campaigning and policy outcomes of elections[4]; some would even say that these matters are more important than the quantifiable results. But at least one must recognize that the quantitative study of elections is a significant element in the discipline of politics.

An extreme 'anti-numbers' position is therefore untenable; and it is probably no longer held. But a somewhat more moderate reaction is equally untenable. This consists of limiting the role of numbers to a small group of fields, such as election analysis, while stressing that most aspects of politics can be handled only by quantitative or normative analysis. Such an 'eclectic' view seems at first to be 'common sense'. While voting behaviour cannot be studied without manipulating figures, administrative studies have to rely on the comparison of cases and policies, yet this division is not acceptable because it is not possible to parcel out fields, or even sub-fields, in such a neat manner. There are areas of administrative studies, as we saw, in which quantitative analyses are useful and are indeed the obvious method; if we want to examine the background or the career patterns of civil servants, or even to discover trends in the policies of local and regional authorities, a purely qualitative approach will be clumsy and unrewarding. And similar points could be made about all other aspects of the study of government.

A third view might therefore be put forward, according to which it is wiser to be wholly pragmatic and to let quantitative studies handle what is quantifiable, while what is not should continue to be treated in a qualitative manner. But this is not an acceptable solution because it is either tautological or based on a misunderstanding of the process of quantification. It is tautological in so far as it says that numbers will not be used where they cannot be used. It misunderstands the nature of the quantification process because it assumes that there are, on the one hand, objects of analysis which may or may not be quantified, whatever the case may be, and, on the other, instruments of quantification waiting, like tools in a garden shed, to be used for quantitative analysis. This is not what happens: the quantification process results from a dialogue between the problem to be studied and the instruments with which it can be studied. Instruments of analysis—statistics, for instance— help to shape the problem, a point which is indeed viewed with suspicion by those who feel that quantification results in distorting the object of study. We shall shortly return to this matter. Conversely, the object of analysis helps to shape the tools; much of mathematics has been discovered by physicists and other applied scientists who needed a technique to study the problems which concerned them, and the same is true in the social sciences. Mathematical instruments are invented in order to study certain problems; consequently, unless one is eager to quantify the problem in the first place, and unless one pursues the attempt in a resolute manner, one cannot find out whether quantification is possible or not.

This is why the development of quantification in political science does depend in part on an 'act of faith', an act of faith which is not instrinsically different from the one which every scientist has to make when he explores a new line of inquiry. This act of faith consists in believing that it will be possible, if one shows enough determination to quantify political problems, to improve significantly, albeit perhaps in ways which are not foreseen, the extent of quantification in political analysis.

But faith alone is not enough; technical competence is required. And technical competence does not merely mean the mechanical ability to apply existing formulas or even to transfer existing mathematical techniques to new fields. The professional competence required must be based on mathematical imagination because, as was pointed out, advances in quantification result from the discovery of new relationships between the problem to be solved and the instruments with which problems can be solved. There has to be imagination to discover the best way in which problems can be looked at in order to be treated quantitatively; and there has to be imagination in order to modify existing instruments or to develop new ones. This means that the development of a quantitative approach in a field such as politics requires that those who use numbers be professionally very well trained, indeed that they be at the frontiers of knowledge in the mathematical fields which they wish to apply to political questions. The advance of quantification depends on there being, not 'number-crunchers' as the 'anti-quantifiers' describe the quantifiers, but 'inventors' of new mathematical tools who are flexible enough to apply highly sophisticated new techniques to the problems in which they are interested.

The development of quantification in political science thus depends both on acts of faith and on the presence of substantial numbers of skilled mathematicians. But the question may be asked: why? What is the point of such a development? Is it necessary to engage in a venture which represents a significant departure from the way political studies traditionally developed? This, indeed, was the debate which agitated political scientists in the course of the 1950s and which has continued ever since, although it is now more muted and quantification has gained a sizeable, although still limited place in political analysis. The answer to the question 'why?' is that, for many political scientists, the study of politics is not intrinsically different from the study of other social phenomena and that it should therefore be undertaken in the same way as other phenomena are being tackled. For those who took this view—the so-called behaviourists—the earlier approach to the study of politics was simply very unsophisticated— as economics was before econometrics appeared. To those who pointed out that politics is littered with unique events or accidents, it was retorted that the only proper way out was to endeavour to look for regularities by abstracting certain aspects and concentrating on them, as had been the case earlier in physics or biology. Unless this was done, the study of politics would remain descriptive, and indeed superficial in its descriptions; there would be little to choose between 'high-class journalism' and the academic study of politics. And those who held this view concluded that it was not surprising that the discipline of politics, unlike economics, should be held in low esteem by politicians and the informed public; what had given scientists and more recently economists recognition and prominence had been their ability to discover deeper underlying relationships among phenomena, and they had been able to do so through a systematic analysis which only quantification had made possible.

Naturally enough, this view was strongly challenged by large numbers of political scientists, in particular in Western Europe where the movement in favour of quantification, and behaviourism specifically, had fewer indigenous roots and where political science was altogether less well established. It was in Western Europe that one mostly found those who felt that the description of political phenomena was too complex to be more than marginally helped by the use of quantitative techniques and who also believed that the normative and philosophical aspects of politics were so important that the effect of quantification was to distort the purpose of the discipline altogether. By stressing the need for a scientific approach, and thereby leading political science towards a 'positivistic' analysis, and by forcing them to undergo a rigorous mathematical training, behaviourists were accused of undermining the long-standing interest in values which should continue to play a major part in the discipline, indeed perhaps be the major concern of political scientists.

Thus begun the 'great debate' over quantification which sometimes seemed to divide political scientists into warring camps. As those who were 'against numbers' tended to uphold the traditional interests and the traditional methods of political inquiry, they came often to be viewed as the 'Ancients', while behaviourists and the most extreme quantifiers appeared to be the 'Moderns'. Over time, the cleavage became more blurred. Many 'traditionalists' were won over to a somewhat more eclectic position, especially since, in a first phase at least, quantification seemed to be successful. Gradually, on the other hand, the pace of quantification slowed down as more difficult problems were being tackled, required more sophisticated mathematical skills, and remained unsolved; disillusionment set in among some of the quantifiers. At the same time, 'positivistic behaviourism' came increasingly under attack, as we saw already in the context of mass political behaviour, by those who felt that the purpose of the study of politics was as much to undertake a general critique of socieity as either to examine traditional values or to describe institutions and behaviour. Meanwhile, quantification progressed somewhat. It became a little more established in some aspects of political analysis; the publication, for the first time in the early 1970s, of a number of texts based on or widely using quantification is evidence of this 'coming of age'. Making fewer claims, quantification was allowed to develop at its natural pace without so much challenge. The slower, but more mature development of quantification begun in earnest.

Statistical tools and the description of the bases of politics in Western societies

The first wave of the development of quantitative politics was rapid and successful. Its main springboard was electoral analysis which, as we saw, was directly relevant to the Western societies emerging from World War II. It quickly led to a mapping of the main social variables which account for voting behaviour; the importance of psychological variables became gradually better perceived and, there too, progress was achieved, although with more difficulty, at a slower pace, and in the midst of greater worries about the limitations of the technical apparatus used by political scientists[5].

Meanwhile, the survey method and statistical techniques had also helped to explore other fields. From the early 1950s, political scientists began to analyse the characteristics of 'elite' groups, ranging from party members to Members of Parliament, ministers and civil servants. There were òccasional difficulties in determining the precise boundaries of these groups (party members for instance, as many of these were so inactive that they scarcely deserved to be called members), or in gaining access to them, especially since it was becoming customary to find out, not merely the social background of political actors, but their views as well. But the picture became gradually more precise: from it emerged comparisons between the various levels of the political pyramid, leading generally to the conclusion that political actors were rather different from and politically 'unrepresentative' of the electorate. The word 'activist' applied to party members came therefore to refer, not merely to the fact that these were more active than the bulk of the population, but also more 'extreme', being on the average located at both ends of the ideological continuum while electors tended to congregate in the middle. It became therefore possible to discover the limits of the representative character of liberal-democracies, limits which could only be found by a systematic inquiry based on the quantitative apparatus provided by statistical tools. Members of the 'political class' were more than occasionally worried by these findings, which they tended sometimes to dismiss as incorrect or misinterpreted. But the conclusion came gradually to be accepted as valid[6].

Analyses of this type were extended progressively to less visible sectors of the 'political elite'. Studies of the civil service, of the upper ranks of the military, of business leaders, provided a firmer base for conclusions about the existence (or lack of existence) of a closed ruling class, about mobility within each group, about contacts between groups. Thus, by the late 1950s, at least for some of the major Western countries, as well as for a number of non-Western countries as well, political scientists had acquired precise information on the attitudes and even influence of most of the important groups involved in the political process (and, in the United States, this knowledge was beginning to be extended to courts as well)[7].

In parallel, but appreciably more slowly and with only patchy results, statistical techniques were helping political scientists to acquire a better knowledge of some of the 'outputs' of political systems. As we have seen in Chapter 3, in the 1960s inquiries began to be made into decisions of local authorities on a general basis; in the United States, some types of decisions made by individual states were also analysed in this way. Meanwhile, for some years already, scholars had attempted to assess the activities of nations at the international level by examining the content of votes at the United Nations; they were able in this way to determine the nature and stability of the various power blocks. Clusters were discovered which provided a mapping of the configurations existing in the world and led to the discovery of the major factors accounting for these configurations[8].

The increased use of statistical tools in a variety of fields led to a refinement of techniques, as scholars using these techniques were themselves becoming more sophisticated. While the first voting studies were based on simple correlations between two variables, the studies of the late 1950s and early 1960s used a wide variety of techniques, some of which had only recently been developed and had indeed been developed for the social sciences and political science in particular. Factor analysis was prevalent at one period.

Multivariate analysis, cluster analysis, path analysis became more and more commonly used. It became possible as a result to measure the precise impact of various 'causes' and to disentangle the ways in which one element played a part alongside other elements in building the overall picture[9].

Statistics thus seemed to enable political scientists to move from the description of a configuration or the mapping of relationships (are Labour or socialist voters primarily working class?) to something closer to a dynamic analysis. But we need to pause a little at this point, because there is here an element of confusion. Some of the statistical techniques which have been in increasingly common use have enabled scholars to discover the direction of a relationship; in other cases, it has been found useful to assess the extent of the relationship between sets of elements, or factors, taking place at different points in time. For instance, in recent years, scholars have looked into the impact of economic cycles on voting behaviour by trying to discover how long it takes for increases in unemployment to affect electoral predispositions[10]; additionally, studies of the Third World have examined the circumstances under which armies stage military coups or the extent to which unfulfilled economic and social expectations lead to rebellions and violence[11]. These studies are not, in the true sense of the word, 'dynamic'. They either examine the relationship in one country at different points in time or look at various countries at the same moment and *assume* that these countries constitute, so to speak, different points on a time scale. In neither case do those studies disentangle the *process* by which the attitudes of the population change; they note the change, and having discovered a difference in the behaviour of two variables, *infer* that a change has taken place during the period in the minds of the populations concerned.

Yet, even if these studies are not 'dynamic' in the full sense, they have at least lent considerable support for the proposition that there is a close relationship between political behaviour and economic movements—short-term in the case of Western cycles, longer term in the case of the rising expectations in the Third World. The degree and the precise extent of the relationship would not have been established without the use of quantified indicators: of this, there is little doubt. More serious doubts about the value of quantification arise when an attempt is made to measure the impact of what we called 'structures' in the previous chapter. In some Third World studies of the 1960s, it was felt possible to assess whether factors such as 'institutionalization' had an impact on the behaviour of populations, and in particular on levels of violence and on the propensity to rebel. This effort followed earlier attempts at assessing precisely the degree of relationship between economic and political development. Authors of these studies felt able to draw conclusions—often very precise ones; T. R. Gurr for instance claimed that the impact of political factors is very small[12]. Yet it will be recalled that these broad political 'structures' have not as yet been defined precisely; it would seem *a fortiori* somewhat premature to attempt to quantify relationships.

Two opposite views can be held, and have been held, with respect to quantitative studies of this type. The sceptical position suggests that these undertakings are at best premature, and at worst counterproductive; an attempt is made to measure objects which are so difficult to define that a false impression of precision is given where it would be more honest to recognize that we still do not know exactly—or even roughly—the contours of the objects which we want to analyse. As long as we are uncertain as to what we mean by 'institutionalization', for instance, it would seem wrong to engage in quantitative efforts whose results could be correct only by sheer accident?

Yet it remains true that only by actually becoming more quantitative can political analysis gradually improve both the definitions and the operationalization of the major concepts which it uses. Quantification leads to greater rigour. If we accept that it is true (and most would accept this point) that the idea of institutionalization, to continue with this example, is important, then it is important to examine it closely and to assess its impact empirically; but the operationalization of the concept will not be improved until we are confronted with the need to find quantifiable indicators because we will not look for these unless we need them in the research which we are undertaking. And gradually better indicators will be discovered. The findings of one scholar will trigger the counter-inquiry of another and progress will thereby be achieved.

There is no 'correct' answer in this debate, except perhaps that there has to be a balance between caution and bold endeavours. Even the short history of the use of mathematical methods in political analysis shows that progress is achieved through such initiatives: we now know more about the behaviour of electors, and much of this new knowledge has come from a succession of 'leaps' into relatively unknown territory on the basis of indicators which were not well tried out. But these 'leaps' were relatively small in the electoral field, at least in the earlier period. Interpretations were given to the responses of electors which were not always warranted but for which there was normally substantial empirical evidence. Generalizations on the broader impact of political institutions are more in the nature of informed guesses; they correspond to intuitive assumptions about what 'institutionalization' or 'legitimacy' seem likely to achieve. They are therefore perhaps unwarranted 'leaps in the dark': our knowledge of the precise structure of politics in developing countries is still too limited.

Yet the major problem posed by the use of statistics in political analysis does not relate to the validity of the findings in the fields in which statistics are already used. What is more worrying is the large number of fields in which statistics are not used, seemingly because they cannot be used. And, more worrying still, those fields are often also the most important, those where politics seems to matter most. While election studies were viewed as particularly relevant in the early post-war period, interest has somewhat subsided; the second generation of studies of mass political behaviour has indeed extended the scope of the inquiry beyond the impact of elections and even outside the electoral context altogether; yet even expanded in this way, these studies are not concerned with the core of the political process, that is to say, with the series of 'operations' which take place between the moment a demand is made and the consequential decision is implemented. We have noticed in Chapter 2 that administrative studies have tended to revert to case studies or to variations on the case method because statistical studies of outputs related these outputs to broad socio-economic, and occasionally political variables, but were not able to handle the political *process* itself. The same conclusion applies to many other quantitative studies, and, in the eyes of some sceptics, to all of them. They feel that these studies are concerned exclusively with the social bases of politics, not with what politics is intrinsically and specifically[13]. No wonder therefore that they should be regarded by those whose main concern is government as useful adjuncts perhaps, but as largely peripheral. Hence the question: is it that the nature of politics, in the strict sense, is such that quantitative methods cannot be applied to its core? Is it only that statistics is not the right method, while other quantitative methods may be better suited to political problems? Or is it that the right method has yet to be discovered?

An important but hitherto unsuccessful endeavour: the attempt to quantify power

As these developments were taking place, endeavours were being made to use mathematical tools of a different kind to measure and analyse a concept which had been central to political analysis for a very long period: the concept of power. Since Machiavelli at least, power had been regarded by many as perhaps the political concept par excellence. It had also been viewed by historians as a crucial factor in the relationships between statesmen. Even in literature, power has often played an important part; Shakespeare was as much concerned to describe and even, in his way, to characterize forms of exercise of power as Machiavelli had been a century earlier. Thus it is not surprising that many political scientists should have focused their investigations on power and had even regarded the concept as the key to the understanding of politics. Some, Harold Lasswell in particular, in the 1930s and 1940s, went as far as suggesting that politics was about power: 'Political science, as an empirical discipline, is the study of the shaping and sharing of power'[14].

This does not imply that the whole of political analysis is about power; it is also about values, about the decisions which are taken on the basis of these values, as well as about the institutions which, as we know, structure the decision process. But, as an empirical discipline, say Lasswell and Kaplan, politics is about power in that the process by which values become decisions and indeed the process by which institutions are established entail relationships between individuals which are based on the exercise of power. Meanwhile, power appears to be a particularly useful concept as it helps to describe, in the true sense of the word, a dynamic activity: it describes the force which contributes to a change of behaviour over time among those on which power is successfully exercised. Thus it is not surprising that some political scientists should have wished to measure power, as indeed Lasswell and Kaplan had proposed: 'Once concepts are formulated in terms of order, of variations in degree, scales and methods of measurement can be developed to suit the needs of the particular problem'[15]. If various levels or amounts of power exercised by individuals could be precisely assessed, the dynamics of politics would *ipso facto* be described precisely. This endeavour was to be an important concern in political science in the 1950s, and for Robert Dahl in particular.

Why did the enterprise seem possible, and why, at least up to now, has it failed? The answer to the first question is relatively simple: indeed it is so straightforward that it is perhaps more difficult to understand why the enterprise was not attempted earlier. A moment's reflection suggests that power as a concept has two attributes which seem to make it a very strong candidate for precise measurement. The first is that it is a truly general concept: everyone knows about it, in an intuitive manner at least;

and everyone can find instances of power everywhere. Indeed, power seems to epitomize all forms of 'unequal' relationships among human beings. Of course, this means that power is 'multi-faceted', and this means that the origins of power can be very different: an individual may have power because he is loved or because he is feared; his power may come from his intelligence or from his beauty; it may be due to his status, class, religious affiliation, or it may be due to his personal skills. Yet—and this seems to be the great value of the concept—all these 'causes' seem to result in one common phenomenon: having power, that is to say being able to make others undertake actions which, as Dahl said, they 'would not otherwise do'[16]. Power seems therefore to be rather like money—and the analogy has not escaped the attention of political scientists, since it has been the driving force behind the move to quantify power. Money, too, is ubiquitous: it may come from a variety of origins; it may be used for an infinity of purposes. Yet it is the common channel through which economic activities are undertaken. Similarly, the origins and effects of power may be so diverse that they cannot be listed; yet politics seems to be 'about power' in the sense that political action results always at some point in the use of power.

This general use of power makes the concept central to political life. But this concept seems also potentially amenable to quantitative treatment because it is naturally viewed as an incremental 'commodity'. We compare the power of different individuals; we remark that Stalin, for instance, had more power than Roosevelt, that Roosevelt had more power than Carter. There is an apparently natural ranking of individuals with respect to power. This seems therefore to mean that we have here a concept which could potentially be measured.

Thus Dahl embarked in a determined effort to undertake the measurement. But, as he began doing so, he discovered a characteristic of power which was to make the matter of quantification appreciably more arduous and clumsier, namely that, if one looks carefully at power, it can, strictly speaking, be defined only in terms of *specific* relationships and, at the limit, in terms of the relationship between two persons only. Of course, it was obvious from the start that power was a 'relationship' but this characteristic is not peculiar to power: all social attributes are ultimately relationships. A rich man is not rich in the abstract; he is rich because his money or the goods which he owns are recognized as 'valuable' by the society in which he lives. Money is thus basically the expression of a relationship between an individual and society. If the rich man is prevented from selling his property, his wealth has little meaning; if someone is prevented from exporting his money outside his country—a common occurrence in the Third World—the rich man is rich in his country alone, and not throughout the world.

Yet money remains, on the whole, a general relationship between individual and society; power, on the contrary, is a specific relationship between an individual and one or a few others. Of course, it may seem at first sight that power, like money, can apply to whole groups, indeed to nations; one talks about Stalin's power over the Soviet citizens. But this expression comes quickly to be seen as an unacceptable short-cut when its content is further analysed. The power of an individual over one man is *never quite* the same as the power he has over another. Each 'amount' of power is different, even if the difference is infinitesimal. The power which someone has over his spouse, his children, his colleagues, his friends, is quite specific in each case. The result is that one has to measure power as the power which A has over X, over Y, over Z, etc., but never the power of A over the whole group, let alone the power of A in general. This is because what gives power to an individual over another is a set of specific characteristics which both individuals have and which relate them to each other: A is loved by X—and therefore X is likely to agree to what A suggests; but A is, meanwhile, feared by Y—and it is fear, not love, which makes Y comply.

This state of affairs has a very unfortunate consequence for the measurement of power: it is simply not possible to find a universal yardstick according to which one can measure the power of A and compare it with the power of B. One can only compare the power of A with respect to X with the power of B with respect to X, knowing full well that the power of A and the power of B with respect to another individual, Y, may have to be ranked quite differently. People therefore do not 'have power' in the way they 'have money'; they have different amounts of power with respect to different individuals. One might of course theoretically be able to rank all individuals with respect to all others and deduce from this a huge league table of the power of all of us. But this exercise would constitute such an enormous task that one cannot sensibly see it undertaken.

This, then, was the fundamental reason why attempts at measuring power failed despite sophisticated quantitative efforts at analysing the concept rigorously[17]. But does such a failure extend beyond the concept of power and does it reverberate on the overall relevance of quantification? Since power is such a central concept, should one conclude, as anti-quantifiers have repeatedly argued, that the role of numbers is peripheral in political analysis because personalized elements are too important and because these personalized elements lead, by their very nature, to variations which are so random that trends cannot in practice be measured usefully? To answer this question, we need to make a little detour into the characteristics of mathematics and the extent to which political activity fits with these characteristics.

Units and assumptions in mathematics and politics

Mathematics is a powerful tool which has enabled scientists to cut through complicated problems by concentrating on a small number of key points. To use mathematics is to simplify. It is to follow a road, well signposted and with well-painted lanes, and thus to be able to progress in the midst of even heavy fog. But progress is possible only if the road has already been built, the signposts erected, the lanes painted. If this has not been done, there is simply no advance and one remains in the middle of the field.

From the beginning of the development of 'applied mathematics', efforts have been made to simplify the environment and, so to speak, to 'signpost' it. Routes have been cut through the maze of the problems raised by calculations of complicated areas and volumes, for instance, by simplifying these areas and these volumes and concentrating on well-known, regular shapes, such as triangles, circles, pyramids or spheres, for which prior calculations had been made. Of course, over the centuries, applied mathematics became increasingly sophisticated: techniques were invented to come closer and closer to reality. The calculus was thus a major discovery for the measurement of shapes and of rates of increase and decrease of certain characteristics. But the need to simplify reality remains. More than occasionally, this simplification results in major distortions; it is then difficult to recognize the reality in the model; the mathematico-physical analysis of colour is based on conventions relating to spectroscopic waves which purely and simply leave aside the feelings which we may have when seeing particular colour schemes in our environment.

The distortion of reality, or at least the ruthless abstraction from reality which mathematics entails and which it entails especially at the beginning of the development of applications of mathematics to a particular branch of learning, is the price which has to be paid if mathematics is to be used at all. And it is a price which political scientists have rarely been prepared to pay because, in many ways like students of literature or the arts, they have rightly been fascinated by the part played by individuals in the development of political life. This meant that political scientists have rarely been ready to look at political life *as if* it was the result of activities of interchangeable units operating under simple general conditions. The world of politics is not, for instance, composed of only two categories, the leaders and the led, with the leaders taking all decisions and the led merely obeying; it is composed of an infinite variety of situations in which the leaders have more or less influence and the led more or less ability to resist this influence. Nor is the context within which these leaders operate viewed as homogeneous: each committee, Cabinet, Parliament, is viewed as different from the others. And, by and large, our intuitive reaction is to say that the stuff of politics is made precisely by the variety of situations and the concrete differences.

This means that the discipline of politics is faced with a vital dilemma with respect to quantification. As we saw, the measurement of power becomes simply impossible when we note that the power of A *vis-à-vis* X is truly different (has a different colour, smell, taste, so to speak) from the power of A *vis-à-vis* Y and from the power of B and Y. Political scientists do not accept the reduction of such 'colourful' concrete differences to one homogenous factor or refuse to concentrate on one characteristic only and, temporarily at least, to forget the individual 'mystery' of the particular relationship between two men. If this is indeed the case, quantification is not valuable either: it remains at the periphery of the study of politics.

The key word is 'valuable'. This is the word which represents the 'act of faith' which we mentioned earlier—an act of faith which is also dependent on the technical knowledge of those who make it. To say that it is not 'valuable' to be prepared to reduce political life in the manner which mathematics requires is to express the belief that as much knowledge will be gained by the use of mathematical tools as will be gained by the use of more qualitative descriptions of political life. Clearly, the validity of this judgement depends upon those making it being fully aware of the capabilities of the tools which mathematics offers; one cannot say whether the mathematical analysis of committee behaviour will be useful unless one knows what problems, for instance, game theory can help to solve. And there is more: one cannot say how much an analysis will gradually progress over time unless one has such a lively and imaginative knowledge of mathematical tools that one can predict how these will improve as one goes along. Yet few political scientists will invest time in acquiring the mathematical expertise required (and the discipline of politics will attract few individuals with high mathematical skills) unless it is believed that, at the end of the day, mathematics will lead to considerable progress. The 'act of faith' and the technical expertise are inextricably linked. By and large, the 'act of faith' has so far not been sufficiently strong among sufficiently large numbers while the technical expertise has been too low among the majority: consequently, mathematical analyses have not been pursued on a wide front. But there is *some* faith and *some* development of technical expertise, with the result that quantitative developments in political science have continued in some areas despite the failure of the measurement of power on a truly global scale.

Why has there been in the midst of a general scepticism and relatively little technical expertise, a continued interest in applying mathematical techniques to some aspects of political life? Because, paradoxically enough, the environment itself, or society—not the political scientists—have in some of its aspects created conditions where the use of mathematical techniques is indeed absolutely natural. This is where we need to return to the point, made earlier in this chapter, that eighteenth-century scientists enthusiastically used mathematical techniques to examine some political situations. In particular, Borda and Condorcet were intrigued by a number of peculiar consequences of the voting process; they discovered, for instance, that one can easily obtain inconsistent results in an electoral college or a committee, if one asks for successive votes for a number of candidates or issues, and they made this doscovery on the basis of a formal, mathematical analysis of the way in which preferences are expressed in the vote[18].

Since the late eighteenth century, mathematicians, economists and, indeed, political scientists have from time to time considered mathematically a number of similar 'paradoxes'; all of these were related to electoral processes and to committee-decision making. Hence a strange situation: in one particular context, that of decisions taken in committees or through elections, it seemed perfectly possible, indeed absolutely natural, to analyse the dynamics of politics in a mathematical manner, while all other aspects of decision-making seemed entirely closed to mathematical treatment. To put it differently: if Stalin had operated within a committee structure, one might have analysed his behaviour mathematically and predicted mathematically the ways in which his committee would have decided; but, as Stalin did not operate in this manner, his behaviour has to be analysed by non-mathematical means. Why should this be the case? And can it not be that, by reflecting on this state of affairs, one might be able to grasp to what extent and under what conditions the application of mathematical techniques to political science becomes possible?

Why, then, did a mathematical treatment emerge so naturally in relation to committee decision-making and to electoral processes? We are not referring here merely to the social background of voters or of committee members; we are not concerned here with the bases of political life or the configuration of the political actors. What we are considering is the 'stuff of politics', namely the framework of the decision process and the conditions under which this process leads to decisions which may be inconsistent with each other or may not provide a conclusion at all. These are studies of political life in its full dynamic reality, not merely studies of the sociological or psychological antecedents of politics.

The reason why mathematics emerged so naturally as a useful tool to formalize the analysis of committee and electoral decisions is a simple one: it is that, in itself, the committee or electoral procedure circumscribes narrowly the decision operation; major assumptions are introduced and these assumptions set aside the concrete characteristics of human beings which political scientists are otherwise concerned to analyse. And it is no accident that this development should have occurred at the end of the eighteenth century, because eighteenth-century writers of the enlightenment period first conceived, and later attempted to implement 'rational' rules of behaviour of a highly simplified character, the first and most powerful of these being that men are equal. What empirical political analysis tells us, on the contrary, is that men are unequal; and the inequalities are usually taken into account in political analysis, not merely inequalities in wealth and status, but also inequalities in political skills, in style, in political involvement. However, for normative reasons, eighteenth-century philosophers and scientists stated that men should be deemed to be politically equal.

They then proceeded to organize government on the basis of this 'unrealistic' standpoint: in Western countries, arrangements were devised which, ostensibly at least, were based on equality. Admittedly, in an early phase, not all adult citizens were awarded the vote, but the most imporatnt point was that those who had the vote were deemed to be equal; and, indeed, universal suffrage arrangements gradually extended this assumed political equality to all adults. Meanwhile, decision-making in electoral colleges, committees, assemblies was based on the assumption that members were equal: consequently, although it has always been clear that there were inequalities under the surface, the belief that political equality was the goal to pursue was strong enough to warrant studies being made on the basis of the assumption of equality. The study of behaviour in committees resembles the study of behaviour in the economic market: economists study the market although it is clear that there are few real markets; but it is believed that the market is a 'good' thing. Similarly, political scientists study committee behaviour in conditions of equality because it is assumed that this is a 'good' means of achieving decisions. In both the case of the economic market and the case of committee behaviour a strong normative assumption ruthlessly abstracts behaviour from reality; it also helps the formal mathematical treatment of the subject.

The norm of political equality is therefore very helpful to those who wish to treat problems arising from voting decisions in a mathematical manner. But this is not the only simplification which the norm of political equality introduces; it also leads to further assumptions which drastically reduce both the range of goals and the opportunities for actors. The ends and the means of committee decision processes are also narrowed down in a very marked fashion.

Individuals have a wide, indeed potentially infinite range of interests; these are ranked in the most complicated manner—indeed, the ranking is so complicated that individuals themselves do not perceive what it is. Our interest in art, in food, in travel, in various social matters belongs to different 'areas' which we are rarely called to compare or contrast. Yet, if one wants to assess the power of an individual over another, one may have to take all these aspects into consideration: the comprehensive analysis of power thus makes us enter further and further fields. But in voting situations or in committee decisions, on the contrary, problems are narrowed down, because a decision has to be made between two or a small number of issues or candidates. The general preference process is, so to speak, operationalized into a choice mechanism which, however difficult it may be in many circumstances, is none the less markedly simplified by comparison with the theoretical choices which might be made. The proof of this drastic reduction of the *ends* is indeed given by the fact that many feel that voting decisions do not leave electors with a 'real' choice, that candidates or parties are too similar to each other, for instance, or that the issues are not clear-cut enough. Be this as it may, that fact is that the effective choice is constrained by the *process* of decision itself.

There is also simplification at the level of the *means* because of a number of rules which the democratic system of voting and of committee decision-making imposes. The reason why it is not very interesting to assess committee decisions in this way if, for instance, someone like Stalin 'dominates' a committee is because Stalin would simply set aside the rules and threaten committee members if these were not to support his views. But a 'regular' democratic committee is one where a number of rules are scrupulously observed and where, in particular, great store is placed on rules relating to the ways in which issues are placed on the agenda, debated and voted on. The voting rules (majority voting, for instance) are of course those which are most conspicuous in restricting the freedom of members to act in an 'inegalitarian' manner, but the whole of the procedure also contributes in 'equalizing' the general framework. It becomes therefore both interesting and possible to analyse the effect of these rules on the decision-making process and specifically to examine the 'paradoxes' inherent in such a system as well as the ways in which one or more of the members can maximize their own interests in the context of the system.

Thus, for reasons which are related to the desire to implement democratic values in the political system, the structure of decision-making becomes constrained narrowly in at least a number of arenas in which decisions are taken in democratic countries. And, consequently, these arenas have come to be the areas in which a mathematical treatment of the *process*, that is to say, of the dynamics of politics, has become possible, and even been able to flourish. But, consequently, too, this area of study has been viewed as narrow, and this 'narrowness' has become more apparent as studies of committee decision-making and electoral processes were being refined mathematically.

'Positive political theory': the mathematical treatment of 'rational' political behaviour

The mathematical treatment of voting and committee decisions thus has an old origin, but it was revitalized in the post-war period, in part because of the greater interest in systematization and scientific analysis, but in part also for more specific reasons: one was the growing interest of economists in this field, economists having a long tradition of formal and mathematical expertise; the other reason was the development of a new mathematical technique, game theory. We have already seen in Chapter 2 that economists were interested in electoral analysis, but that their interests was different from the interest which mainstream political scientists showed for data analysis; economists such as Downs attempted to discover a model of party competition in which the 'rational' preference of electors led parties to adopt gradually an almost identical 'centre' position. But the interest shown by economists was wider: it extended to decision processes in general. Thus Condorcet's and Borda's findings were 'rediscovered' in the early post-war period and presented more systematically by Kenneth J. Arrow who stressed the paradoxical character and indeed the 'impossibility' of basing social choice on individual values in his *Social Choice and Individual Values*, which appeared in 1951. And D. Black published his *General Theory of Committee and Elections* in 1958.

Both Arrow's and Black's work were concerned with the precise determination of the mechanical consequences of majority rule on the outcome of the decision, given different types of preference rankings of individuals. These studies could therefore be said to be connected with the framework of decisions, rather than with the internal dynamics of the decision process; they did consider the way in which the position adopted by one actor could affect the position of other 'players'. Game theory made it possible to advance further into dynamics by providing a tool which helped to assess the best possible outcome for each actor. The analogy between many political relationships—international, national or local—and games is an obvious one. As in games, the rules of procedures and the conventions constrain political actors; and, as in games, it is important to endeavour to anticipate the next move of the opponent before making one's own move. Moreover, the variety of games also corresponds to the variety of situations in which political actors find themselves: political situations of full conflict, or partial conflict, or of cooperation can be easily reproduced in a number of games.

At first, in the 1950s, game theory simply made political scientists aware of the analogy between some political situations and game situations. But gradually game theory truly helped to develop from scratch a theoretical approach to coalition-making, when it became apparent that the majority principle had a definite effect on the 'size' of coalitions for, in a majority context, it is at least theoretically unnecessary to aim at a very large coalition in order to win; it is sufficient to aim at a 'minimum winning' coalition, composed of exactly half the members plus one. In view of the fact that there are many coalitions of various sizes, including so-called 'grand coalitions' which include, for instance, all the main parties represented in a Parliament, the assertion that coalitions 'should' tend towards a minimum size was neither trivial nor indeed obviously correct intuitively. And although the theory has been undermined to some extent since it was first presented by

William Riker in 1962 in his *The Theory of Political Coalitions*, it is still broadly true that, with some amendments (the requirement of 'ideological contiguity' being an important factor), the theory continues to fit best the reality of parliamentary coalitions which occur in the world.

The role of game theory in the development of new models of politics has clearly been significant; and its potential remains considerable, since the mathematical analysis of game theory is far from being fully developed. There are still considerable uncertainties beyond relatively simple 'games', as only theorems between two persons and especially between two persons competing for the same outcome (zero-sum) have been fully developed.

Thus it became possible, in the 1970s not merely to show that mathematics could play a part in a number of branches of politics but even to bring together the different aspects of 'mathematical' political theory into a general framework. In what was the first attempt to systematize such a theory, W. H. Riker and P. C. Ordeshook published *An Introduction to Positive Political Theory* in 1973. This work covers topics ranging from mass participation and electoral competitition to the solution of conflicts between two persons through the analysis of coalitions; it is directly and continuously concerned with the 'stuff' of the political process—decision-making—to an extent and at a level of generality—but also of precision—which few, if any, previous studies had reached. It does therefore seem that mathematical analysis, far from being concerned merely with a description of the bases or background of politics, far from being devoted to esoteric or limited problems (as some aspects of committee analysis seemed sometimes to be), is in fact directly relevant to the examination of a whole range of political questions. And mathematics helps to conduct the analysis better, more rigorously of course, but also more parsimoniously than can the analysis based on the description of a number of cases.

This is in itself no mean achievement. Mathematical analysis has had a profound effect on the way a number of important problems have been approached and subsequently tested empirically. The examination of the calculus of voting has helped to explain at the margin why certain types of voters are more likely to vote and why certain tactics adopted by certain parties or candidates are, at the margin also, quite useful; and we must remember that, in most election situations, marginal gains are those which count. The examination of committee behaviour has shown the difficulties of extracting from a number of individuals a collective outcome which corresponds to the preference rankings of these individuals.

The examination of the characteristics of 'public goods' has shown that the tactics adopted by individuals in order to acquire them are intrinsically different from those which are adopted for 'private goods'. And the analysis of coalitions has shown that it is relatively uninteresting to extend coalitions beyond the size which they absolutely need if they are to achieve a majority. None of these conclusions are strictly 'deterministic': they are 'probabilistic' in that a variety of considerations may, in practice, lead to different strategies on the part of actors; but the 'rational' strategies are followed more frequently than other strategies—and they produce better outcomes for the actors. In the same way as the market gives a structure to economic analysis in the capitalist context (and possibly in large part in the socialist context as well), the analysis of the strategies provides a structure within which the concrete behaviour of political actors can be described and understood more easily.

But the price which has to be paid is some narrowness, narrowness in the types of problems studied and covered— electoral competition, committee decision-making, coalition- making. This is because the mathematical analysis of politics operates, as we saw, on the basis of the assumptions introduced into politics by eighteenth-century philosophers. The problems which are covered in Riker and Ordeshook's text are the problems which arise from the assumptions of political equality and majority rule. As a result, this work, and mathematical analysis in general, have tended to relate to countries which operate under these principles, and not to countries of the Third World nor indeed to the Communist world. It is true that Riker and Ordeshook state that it has been found that the principle of the minimum winning coaltion 'seems to fit the facts of political life in African kingdoms and chiefdoms in Buganda even better than it fits the data to which Riker himself applied it'[19]. But it is also true that the theory of 'minimum winning' coalition only makes sense mathematically and can be tested empirically where the precise numbers in the coalition can be counted and majority rule applies. To take an example from Western countries: where, as in the EEC since 1965, unanimity is required, the idea is simply not applicable.

This last example shows that, even in Western countries, the approach does remain narrow; it does not account for a substantial number of situations where rules and assumptions of political equality and majority rule do not obtain. Moreover, it does not provide an answer as to why these rules are in use, or an idea of the circumstances in which they are more likely to be in use. And from this follows the conclusion that the mathematical theory which has been developed so far is based on philosophical underpinnings which are too narrow and need to be overcome. Mathematical analysis is based, according to those who support its use, on 'rationality', but it is a rationality conceived in limited individualistic terms. As M. J. Taylor puts it: 'Nearly all rational choice or economic theories of politics (and much of economic theory itself) are founded on assumptions about individual preference, including the assumption (usually tacit) that the preferences do not change with time'[20].

It is not surprising that there should be such a close link between the underpinnings of mathematical political theory and of economic theory, since so many economists played a part in the development of mathematical political theory. Nor, indeed, is the idea surprising that the individual should be central to the theory and that this individual should be viewed as static: these were the underpinnings of the philosophical theory which led to the development of Western political institutions from the late eighteenth century. But these views lead to the conclusion that the only 'rational' mode of behaviour for the individual is to maximize his own interest and therefore that the opposition between individuals is endemic, that it cannot be uprooted, merely domesticated. In short, mathematical political theory appears 'Hobbesian' rather than 'Rousseau-ite', let alone Marxist. Not surprisingly, the quantification of politics through techniques such as game theory has been viewed by some as only a very partial approach to political life; and not, surprisingly, the suggestion that politics cannot be truly quantified has continued to linger on.

Can quantification go beyond 'rational' individual behaviour?

There is little doubt that, to date, mathematical political theory has developed almost entirely in fields in which the assumptions of eighteenth-century philosophers obtained and on the basis of a 'narrow' interpretation of rational action. There is little doubt, too, that this is an important, though limited, area of study: we know much better what to expect from majority rule, or how individuals are likely to behave if they wish to achieve their own goals. Since it is the case that much political life is structured by elections and majority rule; indeed, since these procedures are normatively supported by many, either as good in themselves or as the best which have been found so far, it is not irrelevant, indeed it is very important to study the way in which these procedures 'make us behave' and thus to be fully aware of their implications.

But is this all that mathematical political theory can do? Are there grounds for believing that it can move out of the assumptions within which it has been constrained? Can one, as A. Rapoport proposes, 'transcend' the 'paradigm of the strategic decision', 'a strategic decision (being) one that is made from the point of view of a single actor'[21], a question to which M. J. Taylor seems to answer in the negative when he says, at the end of his analysis, that 'the whole of a normative rational-choice theory crumbles when the object which it is intended to justify or recommend modifies the individual preferences in terms of which the object is deemed socially desirable or preferable and indeed it is then not even clear what is *meant* by the preferability of the object' (author's emphasis)[22].

The last point comes to the core of the matter. In order to move out of the constraints within which mathematical political theory has operated, we need to be able to abandon the assumptions which have enabled us to simplify the relationships between individuals. One of these assumptions is political equality; in order to be realistic, for instance about power, we have to accept that individuals are unequal in a large number of ways and that their influence on each other will differ markedly. Another assumption is that these 'equal' individuals operate on the basis of similar types of motivations—that is to say that they wish to maximize their own interests in what Rapoport calls a 'strategic' manner. But, as we saw in relation to power, the abandonment of these assumptions has the effect of so complicating the model that it does not seem possible to find a firm element on the basis of which one can pursue the investigation. Every individual becomes differently related to every other and every individual's preference pattern is so specific that one can only describe individual cases.

It is therefore impractical to relax all the assumptions on which mathematical political theory is based and to attempt a 'general' theory of political behaviour without any postulates. If this were what is being sought, the answer must be that mathematics cannot help and that the quantification of such an analysis is impossible. But this is presumably not what is being asked, and it does not need to be asked. For what is sufficient, if one is to keep 'faith' in the development of a quantitative approach to politics, is to see whether mathematics needs all those assumptions which currently prevail in order to be of use; if other assumptions can be introduced, or if some assumptions can be relaxed, progress can be expected in fields in which mathematical analysis has so far not entered.

There seems to be no reason why at least some progress cannot be achieved. Indeed this is already the case to some extent, as the evolution of coalition models suggests. The first idea which was adopted was that of the mechanical effect of the principle of majority; gradually, it became clear that the ideological dimension was an essential variable: to introduce this dimension means that the preference patterns of actors are taken into account. Instead of simply considering the desire to win at minimum possible cost, the further consideration is now added that men are eager to associate with 'like-minded' or 'congenial' people and therefore that they are prepared to trade-off some of the possible crude gains which they might have had from a minimum-size coalition for the 'pleasure' of being with other men with whom they are (ideologically) at ease[23].

The implication of this new analysis is in the tradition of mathematical development: it entails taking into account one further element at a time and thus building gradually a larger edifice around the original house. One could go further in the same direction and consider more systematically the conditions under which members of a group, a committee for instance, prefer to operate on a majority rather than on a unanimity basis. This would entail broadening the concept of 'pay-off' and moving away from the direct and immediate material advantages which may be obtained, and consider longer-term, emotional pay-offs which may play a part. What would then become important would be the assessment of the conditions under which such emotional pay-offs are viewed to be important—a matter which can be measured at least in some ways by examining the basic attitudes of members of the group; one can assess for instance how far members of the group prefer to remain together in associating with other members or staying on their own. Riker and Ordeshook note that 'grand coalitions occur occasionally [in] total war in the Western European nation-state system'[24]; they then go on to say that these grand coalitions break up after the end of the war, taking the examples of the situation after 1815, after 1918 and after 1945. This amounts to saying that after these wars the desire to be together was felt less strongly than other desires, a situation which may be, and indeed is replicated within nation-states, where 'grand coalitions' of parties occur from time to time. These situations could be examined more systematically and be linked to others, such as that which prevails in the EEC which is, for all intents and purposes, a 'grand coaltition' of the member states.

These modifications may be viewed as merely small improvements within the framework of 'narrow' rational decision-making and therefore leave still undecided the question whether quantification can be applied to the whole range of approaches in the discipline of politics. At this stage, the answer must be left open, as long as a framework as neat as the one presented by eighteenth-century philosophers is not available to those who wish to quantify. For it is clear that a rigorous analysis of power which would be based on strict measurements requires more precise parameters than the ones which we have at our disposal. It is not sufficient to note that the assumption of equality introduced by eighteenth-century philosophers is unrealistic; we have to be able to say more than we can at present about levels and types of inequality between individuals before it becomes possible to measure power.

Similarly it seems too early to introduce quantification on a significant scale in an area in which much progress has to be made and which might indeed lead ultimately to the development of an alternative model to that of 'rationality'—the area of group loyalty. While politics is about power, it is also about loyalty, authority and legitimacy[25]. Yet, as we have seen in the previous chapter, these concepts, and the concepts of institutionalization and integration which are connected to them, are still very vague; their interrelationship has not been assessed precisely; nor has their evolution over time even began to be measured. It would seem that there is scope here for future quantification. Some limited work at the border of these problems has already been undertaken with some success—by D. Rae, R. Rogowski and M. J. Taylor, as well as K. W. Deutsch with respect to communication. Integration is indeed the concept which is most likely to be amenable to quantitative analysis as it appears to be both measurable empirically in a relatively simple manner and as it depends on conflicts between groups which can also be easily circumscribed. An analysis of integration would appear to provide an alternative to the 'rational' decision-making approach, as it stresses groups rather than individuals, cooperation rather than the opposition between individual interests, and a possible change in the values of individuals rather than the presumption that the values of individuals do alter over time. This analysis would also seem to require different types of mathematical techniques (communication theory and diffusion theory) rather than game-theoretic methods which directly or indirectly refer back to a Hobbesian conception of the relationship between the individual and society.

Quantification has not yet made many inroads beyond certain relatively circumscribed fields in the discipline of politics. Its progress bumps against what seems to be the impossibility of discovering and measuring basic political elements or basic political relationships irrespective of constraints. When and as long as these constraints are viewed as narrow, quantification also appears to be a rather specialized endeavour, perhaps an esoteric one. This conclusion is wrong: quantification has a very large part to play, but its increased role depends on there being imaginative explorations of the various ways in which elementary political relationships can be better measured. This, in turn, depends on rather more political scientists than is at present the case being truly mathematically inclined and well trained.

It is commonplace, in some circles, both inside and outside political science, to deny the importance of the quantitative movement. No doubt some quantification is on relatively trivial topics and leads to findings of limited importance, but so are many studies which are purely qualitative and purely descriptive. The main point is that the quantitative approach is not what it is because of mathematics; it is what it is because it has relied heavily on eighteenth-century assumptions which many believe are rather out-of-date, or at any rate rather narrow, about the individual in society. Quantification in politics is interwoven with the principles within which politics has long been studied in the West. Being the most sophisticated form of analytical political theory, mathematical theory can only advance where the level of formalization is itself rather advanced; this is not the case, to a large extent at least, in those aspects of political analysis which go beyond or against the assumptions of eighteenth-century philosophers. It remains to be seen whether political scientists anxious to present alternative models, or simply to broaden the traditional formal models, recognize the value, and indeed the need, for a mathematical underpinning of their analysis.

Notes

1. E. J. Meehan (1968), *Explanation in Social Science*, pp. 5–6.
2. *See* D. Black (1958), *The Theory of Committees and Elections*, Part II, pp. 156–213.
3. *Polimetrics* is the title of a work by T. R. Gurr (1972).
4. One can, for instance, compare programmes in terms of their relative distance. *See* D. Robertson (1976), *A Theory of Party Competition*.
5. *See* Chapter 2.
6. An example of this type of criticism can be found in the criticisms addressed at the time of their publication to S. M. Lipset's *Political Man* (1960), London; Heinemann, and S. E. Finer *et al.*, *Backbench Opinion in the House of Commons* (1961), Oxford, Pergamon, by reviewers from the political world.
7. *See* for instance, M. Dogan (ed.) (1975), *The Mandarins of Western Europe*. An example for Britain is the Report of the Fulton Committee on the Civil Service (1969), quoted in reference to Chapter 3.
8. *See* for instance, B. M. Russett (1965), *Trends in World Politics*.

9. *See* in particular the works of R. H. Alker, Jr.
10. One example is J. E. Alt (1979), *The Politics of Economic Decline*, for Britain.
11. *See* for instance, the works of I. K. Feierabend *et al.* (1972) and T. R. Gurr (1970) quoted in reference to Chapter 2.
12. T. R. Gurr, 'A Causal Model of Civil Strife', in I. K. Feierabend *et al.* (1972), p. 208.
13. This was a view taken by the contributors to H. Storing (1962), *Essays on the Scientific Study of Politics*.
14. H. D. Lasswell and A. Kaplan (1950), *Power and Society*, p. xiv.
15. *Ibid.*, p. xvii.
16. R. A. Dahl, 'The Concept of Power', *Behavioural Science*, 2, July 1957, p. 203.
17. For instance by H. R. Alker, Jr. in H. R. Alker, Jr. *et al.* (1973), *Mathematical Approaches to Politics*, pp. 307ff.
18. *See* D. Black (1958), Part II.
19. W. H. Riker and P. C. Ordeshook (1973), p. 192.
20. M. J. Taylor, 'Normative Rational Choices of Politics', in L. Lewin and E. Vedung (eds.) (1980), p. 25.
21. A. Rapoport, 'Various Meanings of Rational Political Decisions', in L. Lewin and E. Vedung (eds.) (1980), p. 58–59.
22. *Ibid.*, p. 37.
23. *See* A. De Swaan (1973), *Coalition Theories and Cabinet Formations*.
24. W. H. Riker and P. C. Ordeshook (1973), p. 189.
25. *See* P. Blau (1964), *Exchange and Power in Social Life*, New York; Wiley.

References

ALKER, H. R., Jr. (1965). *Mathematics and Politics*. New York; Macmillan
ALKER, H. R., Jr., DEUTSCH, K. W. AND STOETZEL, A. H. (eds.) (1973). *Mathematical Approaches to Politics* Amsterdam; Elsevier
ALT, J. E. *The Politics of Economic Decline*. Cambridge; Cambridge University Press
ARROW, K. J. (1951). *Social Choice and Individual Values*. New Haven, Conn.; Yale University Press
BARRY, B. (ed.) (1976). *Power and Political Theory*. London: Wiley
BLACK, D. (1958). *The General Theory of Committees and Elections*. Cambridge; Cambridge University Press
BOUDON, R. (1971). *The Logic of Sociological Explanation*. Paris; Presses Univ de France (English trans. 1974: Harmondsworth, Middlesex; Penguin)
BUCHANAN, J. M. AND TULLOCK, G. (1962). *The Calculus of Consent*. Ann Arbor, Mich.; University of Michigan Press
DAHL, R. A. (1963). *Modern Political Analysis*. Englewood Cliffs, N. J.; Prentice-Hall
DE SWAAN, A. (1973). *Coalition Theories and Cabinet Formations*. Amsterdam; Elsevier
DEUTSCH, K. W. (1953). *Nationalism and Social Communication*. Cambridge, Mass.; M.I.T. Press
DOGAN, M. (ed.) (1975). *The Mandarins of Western Europe*. New York; Wiley
GURR. T. R. (1972). *Polimetrics*. Englewood Cliffs, N.J.; Prentice-Hall
LASSWELL, H. D. AND KAPLAN, A. (1950). *Power and Society*. New Haven, Conn.; Yale University Press

LEWIN, L. AND VEDUNG, E. (eds.) (1980). *Politics as Rational Action.* Dordrecht; Reidel

LUCE, R. D. AND RAIFFA, H. (1957). *Games and Decisions.* New York; Wiley

MEEHAN, E. J. (1968). *Explanation in Social Science.* Homewood, Ill.; Dorsey Press

NICHOLSON, M. (1970). *Conflict Analysis.* London; English Universities Press

OLSON, M. Jr. (1965). *The Logic of Collective Action.* Cambridge, Mass.; Harvard University Press

RAE, D. AND TAYLOR, M. J. (1970). *The Analysis of Political Cleavages.* New Haven, Conn.; Yale University Press

RIKER, W. H.. (1962). *The Theory of Political Coalitions.* New Haven, Conn.; Yale University Press

RIKER, W. H., AND ORDESHOOK, P. C. (1973). *An Introduction to Positive Political Theory.* Englewood Cliffs, N.J.: Prentice-Hall

ROBERTSON, D. (1976). *A Theory of Party Competition.* London; Wiley

ROGOWSKI, R. (1975). *Rational Legitimacy.* Princeton, N.J.; Princeton University Press

RUSSETT, B. M. (1965). *Trends in World Politics.* New York; Macmillan

TAYLOR, M. J. (1976). *Anarchy or Cooperation.* London; Wiley

WHITELEY, P. (ed.) (1980). *Models of Political Economy.* London and Beverly Hills; Sage

Chapter 6
Whither political theory?

The consideration of the relationship between politics and eternity.

M. Oakeshott

A study of the relationship between principles and institutions. Its focus is analytical rather than causal.

B. Barry

While many political scientists were busy studying mass political behaviour, or elaborating models of the political system, or attempting to quantify basic concepts such as power, there were those who rather gloomily felt that the discipline of politics had lost its soul and who were mourning the passing of 'political theory'. Political theory, it was said, was dead, killed by the endeavour of the new political scientists (Laslett, 1956). This judgement may seem strange at first sight, since what we have so far discussed includes *theoretical* models, mathematical political *theory* and elements of a *theory* of representation and of a *theory* of organization. If, as Sabine says, 'political theory is, quite simply, man's attempts to consciously understand and solve the problems of group life and organization', and if it is, as he further says, 'the disciplined investigation of political problems'[1], it seems difficult to claim seriously that political theory was dead in the 1950s and early 1960s.

Yet those who made this claim at the time were stating rather brutally that something truly fundamental had occurred in the study of politics in the early post-war period. They were making the point that scientific 'professionalism' and positivist 'assertiveness' had taken over; in this climate, old ways of reflecting on politics were viewed as no longer relevant, on the grounds that old methods of investigation were usually too simple, that problems used to be badly presented, and above all that moral considerations were often discussed in the midst of analyses of facts. To many 'new' political scientists, this passing of political theory was, by and large, real progress. But, for the traditionalists, a vacuum was left in the centre of the discipline because the really important problems were now being ignored: political scientists had ceased to be interested in the broad questions relating the organization of society to fundamental moral standpoints; or they arrogantly—and impossibly—tried to fill the vacuum by 'scientific' analyses of behaviour as if 'what ought to be' could be deduced from an examination of 'what could be done'.

The conflict between supporters and opponents of 'political theory' was often acrimonious. Not surprisingly, the 'traditionalists' were more vocal again when, after a few years, disappointment set in among the 'new' political scientists with respect to models which seemed unable to account for reality, or to quantification, which did not result in a steady stream of truly significant results. But the traditionalists did not merely remark that they had always known that it was not possible to quantify politics or that the endeavour to build global models was an unrealistic adventure. They went further and made fundamental attacks against the positivist framework within which political science had flourished, mainly in America, in the 1950s and early 1960s. The 'pseudo-scientific' laws of politics were said to be based on profound misunderstandings about the relationship between 'facts' and those who observed the facts in the human science. The result was narrowness, not of the kind which Easton and Almond deplored because new countries and new systems of government were not taken into account, but a narrowness stemming from what Marcuse was to call the 'uni-dimensional' view of man. The new political science did not only oversimplify, it was felt: it falsified reality.

Yet attacks such as these were more a reaction against the success, however temporary, of the new 'scientific' approach than a positive case in favour of an alternative line of inquiry. The protest did show that 'positivism' had limitations; but what was not immediately clear was what had to be done in practice in order to achieve better results. Perhaps there was a vacuum to be filled, perhaps 'scientism' was too superficial; but the new political science provided a method of inquiry and findings were being made. Indeed, the new developments in political science had transformed the discipline to such an extent that it was not possible simply to return to the past. 'Political theory' may have previously occupied the front, perhaps even the whole of the stage; it did not do so any longer, and no amount of attacks would by itself restore political theory to its previous position. Either political theorists had to accommodate themselves to this situation and learn to live with the new political science, or they had to show that as much progress, and indeed more, could be achieved by their own methods. Hence what sometimes seemed from the outside to be an 'agonizing reappraisal' of the role of 'political theory' in the post-war period—one which appears now to be leading more and more to the recognition that 'scientism' is here to stay and that accommodation is the best and perhaps the only sensible line of conduct. But this conclusion was hard to arrive at; it is still not universally shared by political theorists.

The decline and division of political theory

Political theory has been markedly attacked—or even purely and simply ignored—by the positivists in post-war political science. But this situation came about after a long period of decline and division within political theory. By 1945, indeed already by the turn of the century, many forms of empirical political science had eroded the scope of political theory and undermined the assurance of political theorists; and the diversity of approach was so large among political theorists that it was difficult to find an underlying unity.

In its oldest and perhaps most 'noble' form, political theory was viewed as a grand reflection on man in society. It was felt to be the heir to a long tradition in which an imposing line of great authors constituted major signposts. This line started with the Greeks, Plato and Aristotle in particular, and went through the centuries, St Augustine, St Thomas Aquinas, Jean Bodin, Thomas More, Machiavelli, Hobbes, Locke, Montesquieu (perhaps) and Rousseau being among the main representatives of the tradition. Although, these authors expounded different views about society, they seemed to be united by their common aim—the search for a good society—and by a common approach—the presentation of a global view of political and social life.

From the Greeks to the classical period, political theorists related the facts known to be correct to the many considerations, even allegories, which seemed to give an account of the distant past and which, in the manner of fables, contained a moral for future generations. As little was known about the ways in which societies emerged, developed and changed, it was permissible to imagine how change might have occurred and to draw lessons from this plausible evolution. For instance, it was neither absolutely clear that a social contract between members of the society had ever occurred nor was it absolutely certain that it had never taken place. In this dawn of knowledge, political theory therefore naturally consisted of the sum of the reflections which men made on politics and society. Sabine is right in describing it as 'man's attempts to consciously understand and solve (both aspects are essential) the problems of group life and organization'[2]. Theorists were therefore both concerned with the goals of political organization and the ways politics was run. Morals were intertwined with strategies. There was, on the one hand, emphasis on liberty, justice, democracy, equality, and, on the other on authority, allegiance, legitimacy and the role of the state. The result was the elaboration of 'utopias', mixing appeals to greater morality with precepts for more rational arrangements.

Depending on whether they were more or less optimistic about man's ability to control himself and to strive for the common good by silencing his desires, political theorists proposed blueprints for society of a more or less individualistic and liberal character. If they were very optimistic, they suggested solutions in which individuals could fulfil their own aspirations within the context of a relatively permissive social framework. If they were more pessimistic, and were also ready to see greater restrictions on individuals, they suggested that individual selfishness be tamed by various means. And if, being very pessimistic, they felt embarrassed by such an authoritarian programme, they proposed 'utopias', not in order to see them implemented, but in order to offer guidelines; by a happy accident, some men might be able in some societies to overcome the normal tendencies of the human condition. Throughout these works, the approach was universalistic, and the coverage comprehensive. Writers grabbed what facts were available from every corner of knowledge—from psychology, biology and physics, as Hobbes did, or from the experience of primitive societies, as Rousseau did. This knowledge was then combined with the ideals which the writer proposed, to result in a general theory of political life[3].

In the eighteenth century, however, this 'allegorical' approach to political theory and political analysis became gradually undermined by the growth of knowledge about man's physical, biological and social environment. Rationalism became prevalent; it led to the belief that society could be changed if enough efforts were made to understand its 'mechanics'; the idea of progress became widely adopted. The result was that, when the American and French Revolutions occurred at the end of the century, the role and purpose of political theory altered dramatically. For, before these revolutions, the proposals of political theorists had by and large remained academic. Events in England in the seventeenth century did bring about a change in the political arrangements of the country; but the final outcome resulting from the 1688

Revolution was a compromise between the old and the new society. The break was avoided; there was no fresh start, and theories were heavily diluted by tradition. The American and French Revolutions, on the contrary, were the first large-scale attempts at remoulding entirely the political organization of society. It seemed possible to change the course of the history of mankind; and it seemed natural that intellectuals should address themselves to the examination of the ways in which change could bring about 'progress' in society.

Hence, a number of important consequences for the study of politics and for the status and character of political theory. First, and in an immediate manner, it became imperative that laws be passed to determine specifically what the new organization of society would be. The result was the development of a branch of learning, constitutional law, which could be regarded as the 'right arm' of political theory: it aimed at stating the precise ways in which the principles of government could be put in practice. And, second, the operation of government resulting from these laws led to the emergence of a further type of inquiry, designed to evaluate the ways in which new laws were implemented. Not surprisingly, both constitutional law and the study of political practice developed mostly in the countries which had experienced a break and had moved towards constitutional government; this was especially the case in America and in France where constitutional law, in particular, expanded very rapidly.

For a while, these developments took place at the periphery of traditional political theory and did not markedly affect it. Constitutional law could be deemed to be entirely derivative on the analyses of political theorists, since these had elaborated the principles of state organization on which constitutions were based; it could be regarded as a technical discipline only, even somewhat divorced from the study of politics proper. And the evaluation of the workings of constitutions seemed to be one further step remote from the traditional study of politics; this new branch of study, which was developing slowly, without any theoretical mentors or even academic credentials, was not seen as a threat to political theory.

Yet the effect was to reduce gradually the scope of political theory and probably to divert towards constitutional law and towards the emerging 'political sociology' some of the talent which might have been devoted in the past to political theory. Slowly, it became more difficult to sustain the view that empirical analyses were only descriptive embellishments or mere appendices of studies of constitutions. Political theorists had to take notice of the existence of 'empiricists' as well as of constitutional lawyers.

They had to do so because, during the nineteenth century, two other consequences of the eighteenth-century Revolutions had altered the purpose of political theory. One was, in line with the eighteenth-century rationalist movement, the increased belief that progress could be brought nearer by the development of a 'science of society'. 'Positivism'—as preached in the first instance by Comte in the first half of the nineteenth century—became a new creed; it relegated much of what had been said about society in the past to being infantile remarks of a 'metaphysical' or indeed 'theological' age. It was more important to be concerned with the future, with the evolution of the society in which one lived, than with the examination of the texts of authors whose writings corresponded to entirely different conditions. While Marx's premises and moral stance were very different from those of Comte, his paramount desire to develop a 'scientific' theory of socialism places him within the same broad movemenet—and distinguishes him sharply from the 'traditional' political theorists who were concerned with basic moral vlaues and who did believe in the underlying 'eternal' characteristics of mankind.

Meanwhile—and Marx provides the link between the two aspects—the emergence of the new liberal society led to the rapid development of fundamental critiques of that society. Socialist utopias sprang up almost as soon as 'constitutionalism' and capitalism emerged. In a sense, these criticisms were—to begin with, at least—in the old tradition of political theory, in that they were concerned with the presentation of a global view of what society should be. But they were also very different because they were based on the analysis of nineteenth-century society, not on an eternal view of mankind; and they focused on a 'critique' of the principles of that society, indeed to such an extent that, gradually, and especially with Marx, the 'critique' became the major, if not the only, element of the new theory. 'Utopias' were replaced by a hardheaded analysis of the failings of the current world.

These different movements occurred in parallel throughout the nineteenth and early twentieth centuries. But all of them— constitutional law, empirical 'political sociology', the generation of new utopias, the critique of capitalist liberal-democracy—contributed to a decline of the influence of political theory as it had previously been conceived; and they led also to a climate of soul-searching and internal conflict among political theorists who no longer knew with certainty what their precise function was. They were sharply divided. Some remained close to moral philosophy while others were interested in the philosophy of history; some believed in an endeavour designed to discover the 'eternal' characteristics of man while others felt that man was the product of his concrete environment. In the late nineteenth and the twentieth centuries, these oppositions became increasingly exacerbated by ideological conflicts: socialism, Communism, fascism were attractive to some while they seemed to others to lead to a return to 'barbarism'. The emergence, during and after World War II, of a strong 'positivist' and 'scientist' line among the empirical political scientists was therefore only the least of a long line of events which profoundly undermined the strength of political theory and the self-assurance of those who practised it.

Emphasizing 'eternal' values

As we saw, America was the country where 'positivist' political science was both numerically strongest and qualitatively most distinguished; in Western Europe, on the contrary, the 'new' political science was still relatively weak before World War II and even afterwards. By contrast, the various branches of political theory had always been strong in Europe: almost all the 'great names' of the nineteenth century, from Comte to Marx, had been European. Not surprisingly, the reaction against 'scientism' was to be greater in Europe, throughout the post-war decades, than in the United States.

More specifically, the defence of the most traditional form of political theory was to be particularly strong in Britain. Britain was the country of 'pragmatism' and, as a result, never became the home of massive ideological constructions nor did it champion tightly conceived constitutional blueprints. Ideology did develop to an extent, admittedly; socialist schemes, from Owen to Cole, were elaborated, but they remained at the margin of academic traditions. The absence of a clear break with the past had made it unnecessary for constitutional law to develop as a major discipline; indeed, the visible political achievements of Britain seemed to suggest that piecemeal change, rather than a systematic rethinking of institutions, was the most satisfactory way of handling modern governmental problems. Thus, while an empirical tradition developed in Britain (a tradition which led British political scientists, as we know, to engage successfully in electoral and administrative studies), this tradition was 'narrowly' empirical, so to speak. The justification of empirical studies was, in the main, academic curiosity and, to an extent, suggestions for practical change; this was the same justification as that which can be given for historical scholarship—in which many empirical political scientists were trained in Britain. The aim was not to undertake a 'scientific' analysis or a general reflection on the social and political structure. Political theory could remain pure, very academic; it could also be divorced from other aspects of political studies. Britain was thus the country where the compartmentalization between political theory and empirical analysis was defined most clearly, while being also the country where the status of traditional political theory remained highest—not just before World War II but indeed afterwards.

Thus, when the 'positivist' challenge came to Britain, it came from outside, from the development of American political science. The British traditions of political theory and political philosophy were sufficiently old, however, and the reputation of British scholarship in these fields was sufficiently high, for political theory to remain for a while almost untouched in Britain while elsewhere ideological disputes and 'scientific politics' were beginning to change the discipline of politics.

It is therefore not surprising that, even to this day, Britain should have been the country where political theory of the traditional kind should have best remained most alive, both in the diffuse and general sense that the profession of politics remained relatively sceptical about the 'American science of politics' (Crick, 1959) and in the more precise sense that attempts were made to debunk and undermine the new developments in political science. And the best representative of this tradition in the post-war period has been Michael Oakeshott who endeavoured both to reduce the belief in the overall value of political science and to diminish the role of scientific analysis both for human knowledge and human happiness.

Oakeshott's approach was essentially sceptical about the ability of mankind to rule itself in a 'rational' and satisfactory manner. Consequently, he cast his net widely, not without an occasional malicious twinkle. He was as much concerned to establish the role, indeed the prime importance of poetry, described as the activity of 'contemplating and delighting'[4] as to stress the claims of philosophy which is there to 'listen' to what is going on and to examine the different voices in the 'conversations' of mankind (Oakeshott, 1953). Oakeshott's contribution is one which aims at making political scientists recognize their own limitations as well as the limitations of the activities of politicians. This is why this approach is fundamentally opposed to both 'scientists' and 'ideologues', since the latter are concerned to demonstrate that only because we are unconscious or mystified are we unable to realize that we are continuously manipulated by existing political arrangements. For Oakeshott such an approach diminishes man; it makes him 'boring' (Oakeshott, 1959). But this also means that we cannot expect poetry, or philosophy, to meddle with the practical activities of mankind. Presumably the constant reminder that there are other—higher—forces of thought and reflection is the way in which politicians and practitioners generally are made to realize that they are 'mere' politicians and do not have sufficient authority to rule in a totalitarian manner.

In this approach, the role of political theory and political philosophy is negative; it almost amounts to making sure that politics keeps to its relatively lowly state and does not go 'above its station'. For, while politicians must not pretend to govern the whole of life, political philosophers must not pretend to provide the answer either. The purpose of political philosophy is 'to consider the place of political activity in the map of our total experience'; it is not to provide an end for mankind to seek. The ideologues, not the political philosophers, attempt to provide this end—and they lead mankind to 'bogus eternity'[5].

This view is at one level healthy, in that it fights to prevent politicians and ideologues from wishing to control man's life in general. But it is also so sceptical, and ultimately so negative about the role of politics and political philosophy that the effect of Oakeshott's teaching and general influence—which has been large—has been to reduce the desire of scholars in political science even to undertake those practical studies which, according to Oakeshott, might have some value for both politicians and citizens. Oakeshott's resistance to the movement of 'scientism' and to the pervasive influence of ideology has taken the form of an aesthetic gesture more than that of an alternative approach, perhaps because it was consistent with Oakeshott's standpoint that gestures—poetic or artistic—were more important to the understanding of the human condition than any rational construction. While he therefore helped to maintain the tradition of—or the case for—political theory, Oakeshott did so in such a sceptical manner that it clearly did not contribute to the continuation of the tradition of political theory—rather did he contribute to the continued reputation of the 'museum' of the political theory of the past.

The sceptical endeavour of Oakeshott was only possible because the general context of British political studies was one in which 'science' was never given (except occasionally in the field of administrative studies) true recognition. In the United States discontent and opposition to 'science' had to be less arrogant and to relate more closely to what had been achieved. This accounts for the fact that the resistance to the new political science, of which

Leo Strauss was one of the foremost representatives, was at the same time less precise, less serene and generally less lofty than in Britain. There was little room for scepticism in the United States; the critique of 'modern' political science had to be as enthusiastic as the defence made of it by the 'new' political scientists.

To this extent, Strauss's approach is narrower than that of Oakeshott for whom political philosophy occupies an intermediate position. For Strauss, on the contrary, political philosophy is central and the study of politics can only be truly great if it has once more the characteristics which it had with Aristotle. Strauss is convinced that the crisis of our times comes from the 'positivist' approach, which 'views human beings as an engineer would view material for building bridges'[6]. This is the 'anti-scientific' point which links Strauss to Oakeshott. But whereas Oakeshott ultimately does not provide an answer from within politics because he believes that the answer cannot come from politics or even philosophy, Strauss does believe that political philosophy provides the answer. The close reading and the constant rethinking of the great classics creates an attitude of mind which will lead to what might be called the 'correct' approach to man and his destiny. And, in the first instance, what must be done is to realize the 'oneness', so to speak, of political inquiry, 'oneness' which Oakeshott would not approve of, since Oakeshott is, on the contrary, adamant to maintain each type of inquiry in its place, in its separate compartment. But, in order to come to the conclusion that political knowledge is 'one', Strauss is forced to attempt to show that the 'discoveries' which modern 'empirico-scientific' political science has claimed to make were, in reality, trivial discoveries. This is why the work which was published by Strauss and a number of his followers, the *Essays on the Scientific Study of Politics* (Storing, 1962) is so central to this theme: only if he can prove—and he and his colleagues endeavour at length to do so—that the discoveries are trivial can Strauss seriously maintain that there was really nothing of important in these studies which was not already in Aristotle.

The point that modern political science leads to very little has often been made. To say the least, it is clearly exaggerated[7]. In a sense, Oakeshott's scepticism is more subtle, because it avoids having to answer the question specifically; Oakeshott does not need to answer it because political knowledge can relate 'only' to the world of politics, which is in the inferior realm of practice. For Strauss, the problem is central. Hence the point which he makes in *The City and Man* according to which, while political philosophy cannot 'supply us with recipes for today's use...an adequate understanding of the principles as elaborated by the classics may be the indispensable starting point for an adequate analysis, to be achieved by us, of present-day society in its peculiar character and for the wise application, to be achieved by us, of these principles to our tasks.' The fact that Strauss makes the point in the conditional ('may be the indispensable starting point') *may* be an indication that he has come to realize the fundamental weakness of his stance: his enthusiasm for the classics *may* have led him too far in dismissing modern political science.

The resistance to the 'aggressive' attitude of the 'new' political scientists, whether model-makers or quantifiers, has therefore had in many ways the character of a rearguard action which attempted, in a gallant but somewhat quixotic manner, to contain, almost single-handedly, the advance of the 'battalions' of the 'scientists' and ideologues. But, despite its many qualities, despite its importance in maintaining the interest in the great thinkers of the past, this rearguard action was too negative to be the start of a new movement: neither the Oakeshottians nor Strauss have much to say about society—save to repeat what the classics said. Theirs is ultimately an historical or archaeological interest; although Strauss calls for a reflection about the great problems, and although Oakeshott stresses the need for thought along lines other than 'science', neither makes much progress in these directions. They both state what should or should not be done; neither undertakes the analysis proper. As Brian Barry said:

> To spend one's working life rolling the classics round the tongue like old brandy (as advocated by Leo Strauss and disciples) hardly seems likely to advance the sum of human knowledge. If we really want to imitate the Greeks the first thing to do is to stop looking over our shoulders all the time[9].

Is is not more productive to try and emulate the classics, to play the same game as theirs and to embark on new 'utopias' about man in society?

Political theory as a 'critique' of society

One way of 'defending' political theory was to try to 'roll back' empirical analysis and to maintain it 'in its place'. Those who were more forward-looking or who wanted to keep abreast with modern developments in society could not be satisfied with such a posture. They were often convinced of the failings, let along limitations, of the type of political arrangements which 'constitutionalism' had brought about; they were sure that 'alternative' arrangements would bring mankind nearer to the 'good society'.

By its very aim, however, such an approach was bound to bring those who adopted it in direct conflict with the political scientists who analysed society with an empirical frame of mind; once the idea had become accepted that politics could be studied in a 'scientific' manner, any new proposal made by theorists would have to be 'tested' by the same type of methods as those which were adopted to study current society. If new blueprints could not be tested in this way, they would be dismissed as mere utopias; and if they were, the political theorists who promised them would cease to have the status of 'global thinkers' adamant to carry out the search which the classics had begun; they would be mere 'ideologues' whom empiricists would be able and eager to confront with the many difficulties of the reality.

Thus the political theorists who had an 'alternative' vision of society were naturally drawn to oppose, not just the 'constitutionalist' and 'liberal-democratic' society which empiricists analysed, but the foundations on which empirical analysis was based. They had to undertake a 'critical' examination of the underlying premises of political and social *science*. As one author who surveyed (and approved of) the successive attacks against the 'positivist' mood said: 'It is increasingly evident that in order to gain a critical understanding of the social and political disciplines, we must face not only epistemological but metaphysical issues[10].' In a sense, the 'traditionalists' were right: empirical political science could only lead to limited studies, and these studies were necessarily 'conservative' in outlook, in that they assumed—had to assume—that man operated on the basis of a number of 'rules' or 'laws' of social behaviour which the empirical study of the past could help us to discover. This meant that 'new' laws of social behaviour simply could never be found and indeed would always be dismissed as 'unrealistic'. But the traditionalists were wrong in either idolizing the classics or taking refuge in forms of thought divorced from society; by so doing, they denied themselves opportunities to influence the shape of society.

If an alternative approach was to be substituted for the scientific or positivist school, it had to be based on a more fundamental critique of the scientific approach itself. What had to be shown was that the human mind and human behaviour could be better grasped through different methods based on different foundations. These different foundations existed, it was thought; they were to be found in some of the philosophical movements which had developed on the Continent, mainly in Germany or the German-speaking world. Phenomenology, combined with psychoanalysis and Marxism, seemed to provide the approaches which were needed. These approaches emphasized the difference between the physical and the living worlds. They stressed that while the physical world is observed by us from outside (and indeed even then it is questionable whether we can observe reality without changing it), the living and even more the human world is not 'observable' in this passive manner. In particular, while the physical world does not reflect and take into account its past and its evolution, we not only have a history but can and do spend our time looking at this history. It is therefore theoretically absurd and practically constraining to attempt to discover 'laws' of human behaviour, since by observing and thinking about these 'laws' we may indeed change them.

This is why psychology is both an extremely important—indeed a central—discipline and one which must be used with considerable care. Psychology will be useless if it is based on 'scientific' premises and is predicated on the discovery by 'objective' methods of what 'others' do in given situations. Psychology is essential, on the contrary, if it is based on the fundamental realization of the importance of 'meaning' in human behaviour and of the basic subjective character of any understanding. The way to 'understand' what takes place in society is through an analysis of the relationship between individuals and others; it is through the discovery of the 'meaning' which is given to actions. This is also why 'action' has to be distinguished from 'behaviour', the latter being simply a 'happening' while the former adds the notion of meaning to the way the individual behaves. As Schutz said:

> We want to understand...social phenomena, and we cannot understand them apart from their placement within the scheme of human motives, human means and ends, human planning—in short—within categories of human action[11].

And he adds:

> It is obvious that an action has only one meaning, that of the actor himself[12].

But we must go further: it is not sufficient to recognize that human action cannot be understood without a deep appreciation of the different meanings which men give to these actions, a point which we encountered already when analysing the development of mass political behaviour studies. We must also realize that we are involved, that is to say, that there is no such thing as a disinterested observer looking from outside, in a Lucretian manner, at the battles between human beings. This is where it seemed essential to have a *critical* approach, critical in the deepest sense; we have to 'unmask' all the assumptions of those who had hitherto been concerned with the analysis of man. The so-called 'Frankfurt school' (many of whose members emigrated for a time to the United States) took as their starting point Marx's view that 'we do not anticipate the world dogmatically, but rather wish to find the new world through criticism of the old'[13]. This is a highly sensible position, since, after all, the only world which we know is the one which has existed; but it is also a position which has the effect of creating a climate of thought which is, indeed, critical, rather than constructive. In Marx's view, the consciousness of the conditions under which one lives is the leverage and the linkage, the leverage because it helps to work in the direction of change, the linkage because it makes it possible to understand both one's own 'concrete' situation and the 'concrete' situation of others. And it is on this basis that any sound 'theory' of politics and society must be constructed.

Whether it is indeed true that a sound theory of politics and society must be constructed on the basis of the realization of the specific conditions within which individuals live in a society, no one can, strictly speaking, be sure. What is certain is that, to date, 'critical' theorists have only provided us with a 'critique' of existing societies, and indeed, for that matter, of only that society—the capitalist society—which they chose to undermine, largely because they were not merely motivated by a search for the 'truth', but desperately wanted to demonstrate the 'sickness' of that society. The question remains whether one can really understand any existing society if one believes that one cannot observe when one is involved. Marx and the Marxists seem indeed to believe a little too easily in our ability to discover the 'objective' characteristics of our society; they appear to feel that the problem is merely to adapt our 'consciousness' to those 'objectively discoverable' characteristics. But even if one leaves aside these problems—which Marxists raise in connection with 'positivist' approaches—an even greater problem arises from the suggested methodology: is it in fact permissible to infer what society should and will be in the future from a critique of what exists today?

This is not a problem for the positivist, of course, because the positivist believes that he can find 'laws' of human behaviour which constitute the linkage between past, present, and future.

But if it is asserted that the new society will be altogether new, indeed that the conditions of its operation are, in a sense, not given yet (that what is given is only at most the conditions of the self-destruction of the present society), then it is not clear that one is entitled to extrapolate from the 'critique' of the old to the characteristics of the new. And, specifically, it is not clear that there will be 'progress'—even if it were demonstrated that there was 'progress' in the past. Such a conclusion can be drawn only if one adopts the further assumption that, somehow, mankind always improves, at least in the long run—an assumption which, in turn, has to be based on the general principle that the new, the future, is contained in the past and present. But if this is the case, the 'laws' of human behaviour in the future could also be discovered by an intense analysis of the 'new' elements contained already in the past and present.

The problems faced by 'critical' theorists are at the same time monumental and, so to speak, almost childish. What is to be done is to find a way out of one's conditon, after one has specified that this is not possible because we are constrained by the conditons under which we live. There is therefore a constant critique— critique of one's position, critique of language, critique of the ideological 'mystifications' within which one lives, as Jürgen Habermas attempts to do. As a result, the powers of analysis of 'critics' become so continuously turned in on themselves and on other scholars that the endeavour appears self-destructive, and, at least, not constructive. In a straightforward time-calculus, the intellectual efforts spent on this seemingly indefinite attempt at understanding one's relationship with society cannot be spent on undertaking other activities, and in particular they cannot be spent 'imagining' the framework within which the new society may be organized.

The critique of the 'critics'

It is this impatience with the inability of the 'critical' theorists to provide an alternative model of society, as distinct from suggesting an alternative method of *analysis* of the present one, which is in part at the root of the criticisms which have been levelled against the 'critical' philosophers and political theorists in the course of the second half of the 1970s; but another reason for these (often strident) criticisms is the increasing feeling of 'inauthenticity—or hypocrisy—which seems to surround the 'critical' approach. For instance, Rousseau felt disgusted by Voltaire's double standard, which led Voltaire to become the protégé of the King of Prussia and yet to continue to be engaged in virulent attacks on absolutist regimes. The so-called 'new philosophers' who emerged in the 1970s, in France in particular, have increasingly felt that the rarefied, hypersophisticated and complex critiques of Western capitalist society under the banner of neo-Marxism acted as a huge smoke-screen to cover up the even more unacceptable modes of behaviour of Eastern totalitarian Communist governments. the aim of the 'new' philosophers is to 'unmask', once more, but in the name of common sense, because, to borrow the title of one of the works written in this vein, 'Barbary' has now 'a human face' (B.-H. Lévy, 1977).

Much of the 'critique of the critics' has an emotional base, but much of the critical analysis itself—and that of Marx to begin with—had or has an emotional base—namely that capitalism was unacceptable because of the sufferings it was imposing on human beings and that it is still imposing, in the eyes of the neo-Marxists, on the human race. The anti-Marxist critics also start from the emotional standpoint that, under the cover of Marxism, a totalitarian lead casket is imposed already on part of mankind and is gradually being imposed on an increasingly larger part. Thus the new critics of Marxism write in the same vein as and emulate some of the older political theorists. The contemporary world is in many ways as Hobbesian as the state of nature described by the seventeenth century English writer; the excesses of dictatorship have to be stigmatized and alternatives have to be elaborated and presented to mankind as, otherwise, the dominance of the ruthless will be assured. Political theory started from a disgust with the state of things as they were as well as out of a desire to understand what was going on. Blueprints presented by Plato, Hobbes, Locke and Rousseau were means of getting out of the human predicament; political theory must continue to fulfil this function because, if it does not, mankind will, once more, fall into a barbaric state.

This is the main reason why the nature and role of political theory have to be sharply distinguished from the nature and role of ideology. The nineteenth century had been the era of ideology; it seemed that, when the French and American Revolutions had given the classics their chance, ideologues took over, from Comte through socialists of various kinds to different brands of fascists. 'Eternal' political theory was drowned by the battle between the ideologies, while its status was undermined by the continuous repetition that it was a liberal fallacy to believe that the philosopher could be above the battle. But the result had been the excesses of the Russian Revolution and its aftermath, of fascism and Nazism, and generally the growth of the totalitarian state all over the planet—in the name of mankind but at the price of the destruction of man. Surely it is common sense to realize that not merely is there a place for a reflection on society and for further guidance in order to avoid excesses, but that this role is the most important that can be conceived. And, to fulfil this role, 'empirical' or 'scientific' analyses are not felt to be satisfactory. In fact 'scientific' analyses lead to their opposite—to 'critical' analyses; both can be viewed as rarefied, 'scientism' because it turns mankind into a set of regularities, 'critical' neo-Marxist theory because it sacrifices mankind for the sake of an idea, the idea of not being 'taken in'. Time is wasted in order to 'unmask' the pretensions of an approach which claims to understand mankind and no time is left simply to denounce the obvious monstrous activities which are taking place in the contemporary world. Strauss made the point when he said, in a phrase of voluminous contempt:

...One may say that [the new political science] fiddles while Rome burns. It is excused by two facts: it does not know that it fiddles, and it does not know that Rome burns[14].

But Strauss did not know how to handle the great roman fire either because all he seemed to do, like French generals in 1939, was to fight World War I all over again. To claim that the classics would give the answer was obviously plainly unrealistic. What needs to be done is to denounce what is wrong with society as it is now and try to escalate to a grand view of what change there might be. From the emergence of pre-war fascism and Nazism as well as of Stalinism to the maintenance of totalitarian Communism in the post-war period, the endeavour to present this grand view 'in the name of mankind' has been undertaken by a number of theorists. The point, for them, was not to ape science and to apply it unthinkingly to human society, but to recognize the 'uniqueness and value of man'[15]. The study of the 'human condition' should be the main purpose of the analysis; it must be undertaken without an ideology, Marxism and neo-Marxism being ultimately ideologies since they are more concerned with the progress of 'mankind' than with men as concrete individuals. 'They are ideologies because they are in the logic of an idea. The ideology treats the course of events as though it followed the same "law" as the logical exposition of the "idea". Ideologies pretend to know the mysteries of the whole historical process...because of the logic inherent in their respective ideas'[16].

What Hannah Arendt said in the late 1950s and early 1960s—echoing much of what Raymond Aron said at the same time—has now been markedly more strongly orchestrated by the new French philosophers of the second half of the 1970s; this new generation, which came to adulthood without having experienced the cold war attacks against Soviet Russia and having indeed often concurred in the virulent criticisms of Western capitalist society and of American world-wide interventions, has turned full circle and noted that there was, indeed, no alternative society. Neo-Marxists remain silent about Communist society and this deafening silence is ultimately what led the new philosophers to notice the fundamental intellectual poverty of the neo-Marxist approach. Hence the view expressed by one of them:

I learnt more reading *The Gulag Archipelago* than in many learned treatises on the totalitarian discourse. I owe more to Solzhenitsyn than to most sociologists, historians, philosophers, who during the last thirty years reflected on the future of the West. What a mystery there is in this document, which, no sooner it is written and published, can entirely upset our ideological landscape with all its signposts[17].

The 'new' philosophers—A. Glucksmann and B.-H. Lévy in particular—go on to reintroduce some of the basic notions which neo-Marxists had seemingly been able to throw overboard through their 'critical' analysis, namely, that power is a universal concept, that power is based on the state, and that ideologies—all ideologies, and the Marxist ideology more than the others—have the effect of reinforcing the power of the state by creating a class of men whose function is to oppress intellectually alongside the physical oppression. With the 'new' philosophers, theory has truly run full circle in the space of a few years: those who are attempting to 'unmask' the hypocrisy of capitalism are in turn 'unmasked'. But this turning of the hose on those who wished to do the drowning brings political theory back to the point at which it was in the 1940s and 1950s—and it is perhaps no accident that the 'new' philosophers should provide a link with the anti-totalitarian thought of Arendt, Aron and indeed Friedrich while suggesting an approach, a method of investigation which is in some ways reminiscent of Oakeshott.

For Solzhenitsyn's 'critique' of Soviet society and politics is that of the poet—not that of the political scientist or of the sociologist. B.-H. Lévy, like Oakeshott, discusses the pretensions of academic social scientists by comparison with the insights of the artist. Thus the net effect of this immense detour into methods and techniques designed to debunk the pretensions of 'scientism' is the conclusion that there is indeed much truth in the view that political theory is dead! For, if political theorists commonly complain about what others do (or do not do) and warn about the limitations of their ways, this surely must show that political theory has nothing new to contribute. To warn that power—naked power—is as much present as it always was, indeed is perhaps stronger than in the past, tends to mean that the world escapes our control, and means, by the way, that the efforts of political theorists have been to little avail.

Political theory has to be able to do more if it is to be recognized as a lively element of intellectual endeavour. And this is probably why, below the cacophony of the strident 'critics' attacking each other in a game of words reminiscent of the war-of-words characteristics of the East–West controversy, a more modest, but also more constructive form of political theory has began to emerge, based on two premises. The first is that, even if the findings of empirical political science are unsatisfactory, they have increased our knowledge about society. And the second is that political theory, if it is to survive, has to contribute to a reflection on politics as it is now, including the empirical findings made by political scientists. The more that political theory denies these findings—even if it is to say, as the 'new' philosophers say, that one learns more through novels and art than through academic analyses—the less one will contribute to an improvement of the findings of the empiricists and to the development of political science in general.

Political theory as analysis

One does not know whether the political theorists whose main work concentrated on a criticism of the 'new' political science were indeed satisfied with their own position. But the more 'positive' route which political theorists increasingly took in the late 1960s and in the 1970s has coincided with a dissatisfaction over the barrenness and emptiness of political theory conceived as a mere critique. Provided that political theorists were prepared to study carefully the work of empiricists, learn their techniques and understand their approaches, there seemed to be enough scope for careful reassessment and for an examination of wider implications without having to undertake global reappraisals of the whole 'scientific method' which turned out to be, not only rather repetitive, but ultimately unconvincing to those who felt that there was a need to study society as it is. We have often noticed that many problems of empirical analysis arose from the absence of clear conceptualization; empiricists rush into the operationalization of their concepts without often being clear about definitions. Perhaps they should not even be blamed for proceeding in this way because their concern is to find a practical formula to come to grips with reality and no other or better formula seems to be forthcoming. But it is abundantly clear that empirical analyses would gain—and empiricists would be the first to agree—if definitions were tighter and concepts more precise. Here is therefore an area where political theorists can unquestionably help.

But the concern with definitions and concepts leads inevitably to a broader question—that of the relationship between the concepts, the desires, goals and ideals of the individual who uses them, and the goals and ideals which are put forward as blueprints for the society. The groundwork of linguistic analysis (as practised in Britain and especially in Oxford) can produce, not just dry exercises in very abstract logic, but a valuable, indeed necessary, basis for an effort to understand how men can relate their own goals to those of the society. If one bears in mind what has actually been found, one can return once more to the old moral questions of personal obligation and of the bases for social choice. Rather than by undermining the obvious need for facts in order to establish the supremacy of a political theory in an empirical desert, one can reassert the role of analysis and reflection within the much richer context of a lively empirical discipline.

Hence, a better analysis of political concepts became gradually, from the mid-1960s, the underlying rationale for a number of efforts designed to reinsert political theory within the developing stream of political science. And perhaps the first work in this vein which was truly successful was that of Brian Barry, *Political Argument*, published in 1965. The contribution of Barry's work is fundamental, both by itself and by its influence, in that it did show that it was possible for political theory to add to our *knowledge* without having to be a complete *Weltanschauung*, without being so arrogant as to say that only the classics had something to say and that empirical analysis was pointless, and without wanting, rather viciously but also arrogantly, to undermine the basis of all scientific inquiry. This was indeed to be a continuous endeavour of Barry in the course of the coming decade; he thus played a very important part in the 'reconstruction' of political theory and in the 'rediscovery' of its role, independently from the specific contributions—which have been substantial—of his successive works.

Barry begins *Political Argument* with the bland statement that he is concerned with 'a study of the relation between principles and institutions'. By its very nakedness, this statement seems to brush aside the many years of 'worry' about whether it was, or not, worthwhile to study institutions and whether the function of political theory was to discover principles, look for eternal principles, or indeed guard us against exaggerations of 'scientists' or 'ideologues'. And Barry then goes on to say—in a common-sense manner—that political principles are inextricably linked with the state of society in its most basic structure because 'until some minimum amount of order and material welfare has been secured there are technical difficulties but not philosophically interesting problems'[18]. What Barry aims to do is to find out, extricate and carefully describe, the implications of the various types of arguments which are made in politics. He is concerned with rhetoric because 'the limits of language are also the limits of philosophical analysis'[19]. It may theoretically be interesting to know 'deep down' why individuals choose a course of action, but, as a matter of fact, what we can know is the justification and the argument which is made, not the fundamental evaluation, because an evaluation which is not expressed may be theoretically interesting, but is simply inaccessible.

Having carved for himself an area of study of principles which can be explored practically—and the only one in which principles *can* practically be explored—Barry goes on to assess the limits of our justification: we cannot, and need not, find one common overriding principle under which all justifications can be subsumed. But he also shows that, although the whole landscape is not unified, it is possible to draw some distinctions between types of principles, his main distinction being between 'want-regarding' and 'ideal-regarding' principles, that is, those principles through which some 'happiness' is obtained and those through which some 'perfection' is achieved. With these tools, he is able to examine the whole series of value standpoints which have been and are held (in principle, in the United States and British context only, but in practice in other societies as well) with respect to matters pertaining to government. And this analysis has a very satisfying blend of generality and specificity, a large number of cases being examined under each of the principles—such as justice, equality, freedom or equity. Barry can then end by building from this review of the problems attached to each of these aims a synthesis which leads him to the examination of the ways in which the 'public interest' can be served, and best served; that is to say, by setting up institutions and procedures, such as voting, which help to transform in a concrete manner the wants and ideals of individuals.

Thus Barry is justified in proudly suggesting, at the end of his work, that he, rather than Strauss, is in the tradition of the Greeks: they must be followed, not merely admired as great pieces of art. But his contribution in *Political Argument* is still relatively modest in that he does not attempt to provide a comprehensive basis for political thinking; rather he indicates what are the main tendencies, and the consequential practical 'languages', among those who are concerned in political thinking. Much less modest was the effort of John Rawls whose *A Theory of Justice*, which appeared in 1971, was an almost Herculean attempt at bringing under one roof morals and logic, the study of political goals and the analysis of the best types of arrangements to bring about these goals. As a commentator was to say, Rawls had in fact three purposes: 'In addition to this conception of rational choice and his settled moral convictions about particular matters of social justice, Rawls also had an extremely powerful commitment to an idealist conception of the harmonious and organic society.' Thus Rawls' work is, first, 'a sketch of a proof of a theorem in the theory of collective rational choice...'; second, 'it is a complicated sort of rational reconstruction of the social and moral convictions of himself and (he hopes) his audience...'; and, third, 'it is a vision of a harmoniously integrated, stable social and political order whose structure is articulated by the two principles of justice'[20].

Rawls is therefore directly and entirely in the line of traditional and classical political theory. He wants to marry 'fact' and 'history'; he wants to link 'morality' with 'strategies' and he hopes to provide a theory which will make moral principles acceptable on grounds of logic. Not surprisingly, Rawls' work was treated immediately in the same way as the classics have been treated. Books have been written on Rawls at a speed which is probably unique in the history of political thought. And the works all seem to conclude—as one would of the great classics—that Rawls is a giant and that he is wrong—wrong because ultimately one cannot deduce morality from 'prudence', wrong also because the public good, the public interest cannot logically be founded on the self-interest of the individuals. Thus Rawls no more avoids the leaps into subjective standpoints than his predecessors.

His overall contribution for the development of political theory is therefore mixed. He plays a major part and constitutes a huge signpost in that, first, he shows that political theory is still possible, and on a grand scale at that. Because great works had not been written for years, decades, perhaps even more, it seemed that it was simply impossible to undertake successfully inquiries of this type; and, as was said at the beginning of this chapter, it seemed that the reason why such works did not appear was because empirical or 'scientific' political science had made the approach redundant. Pessimism or disillusionment among political theorists was clearly due to what could be viewed as the 'poverty' of political theory. The publication of Rawls' *A Theory of Justice* showed that there was no ground in principle for such a pessimism; his work is a 'moral-booster' for classical theorists.

But Rawls' work is a modern classic in that, far from rejecting 'scientific' political science, he apparently draws from its findings in order to buttress and indeed build his own theory. He therefore transcends the argument; he proves that one need not attack scientific political science in bulk in order to write a classic of political theory; nor does one need to ignore the findings of the empiricists (or indeed claim that they are trivial). One can carefully draw from these findings, and work on a different plane, that of the ultimate goals of man and of the most appropriate line of conduct that individuals should take.

For Rawls does indeed both transcend the debate about the value of scientific political science (simply by ignoring the debate, quite refreshingly as it turns out) and develop his thoughts on a plane which is emphatically not the plane of the 'scientists'. This cannot be shown more conclusively than by contrasting the scope and purpose of works of 'formal' or 'mathematical' political theorists, such as those whom we discussed in the previous chapter, and *A Theory of Justice*. While Downs, Olson, Riker and many others are concerned with what is (in their view) true about human political behaviour, Rawls is concerned with bringing about a *better* society, one which is just, or at least the one which is the most equitable possible. Thus, while much of Rawls' analysis is based on game theory and takes the form of a 'maximin' problem (how to achieve a situation in which no one is worse off than the worse expectations which one would tolerate), the overall purpose is not to state what will occur in the game, but to discover an arrangement which is indeed acceptable, and (in Rawls' opinion) acceptable to all by comparison with what they have currently. Thus Woolf is right in stating that Rawls' objective is not merely to elaborate 'a theorem in the theory of collective rational choice'; there is also the vision of a 'harmonious, stable social and political order' which Rawls hopes to bring about by using the tool which the theory of games does appear to provide.

Thus the enormous contribution of Rawls is that he provides the long-awaited evidence that political theory is not dead and can stand on its own without having to demean itself in trying 'to pose itself in opposition' to the new developments in political science. But it does remain also true, as countless works have shown throughout the 1970s, that *A Theory of Justice* does not solve the problem which Rawls had set for himself: the question of the justification of morality remains as difficult as ever; and the linkage between private ideals and public interest remains unsettled. But, while this conclusion makes it imperative for political theorists to continue to engage in 'post-Rawlsian' analysis, as part of a continuous search for the truth, it shows also that the role of political theory is essential, alongside 'scientific' inquiries, from which political theory can indeed greatly benefit.

What the comparative 'failure' of Rawls also shows, however, is that it would be prudent for political theorists not to engage too frequently in 'whole' analyses. Those are best left to the very exceptional case of the truly great. Is there, then a place for what might be called a 'second-order' or 'middle-range' political theory, of a constructive kind, which, without attempting a total presentation of man in society, nonetheless contributes significantly to the improvement of our understanding of the bases and goals of politics? It seems that this level exists: so far the area in which political theorists have made their most interesting contributions have been broadly speaking in the field of democracy and participation, including the question of the size of the unit required for real participation to occur. Perhaps the most seminal work in this field is that of R. Nozick, *Anarachy, State and Utopia*, published in 1970; this work is in line with traditional theory, as Rawls' is. It begins by asking the type of questions which the classics asked, and specifically the question whether the state need exist at all: 'The fundamental question of political philosophy, one that precedes questions about how the state should be organized, is whether there should be any state at all'[21]. And this analysis leads Nozick to conclude that the state has to exist, but that the only justifiable state is what he calls the 'minimal state'. He does recognize that this is perhaps not a way of 'inspiring people to struggle or sacrifice'[22]: his solution is no utopia in the conventional sense, although he does believe that it is in fact the best utopia that there can be because such a 'minimal state' is the one which respects our rights.

The point is not to suggest whether Nozick is right in his assertion; indeed, whether the minimal state is the only justifiable one or not, Nozick is probably correct in pointing out that his proposal is not likely to bring about as much enthusiasm as pure anarchistic schemes or schemes which praise collective action and cooperation; this is perhaps why M. J. Taylor's attempt to link 'anarchism' with 'cooperation' (1978)—which is also based on a combination of the classical and the empirical approaches, while being in large part mathematical as well—corresponds more closely to a deep-seated desire to reconcile the urge for self-expression with somewhat romantic hopes for freely-accepted collective action. But Nozick's work is very important in that it contributes (as M. J. Taylor's does) to the rejuvenation of political theory; this rejuvenation is in fact a return to the true tradition of the classics, in which normative analysis uses empirical findings rather than insists on a lofty purity or a somewhat bitter denunciation of those who search for the facts.

Since the early 1970s a similar approach can be found in the renewed interest of the theorists in the analysis of democracy and participation. These questions are viewed as theoretical problems which need to be considered in the light of the findings of the empiricists and, where necessary, in the light of the different conclusions of the empiricists. Such was the endeavour of Plamenatz in *Democracy and Illusion* (1973): his aim was to attempt to extricate some broad conclusions in the midst of the major opposition between 'pro-Western' and 'anti-Western' supporters of democracy; and he concluded that the result 'is not quite the Tower of Babel that it seems to be'[23]. But more recent analyses go beyond summaries, as is shown by the contributions in *Democracy, Consensus and Social Contract* (Birnbaum, Lively and Parry, 1978) which demonstrate that empirical analyses and reflections of a logical *and* moral character can, and need to, coexist.

To say that the fields of democracy of participation, and of the relationship between the individual and the state are those which are currently being investigated by political theorists also means that other aspects—such as sovereignty, legitimacy, allegiance—are still relatively understudied, despite some brilliant exceptions, such as P. Blau's *Exchange and Power in Social Life* (1964), or A. O. Hirschmann's *Exit, Voice and Loyalty* (1970), both of which are more in the tradition of empirical analysis than in that of political theory. It seems that the concentration of political theorists on democracy and participation is not accidental; it corresponds to the fact that, among empiricists, these were the topics which first attracted attention in the post-war period, as we have seen. Thus political theory, far from being killed by empirical analysis, can thrive better in those fields in which empirical work has also been most successful: empiricists identified the difficulties and the 'paradoxes' which political theorists came to find increasingly intriguing. Political theory conceived as an analysis based on or triggered by empirical findings leads therefore to significant results and can find a new *raison d'être*.

Political theory does exist. It seems to know a little better, in the

1980s, where it is going and how it should proceed. Not that political theory as a critique of empirical political analysis has ceased to exist; what might be described as its 'civilized and sceptical' form still interests thinkers whose main ambition is to continue the tradition of 'historians of political thought'—a tradition which has its importance. 'Critical' political theory is also alive, but it is in constant danger of becoming an ideology highly charged with emotion but covered with a strong layer of abstract vocabulary; and it is even more in danger of concentrating on the past and present while leaving the delineation of the promised land for future generations. It is often content with apocalyptic and convoluted descriptions of the current land; by doing so, and on the basis of its own 'action-oriented theory', it ensures that the promised land is truly remote. For it is by talking to men about ideals that one can make these ideals come nearer.

In the past the role of political theory has always been to try by various means to bring about these ideals; in the 1770s and 1780s it seemed closer than ever to realizing this goal, although the realization soon appeared to have been only partial. The fact that political theory has been able, in recent years, in the middle of the battle over 'scientific' politics, to find a more serene posture is a hopeful sign for the maturity of political studies as a whole. The 'problem' of political theory may cease to be a problem for the coming generation, with political (logical and moral) theory contributing jointly with 'empirico-scientific' political science to the gradual unravelling of many of the aspects of the mystery of politics.

Notes

1. G. H. Sabine and T. L. Thorson (1973), *A History of Political Theory*, p. 3.
2. *Ibid.*
3. *See* the distinction in M. Seliger (1976), *Ideology and Politics*, who discusses K. Mannheim and his influence. *See also* R. Mullins, 'On the Concept of Ideology in Political Science', *American Political Science Review*, **66**, (2), 1972, pp. 498–510.
4. M. Oakeshott (1959), *The Voice of Poetry in the Conversation of Mankind*, p. 31.
5. M. Oakeshott (1946), Preface to *Leviathan*, p. 1xv.
6. L. Strauss, 'Political Philosophy' in Storing, H. (ed.), (1962) *Essays on the Scientific Study of Politics*, p. 310.
7. P. Lazarsfeld, 'The American Soldier: An Expository Review', *Public Opinion Quarterly*, Fall 1949, pp. 377–404.
8. L. Strauss (1964), *The City and Man*, p. 11.
9. B. Barry (1965), *Political Argument*, p. 290.
10. R. J. Bernstein (1976), *The Restructuring of Social and Political Theory*, p. 117.

11. A. Schutz (1964), *Collected Papers*, **2**, p. 85.
12. A. Schutz (1970), *The Phenomenology of the Social World*, p. 32.
13. Quoted in R. J. Bernstein (1976), p. 181, from L. D. Easton and K. H. Guddar (eds.) (1976), *Writings of the Young Marx on Philosophy and Society*, New York; Anchor Books, p. 212.
14. L. Strauss (1962), p. 327.
15. E. Goodman (1975), *A Study of Liberty and Revolution*, p. 35.
16. H. Arendt (1951), *The Origins of Totalitarianism*, p. 464 (in 1962 edn). New York, N.Y.; Harcourt.
17. B.-H. Lévy (1977), *La barbarie à visage humain*, p. 179.
18. B. Barry (1965), p. xviii.
19. *Ibid.*, p. 3.
20. R. P. Woolf (1977), *Understanding Rawls*, pp. 190–191.
21. R. Nozick (1974), *Anarchy, State and Utopia*, p. 4.
22. *Ibid.*, p. 127.
23. J. Plamenatz (1973), *Democracy and Illusion*, p. 212.

References

ARENDT, H. (1951). *The Origins of Totalitarianism*. New York; Harcourt

ARON, R. (1965). *Démocratie et totalitarisme*. Paris; Gallimard. (English trans. 1968: London: Weidenfeld)

ARON, R. (1969). *Les désillusions du progrès*: Paris; Calmann-Lévy

BARRY, B. (1965). *Political Argument*. London; Routledge and Kegan Pual

BARRY, B. (1973). *The Liberal Theory of Justice*. Oxford; Oxford University Press

BENN, S. I. AND PETERS, R. S. (1959). *Social Principles and the Democratic State*. London; Allen and Unwin

BERNSTEIN, R. J. (1976). *The Restructuring of Social and Political Theory*. Oxford; Blackwell

BIRNBAUM, P., LIVELY, J. AND PARRY, G. (eds.) (1978). *Democracy, Consensus, and Social Contract*. London and Beverly Hills; Sage

BLAU, P. (1964). *Exchange and Power in Social Life*. New York, N.Y.; Wiley

CRICK, B. (1959). *The American Science of Politics*. London; Routledge and Kegan Paul

GERMINO, D. (1967). *The Revival of Political Theory*. New York; Harper and Row

GLUCKSMANN, A. (1977). *Les maîtres penseurs*. Paris; Grasset

GOODMAN, E. (1975). *A Study of Liberty and Revolution*. London; Duckworth *Government and Opposition*, 1980, **15 3/4**, A generation of Political thought

HIRSCHMANN, A. O. (1970). *Exit, Voice and Loyalty*. Cambridge, Mass.; Harvard University Press

LASLETT, P. (ed) (1956, 1962, 1967, 1972, 1979). *Philosophy, Politics and Society* (5 volumes). Oxford; Blackwell

LÉVY, B.-H. (1977). *La barbarie à visage humain*. Paris: Grasset

MARCUSE, H. (1964). *The One-dimensional Man*. London; Routledge and Kegan Paul

NOZICK, R. (1970). *Anarchy, State and Utopia*. New York; Basic Books

OAKESHOTT, M. (1946). Preface to *Leviathan*. Oxford; Blackwell

OAKESHOTT, M. (1953). *Experience and Its Modes*. Cambridge: Cambridge University Press

OAKESHOTT, M. (1950). *The Voice of Poetry in the Conversation of Mankind.* Chester Springs, Pa.; Dufour

PLAMENATZ, J. (1973). *Democracy and Illusion.* London; Longman

RAWLS, J. (1971). *A Theory of Justice.* Cambridge, Mass.; Harvard University Press

SABINE, G. H. AND THORSON, T. L. (1973). *A History of Political Theory* (fourth edn). New York; Holt Saunders

SCHUTZ, A. (1964). *Collected Papers.* The Hague; M. Nijhoff

SCHUTZ, A. (1970). *The Phenomenology of the Social World.* Evanston, Ill.; Northwestern University Press

SELIGER, M. (1976). *Ideology and Politics.* London; Allen and Unwin

STORING, H. (ed.) (1962). *Essays on the Scientific Study of Politics.* New York; Holt, Rinehart and Winston

STRAUSS, L. (1962). 'An Epilogue' in Storing, H. pp. 307–327

STRAUSS, L. (1964). *The City and Man.* New York; Rand McNally

TAYLOR, M. J. (1976). *Anarchy or Cooperation.* London; Wiley

WOOLF, R. P. (1977). *Understanding Rawls.* Princeton, N.J. Princeton University Press

Chapter 7
Middle-level comparisons

Politics is the art of the possible.

Bismarck

Often the most natural developments are those which take the longest to shape and mature. There is no other way of interpreting the belated resurgence, from the 1960s and especially from the 1970s, of studies of political institutions and of comparative studies of institutions in particular. Traditionally, political science has two main components: theory and institutions. But, while, as we saw, there was much struggle and soul-searching in the field of political theory, the study of political institutions suffered a major decline in the early post-war years. While institutions seemed to be, and had been, central to the analysis of government, they came to be regarded as relatively unimportant and as peripheral to the 'behavioural' concerns of the new political science. Of course, many monographs on individual institutions continued to be published, but this seemed to occur against the prevailing 'mood'. By and large, the more the studies were institutional, and, *a fortiori*, the more they were concerned with constitutional aspects of politics, the more they were felt not to be relevant to the real purpose of political science. This was especially true of comparative studies of institutions, which had been for at least half a century one of the mainstays of the growth points of the discipline of politics; it seemed that 'old-fashioned' comparative government, which was concerned with the description of institutions, would simply be replaced by a behavioural analysis in which 'general models' would play the major part.

Yet, in earlier generations, the description, indeed the close description of institutions had given comparative government its value and its importance. Clearly this was in large part because constitutional government, and liberal-democratic government in general, had led to the setting up of new institutions which it seemed important to monitor. But, by and large, specialists of comparative government had appeared to perform this task effectively. Starting from constitutions and from the bodies set up by

162

constitutions, such as legislatures, executives and courts, they had gradually become concerned with newer political institutions such as parties as well as with the role of business, labour and other interest groups in the political process. They had looked at the 'theory' and at the 'practice' of these institutions, often contrasting the first with the second; and they had examined, on a comparative basis, the variations both of the constitutional blueprint and of the practices.

This interest in the relationship between theory and practice had led specialists of comparative government to cast themselves in the role of watchdogs and scutinizers of the activities of politicians who claimed to be abiding by the rules which constitution-makers had devised. Often noting the gap between the ideals of liberalism, representation, democracy and, indeed, justice, and the reality of many governments, specialists of comparative government could be said to have developed a branch of study which had a clear purpose and at least a broad methodology: the purpose was to relate the 'facts' of institutional practice to the 'theory' of institutions, and through these, to the political values of the society; and the method was to study the 'facts' in the closest possible way.

By the time of World War II, however, the study of comparative government had become rather stale. The concentration on Western European countries and on North America, perhaps acceptable before 1914, was difficult to justify at a time when Communism and fascism were controlling Central and Eastern Europe; but comparative government had been so closely associated with the analysis of liberal government that it seemed unable to expand markedly the scope of its inquiries. A broadening of the approach was necessary, but this broadening of approach only came about after comparative government seemed almost to disappear under the impact of the rapid, indeed sudden, enthusiasm for studies of global models, in which there was little interest in the study of institutions and in what J. La Palombara came to call 'middle range' or 'partial systems' comparisons[1]. Only when the enthusiasm receded, when it became clear that global models still left unexplained the persistent problem of political institutions, did comparative government become once more, though on a broader basis, a major growth area in political science.

Comparative government and the comparative method

By the 1970s, the importance of the comparative study of institutions was once more recognized. This also meant that much of the earlier methodology of comparative government was also recognized to be valid, despite an endeavour, very noticeable at the time of the enthusiasm for global models, to bring the methodology of comparative government in line with the comparative methodology in sociology and anthropology. These disciplines were felt to use a more sophisticated methodology, while, as R. T. Holt and J. E. Turner said in *The Methodology of Comparative Research* (1970):

> In political science few studies in comparative politics have employed the comparative method, as envisaged and used, for example, by Durkheim, Nadel or Murdock. Nor have political scientists produced any writing on the method of comparative analysis that even approaches the methodological work done by sociologists and anthropologists. This is somewhat surprising because the common-sense meaning of the term *comparative*, unadorned by any scholarly tradition, generally refers to a method of study and not to a body of substantive knowledge[2].

Why should it be the case that comparative government did not rise to sophisticated methodological analyses as comparative studies did in anthropology and sociology? Holt and Turner believe that it is because comparative government is a substantive field, while comparison is a method in other disciplines. And they also believe that it is wrong to distinguish such a comparative field in government as they feel that 'in principle there is no difference between cross-cultural research and research conducted within a single country'[3]. Because comparative government is viewed as a field, a systematic analysis of the methodology required is not undertaken, they believe. If, on the contrary, political scientists were to realize—as sociologists and anthropologists do—that comparison is a method, they would undertake their comparative work more systematically and rigorously. Holt and Turner then proceed to state how comparative research should be undertaken: they stress the need for hypotheses before the study begins; they examine the ways in which these hypotheses can be tested and consider carefully the difficulties which face political scientists; they conclude that the answer can be found only in better 'theory' in political science. This seems to be also the conclusion of L. C. Mayer who, in *Comparative Political Inquiry*, after having pointed out that 'comparison as a method is inherent in the scientific method' and that 'political science in the modern sense of that term becomes synonymous with comparative politics', states that 'the effort in comparative politics to build empirical generalizations applicable to the widest possible variety of cases leads naturally to the search for paradigms which are similarly broadly applicable'[4].

The difficulty with these conclusions is that these can only be drawn if one also rejects almost all the comparative government studies which have taken place in the past—certainly up to the 1960s. The advice which Holt and Turner, as well as Mayer give, goes in the direction of the model-making efforts of the late 1950s and 1960s; we know that the discipline of politics benefited from these models, but also that there was much dissatisfaction with them later. We need therefore to ask the question, which Holt and Turner do not ask: why is comparative government a branch, a field of the discipline, and a very important one at that, rather than a method of inquiry? Why have political scientists proceeded for so long with an 'unrigorous', 'unscientific' effort? Is it merely because they are inherently 'unscientific'? Is there not something in the nature of the subject-matter which forces them to inquire into government in the way they do?

It is broadly speaking true that the study of comparative government has long been conducted on a 'haphazard' basis and is like a recipe designed to look rather casually at what two or more organizations, procedures, personalities may have in common; it seems closer to the somewhat unsystematic efforts of the collector than to the endeavours of the academic analyst. Instead of looking systematically for 'hypotheses' which would then be tested after careful operationalization by controlling for specific variables well-defined in advance, specialists of comparative government often seem to be guided by chance, by what happens to be observed or be observable relatively easily. They also often do not seem to know exactly what criteria help them to build up their comparisons. They know that they need some criteria, for it is not possible to compare in general; they know that they are looking for common elements among the subjects which they are trying to compare; but they often seem to find the common elements as they go along.

Of course, as knowledge increases, as the experience of undertaking comparisons becomes larger, political scientists begin to discover common elements and identify criteria of comparison; but they never seem sure that they find all the relevant criteria and that some element, hitherto undiscovered, will not provide a significant clue to the comparison which is undertaken; a place has therefore to be left for unforeseen elements which, beyond the usual variables, may become the main 'explanatory factor'.

Why is this 'unsatisfactory' situation—unsatisfactory, that is, from the point of view of 'scientific' research—perpetuated? Why is it that, despite the development of models in the 1960s, comparative government seems to be returning, at least to some extent, to an approach which bears considerable similarities with the traditional method? Why are students of comparative government so reluctant to use 'deductive analysis' on a broad scale?

The answer lies in the specificity of government, a specificity which, if not stressed sufficiently, leads to a misunderstanding about the difference between the study of government and the study of other aspects of society. We have indicated many of these aspects in the course of this work, but it is worth remembering them at this point; it is especially worth noting that the 'units of observation'—institutions, leaders and countries—have peculiar characteristics. Only in relation to the study of government have institutions and individuals a major, unique importance which makes them, not just objects of curiosity, but the unavoidable objects of the analysis. While, in other disciplines, the personality of a leader or the idiosyncrasies of a committee are bases for examples, or even for gossip, they are the stuff of the study of government and those who study government have to make them the centre of their observations.

The study of government is the study of a relatively small number of countries (less than 200 even after the great independence movement of the 1950s, 1960s and 1970s), in which there are few political institutions (a few parties, a small number of truly relevant groups, one legislature, one executive, a few ministers, one army, one supreme court) and at the head of which there are only very few men who have a crucial part to play. These few countries display considerable variations in size, ethnic, racial and class composition, in historical tradition and culture; the institutions are also markedly different, as are the leaders. Leaders have idiosyncrasies which are such that they cannot be deemed to lead to identical reactions and affect in an identical manner the institutions and the countries which they run. Clearly, one of the major problems in need of examination is the effect which these differences—in background, outlook, psychological characteristics—may have on the development of the policy-making process; and the importance of at least some of these leaders (for instance Presidents or Prime Ministers of very large countries) for their own and other countries' citizens is such that it is not possible to brush aside the study of these men as being of little relevance to political life. They are central to the study of the operations of government, both in themselves and in the interplay between the leaders and the institutional positions which they hold.

Yet, while these differences exist, while there is an urge and indeed a need to look for idiosyncrasies in countries, institutions and leaders, while, as we have noted in Chapter I, 'accidents' seem to play a major part, the urge for comparisons is also very strong—and equally unavoidable. It is unavoidable for reasons ranging from sheer curiosity to vital necessity. And it is from this peculiar state of affairs that the characteristics of comparative government follow. Unique events or situations are built into the study of government. Contrary to what Holt and Turner or Mayer may say, it is not absurd to want to study one institution, one leader, one country; there are enough idiosyncrasies and these are sufficiently important to warrant a detailed analysis. Furthermore, as we shall soon see, there is need for a very detailed knowledge of structures and behaviour in individual countries in order to be able to build comparisons. But it also appears that studies of unique events, individual countries or institutions are not sufficient: this is not merely because, in some deep philosophical or methodological sense, it is possible to discuss a case or an institution only if some comparative scale or yardstick exists; it is also because what one wants to know is how differently the puzzle of government is pieced together in various countries, both because the pieces are differently assembled and because they are somewhat different.

The only way to understand fully what comparative government is about is to draw an analogy with criticism in literature or art. This is not to disparage the efforts towards a more rigorous and scientific approach to political analysis; the endeavour must be continued and it will be, as it has always been since Aristotle. But the point of departure is that leaders and institutions are relatively different from each other, and each has a life of its own, as have writers or painters. Leaders or institutions have to be considered as large elements in the fabric of the political system of the world, and compared accordingly: they are not merely 'illustrations of a trend'.

If it is appreciated that leaders or institutions are like the literary or artistic figures which are dotted about the stage of mankind, one can see that there are, so to speak, three ways of looking at these figures: one is to examine them very closely, and to undertake a special analysis of each of them; another method is to look at them at considerable distance, and try and discover general characteristics about them; and the third is to stay relatively close and yet look for the similarities and differences which are apparent. The first method is that of individual studies; the second is the one which is called for by those who believe that a theory or a general model is required before undertaking studies of comparative government; and the third is the more modest, but also richer appraoch which suggests that we are not likely to be able to discover in advance a 'theory' which will account for the immense variety of situations, but that it would nonetheless be absurd not to try and compare men, institutions, countries, all of which contribute to the political life of mankind. It is the third approach which characterizes comparative government—or comparisons at the 'middle range'.

Of course, it is quite sensible to conclude that the comparative 'approach', as we described it here, is 'messy' and somewhat unscientific; and it is further permitted to say that, in these circumstances, the only truly 'pure' answer to the problem consists in either completely refraining from comparisons and in describing 'unique' situations as they occur or, at the other extreme, to undertake only those comparisons in the few, exceptional cases, where one can operationalize precisely a set of variables and look at their relationship on the basis of hypotheses deduced *a priori*. But such a refusal to undertake 'messy' analyses not only impoverishes us; it will simply not be followed because it is practically so important to understand how others try to achieve broadly the same governmental aims in a different manner that there always will be some scholars eager to undertake studies of comparative government of a 'middle-range' character.

What, then, is the comparative approach in the field of comparative government? It is a multi-pronged effort designed to come as close as possible to the many facets of the reality of the institutions, people and countries which constitute the context within which government acts and develops. It is an approach rather than a method, in that it is certainly not based on the rigid determination of what is 'allowed' and what is 'forbidden' in order to come to the truth. And it is a field as well as an approach because it consists in an effort to look at concrete arrangements, real countries, specific leaders, at a middle-range level. Some may wish to describe the approach as being closer to an 'art' than to a science—if it is necessary for an analysis to rely on predetermined methods, indeed techniques, in order to be scientific; this is a matter, however, on which there may be disagreement. What is clear is that precise techniques are being used only in relatively limited fields, and that, elsewhere, there has to be greater reliance on the imagination of the scholar to find ways of handling the problems which he wants to tackle. Some guidelines exist: the comparative approach relies heavily on classifications and, to a lesser extent, on typologies and taxonomies as well as dimensions, in order to find similarities and differences[5]. But these are no more than guidelines. The value of comparisons is ultimately judged by the results of the efforts made by the scholars. 'Politics,' it is often said, 'is the art of the possible': with so many accidents, so many idiosyncrasies among leaders, so many subtle differences among similar institutions and similar countries, the study of government has also to be content with what is possible, and the best that is possible is what the comparative approach offers to political scientists wishing to study government.

The emergence of comparative government: the role of Bryce, Lowell and Ostrogorski

Comparative government analysis has very old credentials, since it dates back to Aristotle who embarked on a study of constitutions and practices in what he and the Greeks generally regarded as the civilized world—the Greek cities—with an occasional look, more as a counterpoint, at politics in 'barbarian' states. Most of Aristotle's comparative work was lost; yet the distinctions between monarchies, oligarchies and democracies which the Greek philosopher made had a major influence throughout the subsequent centuries. But the idea of comparative analysis was not pursued, for there was more interest in expounding formulas for improvement than in an examination of realities of government. Although Machiavelli was concerned with 'facts', it is only with Montesquieu, in the middle of the eighteenth century, that the 'empirical' approach was revived.

Indeed more than another hundred years had to elapse before comparative government analysis was firmly established. Montesquieu was a precursor; but those who immediately followed him were mostly constitutional lawyers who, as we have seen in Chapter 6, were still primarily concerned with the theory of institutions and not with the way these were implemented. Tocqueville was almost unique in the 1830s in showing an interest for an analysis of both the theory and the practice of American government, which he contrasted with the European situation at the time; even a generation later, Bagehot was exceptional in depicting a subtle and insightful account of the British Cabinet which he compared at many points with the American executive. Comparative government only really developed as a branch of study in the last quarter of the nineteenh century: its true founders were Bryce and Lowell, Ostrogorski also playing a major, if somewhat less central, part in the new field.

Bryce and Lowell are the true founders of comparative government because they realized the originality, the difficulties, but also

the challenge of the type of analysis on which they were embarking. Specifically, they saw that, to be successful, comparative
government analysis had to incorporate elements from a number
of contradictory, or at any rate opposite, trends. First, they saw
that comparative government would be successful only if equal
importance was given to both the study of constitutions and other
institutions and the study of the practice of government. Merely to
look at constitutions, as lawyers tended to do, was insufficient
because problems of implementation were often, perhaps almost
always, very serious; but merely to look at the practice without
looking at the constitutional framework was also unsatisfactory
because the context, or the aim of practices, would be lost sight of.
Thus comparative government should be the study of the 'theory
and practice' of government, to use an expression which was to
become fashionable in the years and decades after Bryce and
Lowell.

To study the practice, however, one needed to discover, indeed,
amass, the 'facts'. On this both authors were extremely assertive,
and assertive to such an extent that they seemed sometimes to
suggest that 'facts' were paramount. What was needed, said Bryce,
was 'facts, facts, facts. When facts have been supplied, each of us
try to reason from them'[6]. As we have seen in Chapter 5, this view
was criticized in the 1950s, by D. Easton in particular, who felt
that Bryce's approach was mere 'factualism', indeed
'hyperfactualism'. This was an incorrect interpretation of Bryce's
stand: the facts were needed in order 'to reason from them'. But
what Bryce said—and correctly said—was that 'facts' were a
prerequisite: analysis without data is mere speculation. And Bryce
and Lowell realized that data were very difficult to acquire, not
because we did not know what facts to acquire or did not have the
methodology to acquire them, but more simply because governments and politicians often hide or at best are unwilling to clarify
what the real situation is. Bryce and Lowell therefore preached by
example: more than anyone before them (save perhaps Tocqueville) and more than most after them, they engaged in a vast
endeavour of 'data collection' about almost every aspect of
political life, from parties to executives and from referendums to
legislatures. They were, for instance, the first to attempt to assess
systematically the role of legislatures by looking at the calibre of
the members of these bodies and at the values of the laws which
were passed, a point to which we shall return.

The search for 'facts' also led Bryce and Lowell towards the use
of quantitative 'indicators', on the basis of an instinctive realization that, in the study of government, qualitative and quantitative

types of evidence have to be balanced. Bryce and Lowell were among the first to realize that it is more satisfying to be able to provide quantitative support for the conclusions which are drawn; but they also knew that it was often impossible to find indicators which were both truly relevant and quantifiable. And, when this was the case, judgements would have to be supported by a mixture of qualitative assessment and quantitative 'data'. Only such a mixture would give a true impression of the reality; it was therefore simply imperative to use, in a careful manner, both types of evidence.

Finally, Bryce and Lowell felt that conclusions would be firm if they were based on as wide a range of governments as possible; therefore, their studies extended geographically to a large number of countries, indeed to all the countries which at the time had institutions of a constitutional or near-constitutional character. Thus, far from being restricted to 'major governments of Europe', as the practice tended to develop later, in the 1930s, 1940s and often since, their analyses covered countries of Western, Central and Southern Europe, and were based on evidence from all countries to the same extent. They were not merely concerned to show how governments had developed in a few 'typical' or 'model' nations, they were concerned to identify the range of developments which were taking place. They could therefore draw conclusions about what seemed to be possible, or not possible, and about what was likely to happen or not happen in the future. They were anxious to discover patterns, in the true sense of the word—that is to say, not in the form of a number of 'ideal types' but in the concrete manner in which governments were run. Their aim was to discover and show the wide variety—the richness—of governmental practice as much as the broad contrasts which can emerge from typologies.

Thus Bryce and Lowell had a deep-rooted belief, an instinct even, which made them realize the complexity of government, a complexity which is both institutional and behavioural. The methodology which they adopted was aimed at grasping this complexity, being both general and specific, quantitative and qualitative, allowing for historical idiosyncrasies as well as for constitutional 'logic'. They felt that the ultimate aim of the study of government was to unravel the mysteries of political reality; but they also felt that such an aim could be achieved only gradually and provided they were careful not to forget any aspect of the reality. To adopt a simpler methodology which would be 'purer' would leave us empty-handed or, even worse, would leave us with the mistaken belief that we understood government, while we merely had a one-dimensional vision of the reality.

Bryce and Lowell were therefore the true fathers of modern comparative government; they have influenced it ever since. The tradition was established to write treatises or texts of a comparative character; this was followed in the 1930s and into the 1960s and 1970s (for example, by P. Merkl, J. La Palombara and indeed, one hopes not too immodestly, by myself, 1969).

Meanwhile, at the same time, comparative government analysis also began to develop in another direction, that of the study of specific institutions on a comparative basis. This tradition was due in large part to Ostrogorski who, in 1902, published a detailed study of political parties in Britain and America. By the last quarter of the nineteenth century, political parties had become one of the major political institutions of modern constitutional government; they were helping to reconcile to liberal-democratic rule many of the newly enfranchised workers whose predecessors, in the first half of the nineteenth century, had opposed capitalism and liberalism on grounds of its lack of concern for the proletariat. But parties were also an interesting field of study because they had developed naturally, that is to say, outside the framework of constitutional theory—indeed against this framework, since many of the political theorists—Rousseau but also the more practically inclined authors of the *Federalist Papers*—had denounced the development of parties as one which would break the necessary consensus in a democracy. Yet, in fact, against these gloomy prognostications, parties provided a successful means of implementing democracy; they helped to create links between government and people and gave the electorate—at least the active fraction of the electorate—a means of participating in the national decision-making process.

A theory of the role of parties was therefore needed; this was the task which Ostrogorski set for himself. But he undertook this effort by using the method which Bryce and Lowell had used for the governmental process as a whole. Ostrogorski did admittedly restrict his detailed analysis to two countries, Britain and America, and his exposition did even take the form of two successive monographs, one for each country. This was because he felt the need to study the activities of parties with great precision and 'data' turned out to be so numerous that only a two-country study would be truly satisfactory. But the overall aim was broader: it was to 'test the hypothesis', so to speak, of the 'democratic' or 'oligarchical' character of the political parties. He concluded that there was little evidence—quite the contrary—for genuine democracy; indeed, there seemed to be inherent, unavoidable oligarchical tendencies among parties. Internal party democracy was mere propaganda.

Ostrogorski thus started a debate about the nature of political parties which has continued to be carried out ever since, with R. Michels, (1915), M. Duverger, (1950), and many others having made many important contributions, all of which reinforced Ostrogorski's views. But Ostrogorski also started a very important segment of the study of comparative government. Comparative government could progress through the study of individual institutions, in two or more countries, of a very detailed character: thereby both our knowledge would increase and the elements of a 'middle-range' theory would gradually be elaborated. In this, Ostrogorski was following a path which Bryce and Lowell had already opened to some extent and in which they were to continue to excel in the early part of the twentieth century. Lowell was to study the impact of referendums in this way *(Public Opinion and Popular Government*, 1919). Bryce's views about the 'decline of legislatures' in *Modern Democracies* has remained a source of controversy ever since. Meanwhile, it seemed that the study of interest groups was beginning to be a subject of important concern, Bentley's *The Process of Government* (1908) constituting a call for an analysis of the detailed role of these organizations in the context of an 'institutional theory' which gave to groups the major part in the development of policy-making. In the 1940s and 1950s, studies of parties and groups did seem to emerge as the main 'problem-areas' where progress could be achieved most rapidly and most fruitfully. It was this tradition of 'institutional' theory and analysis, close to facts and yet concerned with the discovery of broad trends that the sudden interest in developing countries at the end of the 1950s seemed to wish to arrest and even to break—on the grounds that the tradition was geographically too narrow and intellectually insufficiently systematic and 'unscientific'.

The critique of 'traditional' comparative government in the late 1950s

Writing in 1955, Roy Macridis said that 'the traditional approach and emphasis in the comparative study of government will reveal the source of the current dissatisfaction and will point to the need for reorientation. Comparative study has thus far been comparative in name only'[7]. He then went on to say that this traditional study was 'non-comparative', 'essentially descriptive', 'parochial' (that is to say based on Western countries only), 'static' and 'monographic'. And under the 'descriptive' criticism it was stated that the analysis was historical or legalistic, and therefore rather narrow[8].

Two years earlier, in his *The Political System* (1953), David Easton made a strong attack against Bryce whom he blamed for the condition of political science. The attack was made on the grounds that Bryce had influenced American political science in the direction of what Easton called 'hyperfactualistm'. Easton recognized that Bryce did not neglect 'theories' but he stated that, because Bryce was averse to 'system-building'[9] he had led American political scientists on to an entirely wrong path. Easton criticized Bryce for having demanded, first and foremost, that political scientists should obtain facts (quoted above) and he concluded, having surveyed the condition of the discipline at the time, that 'this theoretical malnutrition and surfeit of facts (had had) serious consequences for the maturation of political science as a discipline'[10].

On the basis of these remarks, political science embarked on the development of models, and comparative government of the traditional kind was felt to be redundant. What, then, happened to lead some years later to a counter-movement? Writing in 1970, Joseph La Palombara could say:

> Time was when political scientists looked sheepishly toward their colleagues in other social sciences, apologizing for their own discipline's lack of theoretical sophistication and envying the presumably powerful theories that informed the work of others, particularly the sociologists[11].

And he went on to examine the shortcomings of the models which we discussed earlier, stressing the need for what he calls a 'segmented or partial-system approach to comparative analysis'[12].

But the return to a more classical view of comparative government did not only arise from the shortcomings of models. It arose from the fact that those who supported the model approach did not realize the true importance of the study of institutions. They not only mistakenly believed that these studies were condemned to have a narrow geographical scope, they were to some extent mesmerized by the growth of election studies, and they consequently adopted a rather superficial view of behaviourism according to which the study of institutions and of constitutions was superfluous and merely old-fashioned.

It was, of course, accidental that election studies, based on surveys and involving a sophisticated quantitative apparatus, should have emerged at the time when developing countries became independent and therefore needed to be studied. There is no logical connection between behaviourism, as it was conceived and grew in the United States in the 1940s and 1950s, and the recognition that liberal-democratic institutions played only a minor part in the Third World. But while the coincidence may have been accidental, the result was a considerable amount of linkage between the two aspects: the criticisms made of traditional middle-range studies were therefore not based on a 'clear' appreciation of the characteristics of comparative government, and especially of the role of 'facts' and of institutions in the fabric of government. For, while it was true that comparative government needed to include Communist and Third World countries in a major way, it was not true that the discipline of politics had a surfeit of facts—indeed it should have been realized that the plea to consider Communist and Third World countries meant that many more facts were needed about these countries—nor was it true that 'legalism' was unimportant, as it should have been noticed that 'laws' were merely 'facts' of a special kind.

With respect to 'factualism', the criticism was doubly wrong, wrong (without playing on words) because the critics had their facts wrong and wrong because they misinterpreted the role of facts in the development of comparative government. Easton had 'his facts wrong' because it was not true—it still is not true—that we have too many facts at our disposal in the field of comparative government; in reality, very little is known about the structure and activities of the major institutions of most countries, and in particular of the Third World. Despite considerable efforts on the part of some comparative government specialists, the knowledge which we have of parties, legislatures, the organization and activities of executives, the structure and role of courts, is very limited indeed outside a small number of (primarily Western) countries. Easton could only have made his statement because his interest and knowledge was concentrated on North America, where it may perhaps be said with some justification that there have been large numbers of studies on most aspects of the political process. But the situation with respect to the Third World and even the Communist world—and indeed some Western countries—is radically different: the first modern studies on British political parties appeared in the mid-1950s; the first general studies on interest groups in Britain also appeared in the 1950s[12]. Similar studies on European continental countries appeared only somewhat later.

Thus the problem—in the 1950s but also currently—is still that there are too few facts at the disposal of political scientists, not too many. The trouble has also been that there has been a marked tendency to generalize without the appropriate factual basis for generalizations. Writing in 1971 on Latin-American legislatures, W. H. Agor remarked that there was a tendency to assert that legislatures in that part of the world were very weak; he added: 'It is appropriate to note that this and other similar statements are usually based on extremely impressionistic evidence'[14]. For anyone writing in the late 1960s a text on comparative government which would truly be concerned with patterns of government across the whole world, the reality was that there was a surfeit of models, not a surfeit of facts. There were then and still are very few facts at the disposal of political scientists for the large majority of countries and the large majority of institutions in these countries. This is the gap which comparative government has begun to fill from the late 1960s—in many ways by turning away from the precepts of the model-makers.

For it is not the case that political scientists can 'deduce' the variety of patterns of government from a small number of general principles. What model-makers did not seem to appreciate—but Montesquieu had noted at the outset of the *Spirit of Laws*—was that the richness of the characteristics—economic, social, cultural, institutional, behavioural—of the countries of the world is such that only when the facts are amassed does it become possible to acquire an idea of the patterns which may be found. To take but one example: the characteristics of the French political system are known to be peculiar in a large number of ways. For instance, France is the only Western European country which has had twenty constitutions in the past 200 years; it resembles more, in this respect, a number of Latin American countries (not *all* in reality) than other European countries. This 'fact' cannot be deduced from our general knowledge of political life; no model will enable us to discover it, at least at this stage. Yet the fact that France has behaved in this peculiar manner is important, not just because we may be curious, not even because France is a relatively important country about which much needs to be known in practice, but because, theoretically as well, this knowledge makes us realize the rich variety of experiences which mankind has been and still is undergoing. Our theory of comparative government will only be comprehensive and therefore realistic if we take this richness into account.

Thus the critics of the earlier approach to comparative government failed to realize the importance of 'facts' in order to provide the material required for the development of a theory of government. They did so because they also failed to realize the difficulties encountered in obtaining these facts. Contrary to what the model-makers probably believed, it is easier to build a model than to acquire patiently the 'data' relating to substantial numbers of countries and institutions; the gathering of information on the membership, organization, programmes and decision-making processes of political parties, for instance, is a major operation which, as Ostrogorski's early study showed, entails a careful and prolonged effort. This is in part why the analysis of political parties did not develop on the scale which had been hoped after Duverger's work which was published in 1950. And it is also patent that the hopes which had arisen in the early 1950s to include groups in the study of government were dashed by the difficulty in collecting data for substantial numbers of countries. The compendium on *Interest Groups in Four Continents* edited by H. Ehrmann and published in 1958, was not followed by truly broad empirical studies for one main reason—namely, that the data could not be gathered without a large team which political scientists simply did not have at their disposal. The supporters of the model-making approach appeared not to have appreciated that the 'facts' are often so secret, or at least so carefully hidden, that the problem of collecting data can be the major stumbling block in the progress of comparative government studies, especially outside Western liberal-democratic countries.

But the error of judgement made by the supporters of the more global approach was not related to facts alone. The role of institutions and of legal arrangements was also underestimated or simply misconstrued. The model-making approach was based on 'behaviourism'—in reality, a partial or narrow view of what behaviourism meant. It was a reaction against the overemphasis on legalism in some pre-war and early post-war studies; indeed, to this day, there is still too much emphasis on the constitutional framework in many French political science studies (possibly because laws can be studied without having to undertake empirical research). But it is no more reasonable to conclude that it is not useful to study laws and institutions. Laws and institutions are the means by which—the constraints through which—behaviour occurs. They have therefore to be studied and compared to other 'facts' in the political system. Thus it is right that studies of comparative government be based both on an appreciation of the specific historical dimension and of the legal (and more general institutional) context in which governments operate. This is true even if the laws are not implemented or partially implemented (assuming that we are clear what implementation means in all situations): one of the major aspects of comparative government analysis consists therefore in examining degrees of implementation of constitutions and laws, as well as of other procedures, in order to assess, ultimately, whether certain types of laws and procedures are more likely to be implemented than others, and under what circumstances implementation is likely to be higher.

Of course, it is true that model-makers recognized the importance of structures and institutions in government, but they did so—and increasingly did so, as we have seen—in terms of a 'process of institutionalization', of integration, of legitimization, rather than in terms of the concrete characteristics of specific institutions and specific procedures[15]. This had the apparent advantage of enabling political scientists to grasp problems of development and to give their approach a dynamic character. But it had also the drawback of making it impossible to appreciate the particular ways in which institutions and procedures constrain the behavioural patterns of leaders and citizens. And these differences in the shape of the constraints are at least as important as the extent of the constraints.

Thus the model-making approach seemed increasingly unable to meet the requirements of those who wished to study comparative government. But model-makers had been important in making it patently obvious that comparative government could not justifiably be restricted to the study of 'liberal-democratic' countries; a major effort had therefore to be undertaken to introduce the study of Communist and Third World countries in the analysis. The model-makers also made it patently clear that constitutions, laws, institutions, could not be studied as ends in themselves but had to be viewed in constant relationship with modes of behaviour: this meant, in fact, returning to the traditions of Bryce, Lowell, Ostrogorski, a tradition which was sometimes lost sight of by those who had undertaken comparative government studies in the 1930s and 1940s and who sometimes had been satisfied with formal institutional analyses (in this, model-makers were right) usually because the facts are very, truly very difficult to discover.

Comparative government as a world-wide, but middle-range analysis

After a short eclipse, comparative government of a 'middle-range' character experienced a real 'boom' in the 1960s and even more in the 1970s. Progress has been made, and is increasingly made, in fields which had been abandoned for some time as being rather less interesting because they were 'institutional' while, paradoxically enough, some of the fields which were felt to lead to 'behavioural' studies in the 1950s still await a real breakthrough. For it would almost certainly have seemed more reasonable in the

1950s to expect a substantial development of studies of parties and interest groups than of studies of legislatures, executives or courts. Yet while comparative studies of interest groups are still almost non-existent and while studies of parties have not as yet gone beyond the stage of broad generalizations with respect to the Third World, the military, legislatures and, more recently, executives and even courts have become or are becoming the main preoccupations of comparative government specialists.

For this to occur, what was needed was a desire to return to the study of government in the strict sense of the word, that is to say, to return to the examination of the structure and behaviour of the central decision-making machine of the state. This desire had been undermined by the concern for the analysis of the broad conditions of the development of political systems characteristic of the 'model-making' approach. But events in the world at large began to show that one institution at least, the army, could have a considerable impact on governments and change the structure of politics. From the 1950s, the military began to appear as important as, if not more important than, political parties in the development of the Third World. By a 'happy' accident, it happened that military intervention and military rule were relatively easy to document and analyse on a comparative basis. The phenomenon was widespread; it occurred in a relatively similar manner everywhere; it involved an institution—the army—but it was also a behavioural pattern. Military *coups* could be counted, but the description of individual cases was also interesting. The success or failure of military intervention could be related to the strength or weakness of other institutions. It seemed therefore possible to assess, even to measure, the 'propensity' of countries and of types of countries to come under military rule; it seemed also possible to examine the evolution of military governments and see whether these maintained themselves in office for long periods without difficulties.

Hence a substantial number of important studies of military intervention and military rule; among these, perhaps the two most successful are those of S. P. Huntington, *The Soldier and the State* (1957) and of S. E. Finer, *The Man on Horseback* (1962). Both are relatively old studies, written before the independence of Africa either had taken place or had had time to make an impact. But Huntington based his analysis of the role of the military as much on the examination of events in nineteenth-century Europe as on contemporary development. He concluded that the theory of 'civilian control'—a cornerstone of liberal-democratic theory—had been applied in the nineteenth century through the accident of the maintenance of the legitimacy of monarchs all over Europe, almost alongside the new legitimacy of the people's representatives. But this gave civilian governments only a shaky hold over the military; and, quite naturally, this hold was swept away when economic and social difficulties piled up on countries which had, perhaps too quickly, turned to become republics. There was therefore little hope of avoiding similar difficulties in Third World countries, a point which S. E. Finer showed extremely well a few years later, and yet also before 'patterns' of military intervention had emerged in Africa.

For S. E. Finer, the 'common assumption', the 'unreflecting belief that it is somehow natural for the armed forces to obey the civil power' was mistaken because no reason is adduced for showing that civilian control of the armed forces is, in fact, 'natural'. On the contrary, 'the political advantages of the military *vis-à-vis* other and civilian groupings are overwhelming. The military possess vastly superior organization. And they possess arms'[16]. On this basis, Finer develops a 'theory' or 'model' of military strengths and weaknesses which is in the best tradition of comparative government and elevates his relatively slim volume to the level of one of the major and most elegant studies written in the discipline. Much has been published, and at much greater length, on the military before and since *The Man on Horseback*; but no work on the subject, even that of Huntington, is so parsimonious in the presentation of the analysis and so pungent in the insights. The existence of such a work is the proof that comparative government at the middle-range not merely can be done, but also can provide a true blending of 'theory' and 'descriptive analysis' and therefore account for developments in the real world on a truly general basis without having to rely on a highly abstract conceptual framework which is—or at least overtly seems to be—quite divorced from political life.

Studies of the military began to be published at the very moment when the search for models was at its height in political science; because the analysis of military intervention was 'behavioural' rather than 'institutional', it seemed to be—indeed was—in line with the general approach of the 'new' political science. But students of the military also had different aims from those of the global model-makers: they were concerned with the structure and life of governments in an appreciably more specific manner. Their work constitutes therefore an intellectual link with the studies of other institutions which were to come, while providing also a method, as the new 'institutional' studies were also markedly 'behavioural' in character.

At first sight it might seem surprising that there should have been a renewed interest in legislatures, both Western and non-Western, at the end of the 1960s. If one institution appeared everywhere, or almost everywhere (except in the United States in fact), to be in decline, it was the legislature. Bryce had said so a long time ago; he devoted a substantial amount of his work to showing that legislatures and legislators were not fulfilling the hopes which had been placed in them. It could be pointed out, as I did in *Comparative Legislatures* (1973), that 'legislatures are rarely "strong". Even in liberal-democracies many complain about their impotence, their decline, their ineffectiveness; and if they are strong, they are often blamed for their inconsistency, their squabbles, and thus the same ineffectiveness'[17]. They were obviously very weak in Communist countries; and, in the Third World, in country after country, they were abolished after a few years or completely tamed. Why, then, should they be studied? Is not the legislature the institution which epitomized, more than any other, the 'formalistic' part of government? It is deemed to be strong, to embody the sovereignty of the people—and yet is, almost everywhere, very weak.

The interest which legislatures attracted was at first due in part to the desire of some political scientists, especially of public administration, to increase the role of representative bodies in parts of the Third World. But there soon came to be intellectual reasons behind the interest. Here was an enormous paradox deserving explanation: why should there be such a manifest distance between the claims made for the institution and the reality of power? Why should it be the case that legislatures were weak, not just in the Third World and Communist countries, but in liberal-democracies as well? One might have expected that their influence would be strong in Western government at least. Yet there was a further paradox, in the other direction, as these weak legislatures were also resilient; the 'decline' discovered by Bryce many decades ago seemed to cyclical rather than linear. There was therefore a 'problem' about the legislature as an institution, both an intellectual and a practical problem if suggestions were to be made about possible reform.

These were the questions which students of legislatures began to attempt to tackle from the late 1960s. The result, so far, is encouraging, although no definitive answer has been given as yet to the 'paradoxes' of legislatures. Many collective works have been published, especially under A. M. Kornberg, S. Patterson and the *Consortium for Legislative Research*. We now begin to have a general idea of who legislators are, what are their careers and their ambitions. A corner of the veil has also been lifted with respect to the achievements of legislators. But this knowledge is still not brought together under the umbrella of a fully-fledged model, largely because methodological difficulties remain considerable, especially with respect to the measurement of influence. Large numbers of monographs will have to appear before we have a comprehensive picture of the type and range of activities of legislative bodies and of the conditions under which these bodies become most effective. But we are moving closer to this goal, as can be seen by one of the latest works in the field, M. L. Mezey's *Comparative Legislatures* (1979) which attempts for the first time to provide a sophisticated, and yet realistic, model of the relative strength of legislative bodies.

While legislatures occupied the front of the scene, studies of executives and courts began to emerge from the back of the stage. This may seem the greatest paradox of all, since executives are the apex of the governmental structure and therefore deserve to be studied more than other institutions. Where leaders and ministers come from, how they achieve office, how long they stay in power, what their achievements are, are all subjects of obvious interest and practical importance. Yet, until recently, and with some exceptions (in particular the work initiated by H. D. Lasswell), the comparative study of executives had almost never been undertaken by political scientists[18].

The dearth of comparative work on executives was not due to a lack of interest in leaders and in governments, however; there have, of course, been many important studies on the American Presidency or on the British Cabinet. But, because leadership has often been viewed as highly idiosyncratic, works have been eseentially monographic in character. The only way to approach the study of leadership, it seemed, was biographical and historical. There was considerable reluctance to undertake studies attempting to compare *types* of leadership or to survey the similarities and differences between *groups* of leaders. This reluctance is, but only slowly, being overcome. As G. D. Paige pointed out in his *Political Leadership* (1972), the first general work in the field: 'Methodologically, political science is becoming increasingly more capable of studying scientifically individual human behaviour and of combining individuals through aggregate analysis'[19]. The development of psychological and socio-psychological studies, such as those of the Georges, Barber, Edinger, Rogow and Greenstein gradually provided a basis for the analysis of leaders as 'types' or groups of men with a number of general characteristics. One of the most interesting recent examples of this approach is the study of

Leaders of Revolution, by M. Rejai with K. Phillips (1979), which echoes and markedly systematizes analyses which had first been pioneered by H. Lasswell and by D. Lerner in previous decades. Meanwhile, interest in the institution of the executive and in the personnel of government is beginning to grow. There has not been as yet an important crop of general studies comparable to that which has characterized legislative studies in the 1970s; but, in preparing my study of *World Leaders*, I have noticed the convergence of interests of psychologists, on the one hand, and students of institutions, on the other. The work on executives is becoming increasingly comparative, both with respect to the institutional context within which leaders emerge, and in terms of the social and psychological characteristics of leaders.

But the lack of comparative studies of executives was not merely due to methodological difficulties; it was also the result of the relative paucity of data in some important aspects of the field. The same problem faces students of legislatures and students of executives. The role of legislatures will be well understood only when political scientists have at their disposal a mass of data relating to the activities of legislatures all over the world; studies of executives are so far hampered to a significant extent, first because available data on executives have not as yet been systematically grouped and analysed and, second, because our knowledge of the psychological characteristics of leaders and ministers as well as of the effective power structure within governments is known only for a small number of countries. Information is slowly being amassed, as the study of *Leaders of Revolution* showed and as, it is hoped, my own study also indicates. But much more needs to be covered before the picture of executives becomes clear and the background, duration and activities of leaders and ministers are really understood.

Interest in the analysis of the political importance of courts has grown in parallel to the interest in the analysis of executives. 'Judicial behaviour' studies were pioneered in the 1960s by G. Schubert, first with respect to US Supreme Court decisions, and later in a comparative perspective. In the 1960s and 1970s, the widespread development of administrative courts and tribunals, the rapid expansion of the institution of the Ombudsman, the recognition of the importance of the social background of judges and lawyers on the character and decisions, all contributed to an increase in interest, indeed even to the emergence of an entirely new interest in the political role of the judiciary, although this interest is still confined to a few countries, and especially to the United States. The studies (except those on the Ombudsman) are still mainly devoted to one country only, but it seems worth emphasizing the emergence of this branch of comparative government because what is taking place is a gradual expansion of the concern of specialists about all the institutions which contribute to the governmental decision-making process. It seems now widely recognized that all institutions need to be looked at in a mixed 'institutional and behavioural' manner: they must be examined comparatively (although more specific studies need to be undertaken in order to understand in greater depth an individual leader or a particular institution); and the geographical basis for the comparison must be broad and include, wherever possible, Communist and Third World countries as well as Western examples.

Thus, in the fields of legislatures, executives and even courts, the vitality of middle-level comparative government studies is manifest. The abstract problems posed by the role of institutions are being circumvented by a patient effort which aims at improving the (partial) theories and models as well as at acquiring the empirical data required for the analyses to be firm and concrete. These developments are in the tradition of Bryce, Lowell and Ostrogorski. This is why it is ironical that it should be in the field pioneered by Ostrogorski almost a century ago—that is, political parties—that the advance should have been so limited in the 1960s and 1970s. Duverger's work on parties (1950) seemed to announce a multiplicity of detailed studies leading in turn to comparative syntheses. Given that parties exist, if not everywhere, at least in most countries, and exist in countries with different social structures, different political systems and different societal goals, it seemed that studies of parties could both be world-wide and be highly relevant to our understanding of modern political life.

In reality, studies of parties proved difficult to undertake on a truly comparative basis. Data are difficult to acquire, the area of political parties being politically sensitive, especially in countries operating under a single-party system, as the claims made by party leaders about the strength of their organizations are not just uniformly exaggerated, but almost always difficult to verify: party organizers are usually not keen to let observers find out the reality of party life. This led to some disillusionment among political scientists, which was increased as it became clear that, far from being strong, many parties had feet of clay; the sudden fall of single parties such as Nkrumah's *Convention People's Party*, for instance, seemed to suggest that parties were perhaps not truly relevant to the political process of many new countries, and it was not axiomatic either that, in some Communist countries, the party comes close to the claims which were made about its strength (although its role seemed always important).

Thus the study of parties seemed to lose some of its attractiveness: efforts to go beyond the traditional Western model have not been sustained as much as could have been hoped. G. Satori's work on *Parties and Party Systems* (1976), for instance, remains broadly within the scope of Duverger's work: limited emphasis is given to the Third World and even to Communist countries. Nor has the study of groups developed on the scale which might have been anticipated in the 1950s: interest groups remain the subject of monographs; the cross-national and cross-cultural opportunities have not been explored, except in the most general manner (a good example of this trend being F. Castles' short overall study of *Pressure Groups and Political Culture* (1967)). For groups and for parties, the causes of the relative lack of progress seem to be the same. First, data are difficult to obtain, especially 'real' data which help to check what is proclaimed by the leaders of various countries: empirical studies will only make a breakthrough when a massive effort—probably a concerted one—is made within the discipline. But such a concerted effort is unlikely to occur in a climate in which parties (and even some interest groups) are viewed as inflated organizations behind which hide other institutions such as the army, traditional tribes or ethnic groups, and even small coteries around the leaders. This sentiment does not justify the paucity of studies on parties and interest groups; and a change will no doubt come. But research developments are naturally related to the well-documented decline in the prestige and apparent importance of institutions.

The surge in the number of comparative studies of legislatures, executives, the military, does show that, after a period of soul-searching, the importance of 'middle-range' analyses is now widely recognized. In this new development, the plea for a general and systematic analysis which was symbolized by the 'model-making' movement did play a large part. It is true that the supporters of this movement did not appreciate the importance of 'facts'; this is now redressed, as most comparative government specialists are aware of the need to collect data as widely as possible and know that this difficult collection requires patience and, in many cases, collective efforts. But the supporters of the 'model-making' movement also pointed to essential needs—the need to cover the whole world or at least all types of political systems, the need to develop theory, and the need to look at the practice and not merely at the rules and at the procedures. As a result, albeit unwittingly perhaps, the 'model-makers' did bring comparative government back on to what had been its most successful route in the past, the one which had been pioneered by Bryce and Lowell at the turn of the century, a line which had indeed already begun to be opened by Tocqueville, Montesquieu, and even Aristotle.

Notes

1. J. La Palombara, 'Parsimony and Empiricism in Comparative Politics', in R. T. Holt and J. E. Turner (eds.) (1970), pp. 125–149.
2. R. T. Holt and J. E. Turner, 'The Methodology of Comparative Research', p. 5.
3. *Ibid.*
4. L. C. Mayer (1972), *Comparative Political Inquiry*, p. 95.
5. *See* for instance, L. C. Mayer (1972), Parts I and II, R. T. Holt and J. E. Turner (1970), pp. 1–71; *see also* my *Thinking Politically* (1976), London: Wildwood, Chapter 4.
6. Lord Bryce (1924 edn), *The American Commonwealth*, London: Macmillan.
7. R. C. Macridis (1955), *The Study of Comparative Government*, p. 7.
8. *Ibid.*, pp. 7–12.
9. D. Easton (1953), *The Political System*, p. 72.
10. *Ibid.*, pp. 77–78.
11. R. T. Holt and J. E. Turner (1970), p. 125.
12. *Ibid.*, p. 132.
13. R. T. McKenzie's *British Political Parties* was published in 1955 (London; Heinemann). S. E. Finer's study of pressure groups, *Anonymous Empire* (London; Pall Mall), was first published in 1958.
14. W. H. Agor (1971), *Latin American Legislatures*, p. xxiv.
15. *See* Chapter 4.
16. S. E. Finer (1962), *The Man on Horseback*, p. 5.
17. J. Blondel (1973), *Comparative Legislatures*, p. 3.
18. H. D. Lasswell and D. Lerner (eds.) (1965), *World Revolutionary Elites*.
19. G. D. Paige (1972), *Political Leadership*, p. 7.

References

AGOR, W. H. (1971). *Latin American Legislatures*. New York; Praeger

BENTLEY, A. F. (1908). *The Process of Government,* 1967 edn. Cambridge Mass.; Harvard University Press

BLONDEL, J. (1969). *An Introduction to Comparative Government*. London; Weidenfeld

BLONDEL, J. (1973). *Comparative Legislatures*. Englewood Cliffs, N.J.; Prentice-Hall

BLONDEL, J. (1980). *World Leaders*. London and Beverly Hills; Sage

BRYCE, LORD (1888). *The American Commonwealth*. London; Macmillan

BRYCE, LORD (1921). *Modern Democracies*. London; Macmillan

CASTLES, F. (1967). *Pressure Groups and Political Culture*. London; Routledge and Kegan Paul

DUVERGER, M. (1950). *Political Parties*. Paris; A. Colin (English trans. 1955: London; Methuen)

EASTON, D. (1953). *The Political System*. New York; Knopf

EHRMANN, H. W. (ed.) (1958). *Interest Groups in Four Continents*. Pittsburgh, Pa.; University of Pittsburgh Press

FINER, S. E. (1962). *The Man on Horseback*. London; Pall Mall

FINER, S. E. (1969). *Comparative Government*. Harmondsworth, Middx; Penguin

HOLT, R. T. AND TURNER, J. E. (eds.) (1970). *The Logic of Comparative Research*. New York; Free Press

HUNTINGTON. S. P. (1957). *The Soldier and the State*. Cambridge, Mass.; Harvard University Press

KORNBERG, A. (ed.) (1973). *Legislatures in Comparative Perspective*. New York; McKay

LA PALOMBARA, J. (1974). *Politics Within Nations*. Englewood Cliffs, N.J.; Prentice-Hall

LASSWELL, H. D. AND LERNER, D. (eds.) (1965). *World Revolutionary Elites*. Cambridge, Mass.; M.I.T. Press

LOWELL, A. L. (1896). *Governments and Parties in Continental Europe*. Cambridge, Mass.; Harvard University Press

LOWELL, A. L. (1913). *Public Opinion and Popular Government*. New York; Longmans

MACRIDIS, R. C. (1955). *The Study of Comparative Government*. New York; Random House

MAYER, L. C. (1972). *Comparative Political Inquiry*. Homewood, Ill.; Dorsey Press

MERKL, P. H. (1970). *Modern Comparative Politics*. New York; Holt, Rinehart and Winston

MEZEY, M. L. (1979). *Comparative Legislatures*. Durham, N.C.; Duke University Press

MICHELS, R. (1915). *Political Parties*, 1959 edn. New York; Dover

OSTROGORSKI, M. (1902). *Democracy and the Organization of Political Parties*, 2 vols. London; Macmillan

PAIGE, G. D. (ed.) (1972). *Political Leadership*. New York; Free Press

REJAI, M. with PHILLIPS, K. (1979). *Leaders of Revolution*. London and Beverly Hills; Sage

SARTORI, G. (1976). *Parties and Party Systems*. Cambridge; Cambridge University Press

SCHUBERT, G. (ed.) (1964). *Judicial Behaviour*. Chicago; Rand McNally

Chapter 8
Conclusions

As our predecessors have not investigated the process of law-making, it would perhaps be a good thing to examine it ourselves. Indeed, we ought to go into the whole business of politeia, or constitution, in order that we may round off that part of philosophy which deals with Man.

Aristotle

Every generation that passes is tempted to claim that its contribution is unique, only to be contradicted by the next generation. The point of this book has not been to assert that the discipline of politics has matured so much and has expanded so widely, in the course of the last three or four decades, that earlier contributions pale by comparison and that future developments can merely continue what was recently started. On the contrary, as we often pointed out, the events of the end of the eighteenth century, for instance, led to a change of direction and gave a marked impetus to the discipline of politics; there is every reason to believe that, in the future as well, substantial changes will occur as new problems make a major impact; there is indeed a need to overcome serious problems which have so far been largely overlooked.

What this book attempted to show, first and foremost, was that the discipline of politics, in the years following World War II, has responded actively—enthusiastically—to new world developments and that it has become appreciably more significant as a result. The trials of democracies, their subsequent victory, led to a desire to assess the content of the contribution of 'the people' to the working of government; the fight had been in the name of democracy, but democracy cannot be a reality unless the basis of the pyramid—and in the first instance the electoral process—is firm and well established. Voting behaviour was therefore naturally one of the main *new* concerns of political scientists in the post-war period. And the emphasis on greater participation which characterized the late 1960s brought about a second wave of interest in the problem of the involvement of the people, of its practical limitations and of its possible theoretical extension.

188

At the same moment, the manifest increase in the scope and power of public bureaucracies led to a widespread desire to study these developments in order to prevent excesses, to increase efficiency, and to try and keep the 'New Leviathan' in check. Thus political science expanded the range of its inquiries; and the theoretical underpinnings of these practical developments came naturally to be explored. Thus, in particular, when the emergence of the Third World as a major part of the new international order placed the problem of development high on mankind's agenda, political scientists did not merely feel the need to analyse the specific implications of this new problem; they were also drawn to rethink the overall framework of systems of government and of institutions which had emerged and matured in the 'narrower' context of Western democracies. The interest in 'model-making' may have led some political scientists to be divorced from reality, but the original springboard which produced grand models was, in truth, the desire to cope with the problem of development. And, if political science also became concerned at the time with new methodological explorations and with an altogether more formal and more 'scientific' approach, this was in large part in order to respond more rigorously to the questions which politicians and the public posed about the effect of participation, about power relationships, or about the evolution of political systems.

In attempting to generalize in this way, political scientists encountered many difficulties; and the 'scientific' effort was in part thwarted or at least slowed down by major problems of conceptualization and of method. But, even if one can detect in the 1980s a rather more sober inclination among the majority of political scientists and if this new 'realism' results in greater emphasis on a middle-range study of institutions and of patterns of behaviour, as well as in a return to some of the major value concerns of the past, there was real progress during the grand generalizing period of the 1960s: middle-range analyses go far beyond the pre-war endeavours and the efforts to study policy processes and levels of participation are far more sophisticated than those of the 1940s and 1950s.

The rapid advance of political science and the role of American political science

One thing is certain: political science never had such a rapid development, nor has the quality of the research (*pace* the supporters of the 'great classics') been so remarkable in such a short period. This advance in the study of politics may not be widely recognized as yet; not just the public at large, but even many specialists—politicians, journalists, administrators—may not be conscious of the fact that we have now at our disposal significantly more sophisticated concepts and techniques to analyse the 'facts' than we used to have. Political scientists are perhaps too modest about their achievements; they do not wish to advertise widely what contribution political science makes to our understanding of the world. But, without falling into the opposite danger of exaggerating this contribution, it is evidently the case that our understanding of the problems of old and new political systems, at the level of the masses and at that of the governments and bureaucracies, is now appreciably larger than it was, while middle-range 'theories' relating to democratic and non-democratic systems now provide a valuable framework for analysis *and* for policy-making.

This incomparably greater awareness occurred because, in the space of only 30 years, the discipline of politics truly exploded; it broke its boundaries in almost all directions at the same time. And it did so mainly because of the dynamism of the American political science profession. Whatever may be thought about some of the American contributions, by far the largest part of the important developments of the first two post-war decades occurred in the United States; indeed, the predominance of the American political science profession has continued to this day. Admittedly, political science became a profession earlier in the United States than elsewhere: the American Political Science Association was set up in 1906, long before other national associations were established (the British Political Studies Association was set up only in 1950); admittedly, too, with over 10 000 members, the American association has probably more members than all other national associations put together. But everything cannot be explained by the fact that American political science was organized earlier and had more members: there was, and still is, in the United States, more openness, more desire to inquire into every problem, and a greater belief that these inquiries will have a beneficial effect: there is, in short, both genuine scholarship and intellectual dynamism. These were the qualities which made the early 1960s, in particular, the greatest point in American political science. These were the years when *The American Voter, The Politics of the The Developing Areas, The Civic Culture, Who Governs?, Political Ideology*, were written and published. These were the years when American political science departments in universities, above all those at Yale and Michigan, dominated intellectually the world political science scene and during which there seemed to be indefinite horizons in front of those who entered the profession.

The 'behavioural' whirlwind which spread across the American political science profession was often criticized by Europeans, among whom one could notice a feeling of hurt pride at no longer making the impact which they used to make in the past, not because of their numbers, but because of the quality of the very few 'stars' who had shone in an otherwise very dark firmament. And, with the passing of time, some of the criticisms addressed to American political science have looked prophetic; but what has perhaps not been so often noticed is that much of the criticisms also now looks simple, childish almost, as the American approach to scholarship in political science is becoming increasingly adopted.

What has made some of the criticisms of behaviourism look prophetic has been the realization that the 'individualistic' basis of society is highly questionable. American political science has broadly adopted the assumption of individual rationality according to which members of society attempt to maximize their own interests. This assumption has come under criticism, to an extent at least, because of the gradual refinement of 'rational choice' analyses in the United States itself. The logical and moral difficulties of the attempts to base social action on individual self-interest were discovered or re-discovered: it just does not seem possible to find a clear justification for cooperation and for the promotion of collective goods if it is fundamentally posited that individuals only maximize their interests. Nor does it seem possible to solve rationally problems of decision-making in a majority context if only individual preference patterns are taken into account.

Yet these difficulties remained in the nature of puzzles for most American political scientists and they would probably have remained so, had the European critique not been based on a rather different tradition in which there is individualism, but where collectivism also plays a very large part. For a while, in the early 1960s, many Europeans were tempted by American interpretations, but others were not and these saw their influence grow. The turning point was probably the student revolt of the late 1960s, not so much because of the revolt itself, nor even because of its achievements, but because the revolt developed around the idea that 'imagination' should prevail over rationality and that the solution to societal difficulties was to be found by transcending individual interests rather than by attempting to bring them together. The effect of the student revolt was to make political scientists question more vigorously the assumption of individual interests: older approaches—Marxist, but also Freudian—helped to re-open the question of the basis of political action.

Thus the American 'behaviourist' approach of the 1960s has been seriously undermined by the renewed favour of philosophical and psychological approaches based on principles other than 'rationality'. But, after a period in which some Europeans—as well as some Americans—seemed to think that 'anti-models', alternative paradigms, could provide the answer which had escaped political scientists when individual rationality was the dominant framework, it seems that many of the criticisms which had been directed at the American 'science of politics' have also evaporated. In the fight for or against functionalism and for or against Marxism or neo-Marxism, the once widely respected view that the discipline of politics was an 'art', that it should be descriptive only, that it should be low-key in its approach and suspicious of its potential, seemed simply to vanish. Europeans have perhaps succeeded in undermining the validity of the overall conceptual framework of the early 1960s; but they have also increasingly come to act as if they believed that the discipline of politics was a 'science', at least in the sense that it had to be general and that progress could be achieved only through a rigorous examination of data drawn from a wide variety of experiences. The criticisms against American political science uttered in the 1950s and 1960s were often merely a *cri du coeur*; they were attacks against some of the more unrealistic claims of behaviourism, because Europeans often preferred either armchair philosophical discussions or cosier detailed descriptions which did not pose intellectual problems of analysis. But, gradually, Europeans followed more and more the scholarly precepts of the Americans; they came to believe in generalizations while also realizing that generalizations based on limited data simply would not do. Thus, in the late 1970s, there has been an increasing convergence of methods, even of techniques, and generally in the way in which advances in the discipline can be achieved. One of the most prominent scholars of the neo-Marxist school, N. Poulantzas, became increasingly convinced, shortly before his death, of the value of quantitative techniques in the study of politics; J. Habermas' current attempts at understanding problems of legitimacy in Western societies entail detailed and systematic empirical analyses. It seems that the emptiness or 'poverty' of mere criticism is now being perceived. The desire to make an advance drives all political scientists towards similar methods of investigation. This may not mean using statistics at every point of the analysis; it may not even mean using mathematical techniques at all. But it does mean that the emphasis is on attempting to obtain results by methods based on a rigorous inquiry and that mathematics will be used where it is valuable and when it is possible.

A scientific revolution in political science?

Thus the conclusion which can be drawn from the development of political science in the post-war decades is not so much that it underwent a 'scientific revolution' but that it made its genuine professional breakthrough. Too much was made in the 1960s of the potential for a rapid transformation of the whole discipline through what appeared to be—and indeed was—very real progress in one field, that of electoral behaviour. At the time, the discovery of the survey technique and the simultaneous development of a number of statistical tools designed to analyse the data gathered through surveys with increasing sophistication made many believe that, gradually, the whole of the field of political inquiry could be rejuvenated, indeed completely transformed by osmosis. These views were held at the time when reflection on the development of science became fashionable; it seemed reasonable to conclude that political scientists were helping to fashion one of those 'revolutions' which Kuhn (1970) described for the natural sciences and through which, in a short period of time, by the felicitous combination of techniques and models, the whole grasp of a discipline over the subject-matter is suddenly markedly increased. Thus, without wanting to be overcynical, there was a certain rush among political scientists to be 'Newton' or 'Einstein'; thus, more importantly, many political scientists came to believe that, since the techniques had been discovered or were on the verge of becoming fully 'operational', the main problem was to discover the model, and the bulk of the glory would accrue to the one who would first make the crucial discovery.

Whether 'scientific revolutions' always occur in the manner suggested by Kuhn, especially in the social sciences, is a matter best left for posterity. As we have already noted, following Meehan's remark, social scientists are perhaps over-obsessed with problems of methodology and are certainly more concerned with method than are natural scientists. It seems therefore idle to ask ourselves at this point whether a scientific revolution is about to occur in the discipline of politics. What is clear, however, is that the 'model-making' endeavour of the late 1950s and early 1960s has not led to the transofrmations which were hoped for. The result was, rather, as we already stated, a plethora or 'surfeit' of models, none of which seemed to be very convincing, apparently because these models were so general that they did not solve the real problems to which political scientists (and indeed the politically involved public) addressed themselves. They were like superstructures built before the infrastructure or like the roof of an edifice whose shape was still unclear and whose foundations were not firmly in the ground.

Perhaps the failure of these models to account for the reality has had a salutary effect, however, in that it has dampened the ambitions of political scientists and made them more aware of their condition of 'ordinary' scholars working together for the development of the discipline. In a sense, the model-makers of the late 1950s, as well as some of their 'critics' of the 1960s and 1970s, took postures not altogether dissimilar from the postures of the 'lonely' scholars and philosophers of the past whom they often wanted to displace. The requirements of an on-going discipline suggest, on the contrary, that developments take place in the context of an effort undertaken, if not necessarily collectively, at least on a stage in which there are large numbers of actors working together for the success of the play. The model-makers of the behavioural school were more often adamant to sing their own aria; so were, more recently, some of the most prominent representatives of the 'critical school'. The decline in the prestige of models made the case for these solo performances less overwhelming among the representatives of the 'positivist' or scientific school in political science; the same seems to be occurring among the representatives of the 'critical' school, as it becomes clear that 'solos' in favour of an alternative approach are also empty calls: if too often made, they are repeat performances with few new developments.

Three major stumbling blocks

The problem of facts

Rather than talk about a 'scientific revolution' with the 'all-or-nothing' connotation which this expression seems to entail (unless a 'revolution' occurs, any advance is considered to be trivial or at best relatively insignificant), it seems better to concentrate on the problems which political scientists have to face and which the discipline of politics as a whole has to overcome gradually in order to make further substantial progress. By and large, in the more 'realistic' climate of the 1980s, political scientists seem to be more aware of these problems, but the consciousness is still not as widespread as it should be for enough scholars to work systematically to undermine the effect of these stumbling blocks.

At the end of this survey of the current state of political science, three such stumbling blocks can easily be identified. The most obvious, and the one which could most easily be overcome given enough resources, results from the lack of sufficient 'facts'. I have pointed out repeatedly, especially in the previous chapter, that studies of government are hampered because many aspects of government in most countries of the world have remained insufficiently researched. It may seem ungenerous to emphasize again that the absence of facts, clearly noticed by precursors such as Bryce and Lowell, was, to say the least, markedly underestimated by many prominent representatives of the 'behavioural' school. Perhaps this underestimation made the discipline of politics progress more quickly in some directions; but the effect was serious in general because, in some ways like the traditional political theorists praising the indefinite concentration on the 'literary' analysis of the classical works, the model-makers who denied the need for facts contributed to creating a climate in which the search for facts was viewed as a relatively unimportant effort. Instead of urging political scientists to build the foundations and the walls of the edifice whose roof the model-makers were attempting to design, they seemed anxious to see everyone concentrating on the art of roof-building.

This resulted in a serious overconcentration of efforts on model-making, and on critiques of existing models. To some extent, the discipline of politics became bogged down in the 1960s in endeavour after endeavour to examine in much too great details the value and limitations of the model-making efforts. Just as it can be unrewarding and indeed very dry to dissect and reinterpret Hobbes, Locke or Rousseau, it was unrewarding and dry to dissect, reinterpret and criticize the underlying assumptions of Easton, Almond, Deutsch or Huntington. Very little intellectual profit accrued from these exercises; and very much was lost, as younger political scientists did not sufficiently direct their energies to the acquisition of vitally important data on almost all aspects of political life in the large majority of countries for which little was known. And the danger still exists, to the extent that many of the efforts of those who belong to the neo-Marxist school also consist of reinterpretations and 'critiques' of existing critiques.

This state of affairs was not only detrimental within the political science profession. It had an effect outside as well, as the political public and especially the decision-makers were not aware of the stumbling blocks which prevented and still prevent political scientists from assessing realistically how governments are structured and what governments achieve in the contemporary world. They were not made to realize that our ability to pass judgements was markedly impaired by our relative ignorance of the activities of most governments and that this ignorance was in turn due to the huge difficulties encountered by students of politics when they want to acquire data.

The climate is slowly changing as, in the 1970s, more political scientists have given priority to efforts designed to acquire a better picture of the rich landscape of political life all over the world. Perhaps it may ideally be more elegant to concentrate on a deductive approach, but no natural scientist ever deduced the world: it was there to be seen, touched, measured; deductions came afterwards, as *ex post facto* explanations designed to make sense of what had been seen and touched. This now seems to be the view among those political scientists who aim first at finding out what the military does, what legislatures achieve, what executives decide and what courts are concerned with.

The more quickly this view spread across the profession, the more the public and the political leaders will also become aware of the difficulty of acquiring precise knowledge; and the more quickly they will realize that political scientists cannot reasonably be asked to pass judgements about our society and about other societies unless means are given to them to overcome the 'knowledge gap' which confronts all of us. Contrast the state of affairs with respect to politics with the one which prevails in the social and economic fields. Sociologists and economists have at their disposal teams of researchers whose sole role is to amass knowledge and to present this knowledge in easily usable form, whether it is in UN Yearbooks, OECD Reports, national censuses. Political scientists have no official international or even national organizations at their disposal telling them about the number of military coups and the size of the armed forces involved in these coups, the characteristics of governments and the nature of the decisions which they take, the role of legislatures and their relative involvement in various fields of public policy, the size and detailed involvement of political parties at the national, intermediate and grass-roots levels, the characteristics and activities of interest groups. And, while the views and attitudes of the population are known for some countries (and as a matter of fact only quite recently), we are simply ignorant about the way the immense majority of the inhabitants of the globe think and feel about politics.

The point is not to blame governments or the public for not

enabling political scientists to have *all* the relevant data at their disposal: it is clear that many of these data cannot easily be obtained, for instance because many governments in many countries simply forbid the kind of investigations which are required in order to obtain some of the information, especially information relating to citizens' beliefs and participation and to party or interest group activities. But *much* of the information can be obtained for the large majority of countries—and it has not been gathered. It must be made clear to political leaders and public opinion as a whole that these data cannot be obtained until and unless either resources are placed at the disposal of political scientists for them to acquire these data, or governments entrust organizations (such as OECD or even perhaps special UN agencies) to collect background information on a homogeneous basis in all or the large majority of the countries of the world.

But it is not reasonable to expect the politically active public or even politicians to be truly aware of the magnitude and urgency of the problem unless the political scientists stress the point and stress it repeatedly. And, of course, political scientists will not stress the point unless they are themselves aware of the magnitude and urgency of the problem. The model-makers of the generation of 1960 were not, on the whole, aware of the problem; the 'middle-range' political scientists of the 1970s and 1980s appear to have, to a much greater extent at least, the awareness required. It can therefore be hoped that a change will occur both because political scientists are likely to be increasingly concerned with the collection of data and because, as a result of their pressure, governments and political leaders in general will gradually appreciate what is missing and what needs to be done to correct the situation.

The importance of psychology

A second stumbling block facing political science relates to 'political psychology' or to what G. Wallas called 'human nature in politics'. By and large, it is still the case that political scientists remain unaware of the need for much deeper psychological investigations, probably because, so far, few political scientists have acquired a serious grounding in psychology. There has been considerable emphasis on sociological training, both empirical and theoretical: much of the modern development of political science has rested, as we saw, on sociological analysis. Psychology, on the contrary, has had only limited influence. It is true that some political scientists have been influenced by psychoanalytic approaches, both in its more traditional 'individualistic' forms and in some of the neo-Marxist forms which have become somewhat fashionable on the Continent. Yet this influence has not gone beyond rather limited groups of specialists, while the bulk of the political scientists have continued to be rarely exposed to the conceptual categories, methods of approach and findings of the psychologists.

This is unfortunate, as it prevents political scientists from being at ease in handling many important problems in the discipline, ranging from elite analysis to problems of mass loyalty. Almost at the outset, we pointed out that one of the major problems of contemporary British politics has been the inability to make sense of the apparent contradiction between attitudes of the public towards trade unions and income policies and voting behaviour patterns. By and large, the public, including most trade unionists, condemns the trade unions and supports wage restraint; by and large, too, trade unionists obey the orders of their trade unions; and, even more seriously and more surprisingly, electors have failed to support successive governments which have attempted in various ways to introduce wage restraints. This happened in 1970, 1974 and 1979. It is idle to claim that survey respondents are ignorant of the issues, or are dishonest, or, even less, are unrepresentative of general opinion. What is clear is that the attitude towards incomes policies does not lead to what seems to be the logical consequences—namely, to the support at the polls for governments which attempt to implement these policies. What this means is that the mechanism—the psychological mechanism—which operates in the minds of the electors at large is simply not well understood.

This is not the place to attempt to answer a question which has obviously many ramifications. But it is worth exploring at least some of the dimensions of the problem, as this exploration will help to show the directions which a psychological analysis of mass political behaviour might take. First, it is clear that we do not know the precise characteristics of the commitment, or 'loyalty' of union members to their trade union. As has often been said about survey findings, questions are asked of respondents in an abstract context, not in the concrete reality of a specific situation in which, for instance, workers are involved in a dispute with their employer or with the government. Loyalty to a trade union, when it is put to the test, involves also loyalty to peer groups, to friends, to neighbours: how much pressure such a loyalty can exercise on individuals is something which political scientists do not know, and have not even begun to consider.

Moreover, as was also pointed out, surveys do not provide a means of tapping the precise contours of the dynamics of a given political situation. In the relationship involving trade unionists, the trade union leadership and the government, the progressive effect of the influence, not just of the trade unions as such, but of the environment in which members operate has to be discovered and analysed. What the events of the late 1960s and the 1970s in Britain showed was that governments tended to win the first or early rounds of their battles with the trade unions, only to lose eventually as, seemingly, trade unionists became gradually disillusioned with the inability of the government to produce results which would be (or seemed to be) as satisfactory as those which might have been obtained by following the trade union leadership. But neither the ways in which this change of attitude takes place (if it does take place), nor the speed at which it takes place, nor indeed the specific incidents or reasons which lead to a change have been circumscribed or explained. Each government presumably assumes that it has a better idea than the previous one and that it will be therefore able to avoid the mistakes which were made in the past. But what the 'right' solution is remains unclear as the dynamics of the situation are not understood from the point of view of the psychology of the electors.

The problem relates therefore to far more than a simple dichotomy between 'attitudes' and 'behaviour', although part of it corresponds to this dichotomy. What is required is a systematic exploration of the characteristics of human personality and of the responses which are made by men to stimuli or pressures from the environment. It is therefore evident that only a major involvement of political scientists in psychological analyses can begin to provide an answer to what might be called the British trade union 'paradox', a paradox which is only one example among many of those which even a superficial glance at electoral behaviour in the contemporary world can easily identify. As was pointed out in the introductory chapter, the persistent Communist vote in France also constitutes a puzzle; nor is there any simple explanation of the fact, which has periodically perplexed leaders of left-wing parties in Europe, that a very substantial segment of the manual working class prefers conservative or right-wing parties to the 'natural' or 'official' parties of the working class.

Thus the understanding of mass political behaviour will always be limited, 'uni-dimensional', or static, until political scientists place a major emphasis on the psychological dimension. And what is true of mass participation is as true and as abundantly clear with respect to decision-making processes in small groups and by political leaders. So far, committee decision-making has been essentially examined with the tools of economists: game theory has, by and large, been the substitute for a sophisticated understanding of human psychology. The dynamics of committees are clearly based in part on the universal constraints which game theory helps to 'operationalize', especially in the (relatively rare) cases when members of committees are, broadly speaking, equal. But, when there are, as happens so often, considerable differences in the power and influence of committee members, an understanding of the dynamics of committee decision-making requires a precise knowledge of the part played by different personality 'types'. And while this role is patently obvious in the context of leaders' decisions, while it has been described impressionistically by historians and gradually with greater precision by biographers with a more rigorous grounding in psychology, it is still not studied systematically: political scientists by and large do not find it easy, or congenial, to give a major emphasis to the psychological dimension.

This is quite understandable, for psychology is a specialized discipline, and one which political scientists cannot be expected to be able to use unless they invest a considerable amount of time to undergo a specialized training; the few political scientists, such as R. E. Lane, F. I. Greenstein or A. A. Rogow, who became specialists in psychology, have indeed all devoted years of their 'spare' time to acquiring some of the skills of professional psychologists. Quite understandably, most political scientists have not done so; they cannot be expected to do so as long as the regular training in graduate schools does not entail, as a matter of course, at least some elements of a psychological training. This is too important a matter, however, to be left to the accident that a few political scientists will find the psychological bases of politics important enough to make the investment themselves. Incentives must be given early, together with a taste of the directions which the analysis might take when psychological variables are taken into account.

The need to discover the basic 'unit' of politics

The lack of a good grounding in psychology—and the consequential relative absence of analysis of the psychological dimension—is therefore a major stumbling block which the study of politics must circumvent in the course of the coming years or decades. But the most serious stumbling block lies elsewhere: it arises from the inability of political scientists so far to discover a basic 'unit' of political activity, an element which might be added or multiplied in order to describe and measure differences in political behaviour.

We have examined at some length, in the course of Chapter 5, the efforts which were made in order to discover such an element by means of circumscribing rigorously the concept of power. Not unnaturally, the concept of power has been widely regarded as central in political relationships; not unnaturally too, it seemed that it could be measured. Yet efforts at measurement proved unrewarding, largely because, as we have seen, the power of each individual has to be related to those specific individuals on which it is exercised: one could not therefore attribute 'quantities' of power to different actors; comparisons between individuals were at best clumsy and difficult, and perhaps impossible.

Some success was achieved, admittedly, not so much in measuring power, but in the formal analysis of the conditions under which decisions are taken in some situations; it seemed possible to discover the strategies which were most profitable when actors looked rationally at the problems which they faced. But this analysis has been successful only under rather special conditions. I have pointed out that, by accident, the liberal-democratic ideology which was adopted in the West from the end of the eighteenth century provided a framework of rules (decisions taken by a majority, equality of decision-makers) which simplified the conditions under which decisions were to take place: this simplification helped to formalize some of the analysis. The study of the consequences of majority decision-making developed. And to the extent that individuals were 'rational'—if they had 'utilities' which they tried to maximize—game theory helped to elaborate a decision-making analysis from which one could deduce the best possible outcome for the actors concerned. Yet, even under these conditions, we had also to note that game theory is not sufficiently developed to provide solutions when there are substantial numbers of actors and the game is cooperative rather than zero-sum.

This situation seems to condemn the discipline of politics to remaining essentially qualitative in its hard core. Quantitative methods may be used with some success to describe some of the 'outer' manifestations of political action, for instance, the behaviour of millions of voters, or the patterns of decisions of governments in certain fields; but it seems that, if we want to understand why these decisions have taken place, and to look at the variations in time and space of the types of relationships which exist between individuals or between individuals and groups in societies, we still have to resort to descriptions of specific cases, and these descriptions appear to be nearer to the efforts of historians than to the endeavours of physicists or even economists or psychologists.

The solution to the problem would seem to be closer at hand if, as is the case with voting paradoxes or rational games, political scientists were willing to simplify drastically the conditions under which they analyse politics. But they are here in a dilemma, because the amount of simplification required is so large that they become truly remote from the 'real world'. Hence the unwilling-ness of most of them to go as far; those who have done so have been accused by others of neglecting the rich variety of political life. Indeed, even when the norms adopted by the society intro-duced a 'simplifying mechanism', as with the liberal-democratic model of government, it appeared quickly that the norms were not implemented sufficiently widely to lead to a truly realistic analy-sis—and political scientists were often inclined to look at the 'true picture' behind the formal rules.

This constant need to return to 'real' situations and to break the straightjacket of formal assumptions suggests that the problem faced by the discipline of politics is not merely one of inadequate techniques of measurement of power or other aspects of 'rational' behaviour. It shows a basic dissatisfaction with the concept of power as well as with other 'rational' arrangements because of the assumptions on which these are based. We said that some viewed the concept of power as central to the discipline, but this view is not shared by all political scientists; nor is the part played by rationality equally viewed by all as the most important one. There is a widespread feeling that controversial assumptions lie at the root of these approaches, assumptions which can be termed 'pessimistic individualism': power and rational-choice models are pessimistic because there is always, even if it is hidden, a notion of a clash of interests, which it may be worthwhile reconciling, but which cannot be reconciled without difficulty; and there is indi-vidualism because it is believed that cooperation exists only if, and as long as, individuals find it useful to cooperate in terms of their own interest. In short, these analyses are based on an underlying doctrine of the 'original sin'; or to view power as the central concept is also to consider that coalitions, alliances, bargains, trade-offs occur only to the extent that individuals think that it is in their interest to come together because of some bigger danger. An alliance is the cooperation of some against threats coming from others.

Such an assumption may be widely believed: it is not universally adopted. Some do not believe in it because desires for cooperation, for community, for love appear also to be widespread, and appear to need to be promoted and fostered. Moreover, the existence of cooperative sentiments makes it difficult to decide what precisely is meant by individual 'interests' and by 'rationality'. If someone finds pleasure in his association with others, and in the work he does to help others, it is difficult to decide what is 'rational' for such an individual: in the circumstances, it seems *prima facie* more rational to maximize the warmth of the relationships in which someone is engaged than to concentrate on economic benefits. While it may seem true that much in our lives is 'selfish, brutish, and short', it is clear that in all of us, too, there is an element of 'associationalism' or 'communitarianism' which leads us to make 'sacrifices' for those whom we love, in ways which cannot be justified in terms of strict interest maximization. Clearly, therefore, power and rational decision-making in the narrow sense are not the only aspects of human relationships which have to be taken into account to describe political relationships; and 'optimists' would argue that sentiments such as love, admiration, respect, etc., should be fostered, not suppressed and that politics should become increasingly the politics of love and of cooperation rather than the politics of power.

There is a further difficulty with the analyses based on power and rational choice. These approaches are concerned primarily with individual actors and individual relationships and not with social forces. While political life evidently depends on the interplay between groups and on the effects of social and economic cleavages, power relationships are primarily exercised among individuals. Naturally enough, the politics of power comes to be regarded by some as relatively superficial, even trivial, by comparison with the broader questions raised by the politics of group conflict and the dynamics of this conflict. Hence the view which is sometimes expressed that personal conflicts are mere epiphenomena, that they at best constitute manifestations of deeper social trends. By and large, political scientists have not gone quite as far: for reasons which we have noticed throughout this book, they have always recognized that individuals are important, and that the relationships between individuals are an essential part of the analysis of politics. But political scientists have also generally felt that the analysis of personal relationships does not constitute the whole of the analysis of politics and that a realistic interpretation is one which takes into account the role of individuals and the impact of social forces.

If social forces are to be given a prominent place in the

'explanation' of political life, it becomes impossible to hold the view that power relationships are central to political analysis, unless one is to give to power an altogether wider meaning—a societal meaning—which it does not ostensibly have; some, mainly those with a Marxist orientation, have sometimes considered power in this manner, but this extension of the scope of the concept is rather controversial, probably mainly because it entails giving to groups an active, almost conscious influence on individuals; it entails 'personalizing' or 'anthropomorphizing' the role of groups in an unwarranted manner.

And this extension of power to social groups seems unnecessary because we have at our disposal concepts which help to cover the influence of groups on their members. Concepts such as loyalty, allegiance, legitimacy or, alternatively, alienation, are related to the impact which groups make on individuals while not implying that this impact is the result of an 'effort' of the group to put pressure on the individual. It seems therefore more sensible to confine the use of power to the realm of actions among individuals, while attempting to circumscribe group influences through other concepts.

The search for the discovery and measurement of a basic element of political life could take interesting new directions as a result. Having concluded that power was not truly the central element in political relationships, both because it implies a kind of pessimistic selfishness which is part, but not the whole of political life and because it does not help to cover the relationship between groups and individuals, political scientists might find it appreciably more rewarding to explore group loyalties; they might assess whether allegiance or legitimacy (with their converse, alienation) could provide the basis for the unit of measurement they have been striving for.

This has so far not been the case, somewhat surprisingly: although the importance of legitimacy and allegiance has often been stressed, there have been few efforts to use legitimacy and allied concepts for the purpose of measuring precisely the relationship between individuals and groups. The task may seem daunting, but it is not immediately evident that it is more daunting than the task of measuring power among individuals. And while it may not be easy to measure precisely the extent of loyalty of individuals to groups, it would seem possible to compare broad levels of loyalty and thereby assess the amounts of loyalty which groups so to speak can 'extract' from the part of the population which is loyal to them. A thorough examination of the various components of loyalty might therefore bring political scientists closer to the discovery of the basic 'element' which the discipline of politics needs if it is to describe with precision, and ultimately to measure, the characteristics of political life.

An emphasis on the study of loyalty does relate to the importance of the psychological aspects of politics which we examined earlier. The emphasis which was placed on power does relate to the psychology of politics as well, admittedly, but to an oversimplified form of psychology which gives paramount importance to individual interests. It is true that this approach has often been used with some success in political theory, from Machiavelli to Hobbes and indeed Bentham; and it has been the main foundation of classical economics. But political theory at least did not overcome the problems which 'pessimistic individualism' raised; nor is it entirely clear that modern economics can claim that this assumption provides a full answer. An emphasis on loyalty requires a rather more complex psychological analysis: it entails understanding how far individuals act on the basis of their loyalties, how far they are cross-pressured in their loyalties and how, over time, these sentiments may be eroded or reinforced. It seems therefore that political science requires a combined effort involving greater sophistication in the field of psychology as well as a systematic exploration of the potential provided by loyalty for the measurement of the relationship between individuals and groups. At the same, time, the gradual gathering of more relevant facts about political life should provide an empirical basis for the testing of hypotheses relating to the emergence, development and decline of allegiance of citizens with respect to the groups to which they belong.

The role of normative theory and its relationship to the 'real world'

I stated earlier that one of the major objections to the assumption of 'pessimistic individualism' was that it seemed to foreclose the possibility that political relationships might 'improve' through their being increasingly based on cooperation. As long as what is conveniently regarded as 'rational choice' is viewed as the underlying assumption of all political action, it is simply not possible to regard cooperation as an 'improvement'; and, whatever may be claimed by those who extol the virtues of self-interest, it is a *fact* of human relationships and of political relationships in particular that the self-interest assumption is regarded by many—within political science, but perhaps even more importantly outside—as restricting, as limiting, as basically unworthy of man taken in the plenitude of his achievements. In the same way as art and aesthetics are usually regarded as being limited, if not crushed, by a 'narrow' economic approach (and many of the attacks against classical capitalism have been made on the grounds of the philistinism of the capitalist class), the 'idealistic' desire to bring about the brotherhood of man appears to be crushed by a view of politics which is characterized by 'rational choice' and by an emphasis on the overwhelming role of power.

No amount of pressure exercised by those who believe in rational choice analyses will stop this idealistic desire. This is why 'political theory'—in the conventional sense—re-emerged, as we have seen, despite the heavy concentration of empirical and descriptive analyses characterizing some of the endeavours labelled as 'behaviourism'. And it is because the desire for what can be loosely called 'morality' in politics was crushed so strongly that it came back with a vengeance and unrealistically attempted to reduce the case for careful empirical studies of 'human nature in politics'. It has to be recognized—and it is fortunately increasingly being recognized, Rawls having played a large part in fostering this recognition—that the discipline of politics is based on a combination of empirical and normative analyses, that normative analyses can no more be suppressed by the increasing impact of scientific techniques in the political field than empirical efforts can be set aside by the repeated cry that man is more than a set of variables which can be systematically analysed.

The combination of empirical and normative analyses is at the heart of the discipline of politics. It was at the centre of the discipline in earlier times, when problems seemed to be, if not simpler, at least less numerous and more straightforward; it remains at the centre of political inquiry in a more complex world in which the structures of government have become very numerous and in which citizens are more aware of problems and are more interested and involved in the solution of these problems. This is why there is, not just a case, but a basic need for a general 'political theory' which is concerned, as in the past, with the analysis of values and with the determination of the conditions under which these values can be translated into broad institutional arrangements. But this is also why, more perhaps than before, much of this desire for 'morality', for 'improvements', comes to find its way into detailed studies of political life.

One manner in which this effort to inject normative or value analyses in detailed problems is taking place is through policy studies which, as we have seen, especially in Chapter 3, have become in the 1970s an important and rapidly developing aspect of the discipline of politics. For policy studies are not merely, as they are sometimes described, the consequences of a desire to introduce more rationality in the process of decision-making: they have of course that role; they aim at avoiding inconsistencies between the policies pursued by various agencies; and they aim at discovering the institutions which will be designed to achieve the policies required in the most efficient manner. But the demand for policy-oriented research is not solely based on the desire to offer some suggestions to politicians and to the public in their search for the implementation of goals which they have already decided on.

Policy-oriented research is also concerned with the goals themselves; it proposes to ascertain what the goals are, to begin with, as it is clear that politicians and the public do not have the time or even the disposition of mind to look calmly at the goals for which they strive. And policy-oriented research is thereby inescapably concerned with the examination of the relationship between specific goals in various sectors of government and the overall values of the society. The effect is to link policy research to 'political theory' in the conventional normative sense; it is also, by a feedback process, to reconsider some of the basic values of the society, as a result of a continuous dialogue among policy research specialists and between normative political theorists and policy specialists.

Thus it is not inconsistent to call for more policy-oriented research in the various aspects of political science *and* to call for the maintenance of the (more traditional) concern for political theory. To view policy-oriented research as antagonistic to political theory is absurd; to view policy-oriented research as merely a means of improving the 'system' as it is, and therefore as part of the machinery by which modern social science 'chokes' individuals and builds more and more interconnections between institutions as a result of which new moves are increasingly difficult is, in point of fact, to denigrate individuals and to underestimate the ability of man to respond to the challenges which have to be faced. Policy-oriented research is a necessity, not just in order to monitor inefficiencies and to reduce them in the future, but in order to achieve a better injection of 'moral' principles in the daily development of policies.

The same is true of voting behaviour and of mass participation studies which have often been viewed as the archetype of behavioural research. The investigation of electoral behaviour is but policy analysis of a kind, namely, the implementation of the *policy* of popular participation. To deny that popular participation was and is a policy, and a very conscious one at that, simply because it happens to be one of the central policies of many modern governments and one which conditions or at least colours many of the others, indicates that one is labouring under a misconception.

Mass participation was never a fact: it was demanded by some; it was achieved, usually with difficulty and by small advances, in the course of the last 200 years. And it is still markedly hampered both by ideological disagreements about what its value is, and what its 'proper' scope should be, and by conflicts about the ways in which the policy can best be implemented. This is why the analysis of popular participation contributes, as does the analysis of other policies, to a better assessment of the ways in which implementation can take place and to a fundamental discussion about the values involved.

Those who criticized electoral studies from the 1950s onwards did not do so merely because they thought the findings were trivial, although they often claimed that this was their ground for attack. They criticized them primarily because they felt that these studies led to a reassessment of the values relating to popular participation—a standpoint which was indeed also adopted by those engaged in electoral studies. Through this debate, studies of popular participation broadened and became increasingly concerned, in the 1970s, with the exploration of the many ways in which participation takes place and of the general conditions under which democracy appears to be able to operate in our societies. This had the effect of leading to reflections on the characteristics and purposes of participation—and ultimately to the revival of the ideal of participation as a fundamental 'policy problem' for our societies. Thus, far from having restricted our discussion of the possible scope of democracy, voting behaviour studies resulted in a more informed discussion of the conditions and purposes of participation. Far from having stifled the inquiries of political theorists, electoral studies led to a deeper reflection on the values which need to be embodied through the electoral process and other forms of participation. As we have had occasion to note, the study of participation thus became simultaneously one of the most sophisticated areas of empirical analysis *and* one of the most lively fields of normative inquiry.

The experience which the discipline of politics underwent in the course of the last few decades shows beyond any shadow of doubt that there is no danger that 'imagination' will be overcome by the pressure of technical advance; and it shows also that there is no danger that the mystery of politics is about to disappear. What this experience indicates is that the mystery is at every corner of political life and corresponds to the vitality of this political life. It expresses itself in many forms—through the accident of the idiosyncrasies of individuals, through the numerous 'exceptions' to the general rules which are decreed by policy-makers or to the regularities which are observed, and ultimately through the intrusion of 'natural' forces in the pre-ordered developments designed to dominate these forces. No one ultimately seriously holds the view that it would be better to practise politics in a wholly mysterious context; thus although few politicians and members of the public have so far been prepared to acknowledge their debt to those who engage professionally in the discipline of politics, the effective behaviour of both active and passive citizens shows that they are dependent on political science in order to make sense of the reality of their society and even more of the ways in which this society can be maintained, gently reformed or profoundly modified.

But the element of mystery will always remain; it is because of this mystery that the discipline of politics has to rely on a combination of technique and imagination. For, beyond the mystery of the accidents and of the personalities, perhaps the greatest mystery is the desire of man to look for new ways of mastering his fate, not just as a result of each generation wishing to make its mark on the tapestry of mankind, but because each individual has, within his own self, a peculiar combination of desire for security and longing for the unknown. Very realistically, the discipline of politics embodies both this desire and this longing. And if it is occasionally noted that the cohabitation is somewhat uneasy, let it be remarked that this cohabitation is also uneasy within each society, each group, indeed each individual. The discipline of politics draws its richness and its strength from combining 'realism' and 'idealism', empirical analyses and a concern for values. It has always done so, and it continued to do so in its great expansion during the post-war years. And it is by doing so that it serves the best interests of mankind, as it offers some guidance to its exploding population while it retains scope for experiments and a place for imagination.

References

KUHN, T. S. (1970). *The Structuring of Scientific Revolutions*. Chicago, University of Chicago Press

Index